D0338317

ITALIAN
WINE

ITALIAN WINE

Victor Hazan

For Judee and Bill, with my best wishes.

Vic Hazan

ALFRED A. KNOPF

NEW YORK   1984

THIS IS A BORZOI BOOK

PUBLISHED BY ALFRED A. KNOPF, INC.

Copyright © 1982 by Victor Hazan

All rights reserved under International and Pan-American Copyright Conventions.
Published in the United States by Alfred A. Knopf, Inc., New York,
and simultaneously in Canada by Random House of Canada Limited, Toronto.
Distributed by Random House, Inc., New York.

LIBRARY OF CONGRESS CATALOGING IN PUBLICATION DATA

Hazan, Victor.

Italian wine.

Bibliography: p.

Includes index.

1. Wine and wine making—Italy. I. Title.

TP559.I8H39   1982   641.2'22'0945   82-47831

ISBN 0-394-50266-3

Manufactured in the United States of America
Published November 24, 1982
Second Printing, July 1984

This book is for Marcella,
insostituibile e carissima compagna,
who caused it to happen.

Contents

CHAPTER 5

ITALY'S SWEET WINES
and Other Wines of Special Interest 214

APPENDIX A

When and How to Serve Italian Wine 231

APPENDIX B

The Rules
How Italian Wine Production Is Regulated 239

APPENDIX C

A Glossary of the More Common Terms
Used on Italian Wine Labels 246

APPENDIX D

Three Examples of Italian Labels 249

APPENDIX E

Italy's Controlled Appellation Zones 252

APPENDIX F

How to Shop for Italian Wine 294

BIBLIOGRAPHY 297

INDEX 301

Preface

It has been more than five years since Judith Jones, my editor at Knopf, asked me to do a brief guide to Italian wines, both of us feeling then that a little book would adequately accommodate the dimensions of the subject. As I worked my way into the project, my notes multiplied; it became apparent that for each wine I was familiar with there were a hundred more to discover, beyond that hundred a thousand, and where it ended neither I nor anyone I talked to knew. I had opened the cellar door of a small country and had stepped into a universe.

In the first months after I began work, I visited winemakers in every Italian region, except for Calabria and Basilicata at the southernmost tip of the peninsula. Invaluable as the acquaintances I made and the conversations I had proved to be, it was not long before I chose to conduct the bulk of my research away from the field.

Even if there had been time enough and the means to call on every worthy producer in the country, tasting wines at the source gave a fragmented and partly distorted impression. Wine often tasted so much better under the protective gaze of its maker, and relating it accurately to products of similar grapes grown elsewhere put too much strain on the reliability of one's notes and memory. Therefore I collected and sent for bottles of every wine described in this book, and hundreds more besides, and assembled them in Bologna, my home base.

There I assorted the wines, grouping them usually by grape variety or wine type, sometimes by year, by producer, or by any other significant characteristic they shared. I proceeded to taste each group blind, as often as possible with colleagues and friends. We would, for example, have tastings of Pinot Grigio from every zone where it is produced or of Chianti from all the nine Classico townships; we'd compare Barolo with other Piedmontese reds one day, Barolos of the same year from different vineyards the next day, Barolos of different vintages by the same producer on the third day.

In the course of these tastings, it was not only the individual features of the wines under scrutiny that emerged, but also those components of character that they had in common. What seemed at first to be an unmanageable variety of wines gradually fell into a few distinct groups. Eventually, out of the information gathered, the plan of this book, based on relationships of taste and of grape variety, rather than of geographic origin, took shape.

In the long interval between the time this book was commissioned and completed, Italian wine has made a substantial impact on American drinking habits. After decades of being looked upon with condescension, Italy's wines are beginning to be taken seriously. And well they might, for no other nation produces such a variety, offering so much flavor, at such reasonable price.

Inevitably the ones most widely available are not those that reflect most brightly the glories of Italy's current production. For every thousand cartons of characterless, industrial white wine there may be one from a choice estate in Friuli's Collio. For every Barolo from a superior vineyard, there are hundreds of the name-exploiting bargain-basement variety. There will always be more ordinary wine than good, and it is a fact of commerce that merchants find it easier to sell a bottle that costs a dollar less than one that is worth a dollar more.

But exceptional wines from conscientious producers are no longer as unknown as they used to be. The demand for quality has the power to draw it to the market. For us who write about Italy's wines, the most satisfying accomplishment is to arouse the interest and supply the information that can nourish and strengthen that demand. To those who make fine Italian wines, this can bring the recognition and encouragement they well deserve. To those who will drink them, it can provide an inexhaustible source of pleasures.

New York, January 1982

Acknowledgments

A full account of my debts to everyone whose knowledge and assistance constitute the capital on which I have liberally drawn in assembling this work would produce a list into whose very length my creditors' identities might disappear. To the greater part of my benefactors I shall therefore express my gratitude collectively. Those who have helped me will know that I remember and am forever grateful.

A few, whose contributions have been exceptionally significant, I cannot fail to cite:

Luigi Veronelli, Italian wine's controversial and quixotic arbiter of excellence, whose championship of the small producer over the large has won him adversaries as well as admirers. Through his tireless jousts against mediocrity and anonymity he has done more than anyone else in his country to call attention to the accomplishments of individual winemakers and the intrinsic merits of single vineyards. To Veronelli I am deeply indebted for the generosity with which he has shared his research and his friends.

I am also grateful to Nino Franceschetti in the Veneto; Giorgio Grai in Alto Adige; Francesco Spagnolli in Trentino; Vittorio Puiatti, Mario Schiopetto, and Gaspare Buscemi in Friuli; Franco Biondi-Santi in Montalcino; John and Palmina Dunkley in Chianti Classico; Antonio Mastroberardino in Avellino; and Antonio Vodret and Enzo Biondo in Sardinia; all have been prodigal in giving me their time and their incomparable insights into the wine of their areas.

Renato Ratti of Piedmont has been, through the years, an always accessible and constantly illuminating guide. Anything I may have understood about the production of Italy's preeminent red wine region is largely due to him.

Through Giacomo Tachis of Antinori and Ezio Rivella of Villa Banfi I had my introduction to technically advanced Italian winemaking of the highest order.

Unstinting help in collecting information has come from the Italian Trade Commission in New York by way of the former Commissioner, Lucio Caputo, and Fenella Pearson, the former director of the Wine Promotion Center.

The tasting skills of Harriet Lembeck have been a standard to which I have urged my own more reluctant and careless palate to conform.

Giuliano Hazan, my son, has helped in more ways than I can count, sharing the tedious task of handling thousands of bottles, keeping records, checking my typescript, and lending the invaluable impressions of his unspoiled and gifted palate.

Judith Jones, my editor, has administered, with inexhaustible patience, that perfectly blended potion of guidance and latitude that brings vigor and assurance to an author's lamest efforts.

I am unable to produce adequate thanks for what Robert Lescher, my literary agent and mentor, has done. He has steered me past the first perilous moment of complacency, shepherded me through a much longer and daunting period of apprehension, offered throughout his support and, to the very end, invaluable suggestions beyond enumeration. If I have managed to bring this book in, it is because he has been beside me every step of the way.

ITALIAN WINE

[1]

ITALIAN WINE

How It Has Been Organized in This Book

If we love wine, there is no place more promising to indulge our passion than among the enticingly varied bottlings of Italy. But it can remain a passion largely unrequited unless we find the way among the thousands of different wines that flow from this most prolific and diversified of wine-producing countries. Where do we pick up a thread that will guide us through the maze?

The most logical solution, one that has always been followed when writing about the wines of any single nation, is to begin at the beginning, at the geographic place of origin, fixing the character of a wine through the circumstances of its birth. And of those circumstances, where Italy is concerned, there would be a marvelous story to be told, a story of regions that are more unlike than are most nations.

When in wandering through Italy's wines, one finds in Piedmont the power and authority of Barolo, in the Veneto the charm of Soave, in Romagna the heartiness of Sangiovese, in Tuscany the austerity of Brunello, in Sardinia the fullness and listlessness of Cannonau, it is not only the properties of a grape variety, the nature of the soil, or the influence of climate that are making themselves manifest. It is also the character of peoples whose histories, temperaments, physical features, and very speech are sharply dissimilar, as are their cuisines and their wines.

Enthralled though I was with this approach, I ended, however reluctantly, by putting it aside. For anyone looking for direct answers about Italian wine, whether it is what wine to pick up for Saturday night's dinner or what fine differences there may be between a Pinot Grigio from Friuli and one from Alto Adige, it seemed just too roundabout a way to go. I became convinced that the most straightforward way to organize the subject was to group wines according to the place they occupy, not on the map, but on the spectrum of taste.

All the wines described in the main portion of this book have been grouped into five broad, and I hope easily grasped, categories of taste. The red wine categories are Big Reds, Medium-Range Reds, and Light Reds. The white wine categories are Light and Crisp, and Full and Fruity. This classification makes it possible to deliver rapidly to the reader information that he would otherwise have had to find by picking his way from region to region, from one unfamiliar name to another.

For example, in a conventional arrangement, Barolo, a deep, powerful, complex red, and Grignolino, a light, charming, pale one, both from Piedmont, would be discussed in a chapter on that region. But the taste impressions that Barolo makes are much closer in kind to those of such weightier wines as Brunello from Tuscany or Taurasi from Campania. Therefore you will find Barolo, Brunello, Taurasi in the Big Reds section, with their peers, and Grignolino among Light Reds of different geographic origins, but of comparable interest.

Furthermore, by loosening the geographic bonds, certain significant relationships between Italian wines emerge that would otherwise have been slighted. We can now examine in the same context a group of reds from the nebbiolo grape whether they are made in Piedmont or Lombardy, those sired by barbera in Piedmont, Lombardy, and Emilia-Romagna, the family connections of white wines from Tuscany and Umbria, or the varying achievements of cabernet in seven different regions. (In each category, the wines belonging to a "family" are grouped at the beginning, followed by an alphabetical listing of independent wines.)

Classifying wines by taste also serves to isolate the separate personalities of a wine that has but one name. Thus the reader will find that the three major and distinct styles of Chianti are each described in their appropriate taste category.

The principal portion of the book takes up in varying detail the major "families" of dry Italian wine and those individual wines that seemed to me to have special interest. In addition, there is a section on sweet wines and a brief selection of rosés.

There is an explanation of the D.O.C. law, the wine statute that governs Italy's controlled appellation production, a glossary of terms that you may meet on an Italian wine label, and an illustrated guide to reading

Italian labels. There are nineteen regional maps showing the location of all the controlled appellation zones to date, and scattered through the text are maps in relief that close in on specific production areas, conveying an impression of the terrain.

Since the overall concern of this book and, I presume, of those who will use it, is taste, I have written also a brief essay on tasting.

This book has two objectives. One is to supply straight information, telescoping it so that the focus narrows gradually from the general to the particular, allowing the reader to take in as much or as little as may be useful to him.

The other objective is to characterize as many wines as possible, to catch their likenesses together with some of the emotion they evoke, to call attention to the fact that beneath the inert mass of statistics heaped upon it, wine has a living identity.

In doing these character studies, I have resorted to a variety of techniques, as a portraitist might do a quick pencil sketch or a full oil, suiting them to the subject, using no more than tasting terms sometimes, other times relying on anecdote or on details of landscape.

As models, and it is important that the reader know this, I have taken no single specific wine from a specific year, but out of elements derived from various tastings, I have constructed archetypes that I consider most representative of the features we should expect or hope to find. You should not be dismayed if, when you open a bottle at home, your evaluations do not exactly coincide with mine. Wines—at least the nonindustrial ones—are not stamped from molds, nor are organs of taste.

My characterizations are not meant to encourage an exact duplication of my experiences, but to provoke curiosity, to stimulate awareness, to help set off for my fellow wine drinkers lively and, I hope, satisfying responses to Italian wine and to its innumerable expressions of character.

[2]

TASTING

The Art of Wine Appreciation

Tasting is very different from drinking. Tasting demands involvement and the patient cultivation of our senses. All that drinking requires is a glass in the hand. Since our ultimate objective when we pour wine is to drink it, we may well ask why we should bother with anything else. We don't really have to, not unless we care to understand what we are drinking.

Wine appreciation is like the appreciation of music or any other art. We can turn on music as background and hang pictures on our walls as decoration, letting whatever they have to say slide past our consciousness. Or we can use our ears and eyes to turn to them the undistracted attention of our mind. We can negligently knock back the contents of our glass, or we can try to interest our palate in some of the things that nature, man, and time have put into it.

The extraordinary fact about wine is that we can use it with equal success either to rouse our senses or to numb them. In the case of a few wines, obliviousness might even be a merciful thing, but it is more likely that a heedless palate will permit too many joys, small and large, to pass our lips uncaught.

The most comforting fact in tasting is that virtually all of us possess the right equipment for it, and that equipment is usually more sharply tuned than we suspect. Practically every sensation that we think of as one of taste is one of smell. Anyone who has ever had a bad cold will confirm how short of flavor food becomes when his smelling organ is incapacitated. This organ's place is in the upper shaft of the nasal cavity.

When the vapors of volatile substances, such as those that wine is made of, reach it, their traits are scanned and instantly reported to the brain by a fine frond of nerves. This is one of the oldest of man's senses, one that from the very first in our search for food has helped us distinguish the wholesome from the rank. Because it has been so closely connected with our survival, the sense of smell, although it is as old as man's origins, has never withered. The association of smell and memory is keen, indelible, and capable of producing strong emotion. Who has not relived whole episodes of his life evoked by the smell of a particular perfume, of leaves moldering in the woods, of fresh-baked bread or cake, of sea air, of a wood fire? This miraculous sense can make tasters of us all.

Smell will tell us most of what we want to know about wine. It can tell us whether it is young, mature, or decrepit. Whether it is fine or coarse. Simple or complex. It gives us the measure of a wine and prepares us for the size of experience we are likely to have.

The other organs that we need for the complete appreciation of wine are our eyes and palate. Although their range is more limited, their function is equally important, and we shall soon see how they are employed.

At some point, what our organs tell us must be put into words if we want our mind to hold on to a wine's identity after it is beyond the reach of our senses. Here is where most of the difficulty lies.

The vocabulary of tasting seems very hard to relate to the sensations it arouses in one's nose and mouth. Adjectives such as *round*, *crisp*, *heavy*, *flabby*, *meaty*, *hollow* appear to describe substances very different from the liquid in a glass, while others such as *charming*, *awkward*, *subtle*, *shy*, *austere*, *forceful* seem more appropriate in characterizing human personalities than wine.

Tasting notes must frequently rely on metaphors, on expressions borrowed from the repertory of other senses; yet it is not as high-flown and baffling a business as it sounds. For thousands of people who deal not in metaphors, but in wine as a commodity that needs to be produced, bought and sold, tasting and its language are plain tools of trade. The process of tasting addresses itself to wine's basic attributes: appearance, odors, structure, style, and aftertaste. Certain terms that describe what is disclosed to our senses have gained general acceptance. These terms are useful because they help shape our responses into a conscious pattern of appreciation and touch off awareness by reminding us of what we are

looking for. As we become more experienced in identifying our sensations the appropriateness of the terms that describe them will become
more apparent.

APPEARANCE

We begin to taste wine by looking at it. Appearance is never conclusive,
except in the case of glaringly defective wines. It is the prologue to a
wine's performance, which may provide strong hints of both its failings
and its virtues.

What appearance speaks most clearly about is the state of development and conservation. Age brings darkness to the hues of white wines
and pallor to those of reds. The changes that the color of white wine
undergoes in successive stages of maturity can be compared to those of
silver when it is allowed to tarnish. It becomes a gradually darker yellow
that in the final manifestations of decrepitude deepens to amber and
eventually to dark brown. Dry Italian white wines that improve with age
are very rare, and an unexpectedly deep color warns us that what we are
about to taste may be oxidized and past its prime.

The colors of healthy white wines range from very pale with green
flashes, to yellow, to gold. What we can expect from a pale, greenish wine
is taste that is vigorous, fresh, tart, and slightly underripe.

Gold is the color of white wines that gleam with the luster of that
metal. It may vary from pale to yellow to deep gold. Full taste impressions may be expected, and a rich, glowing, deep gold prepares us for
what is likely to be a sweet wine with a honeyed aroma.

When the flashing lights of gold are missing, the color is called simply
yellow, which may be further described as pale or parchment yellow,
light yellow, straw, deep yellow. It is often the color of fruity wines from
the plains or low-altitude vineyards in warmer climates.

Young red wines should have a bright, purplish, peony hue. The
more intense and brilliant the purple, the more likely it is that we have
a wine from a cool climate, with good acid, and with a substantial period
of development ahead of it. When the tint shades toward a bluish violet,
the wine's road to maturity may be brief and uneventful. As a red wine
evolves, its color will become ruby or garnet and eventually brick red
at the edges or, as in a mature Chianti Classico, orange. In a well-made
venerable Barolo of good lineage much of the color drops out, and a
broad section of the rim will be transparent white. This is not a defect

in a well-rounded wine; we should be prepared for scents not of fresh fruit, but of spices, bark, and leather followed, perhaps, by luscious flavors. A leaner wine may be dried out, however, and what it may have to give us might be no more than the caramelized taste of prunes and tar.

There is often a relationship between the intensity of the color and of the aromas. From light-complexioned wines we may expect fresher, fruitier smells, while the deepest reds generate denser, heavier aromas.

Clarity and brightness are qualities required of all wines, white or red. Cloudiness is a defect except when it can be traced to shaken-up sediment, which, in Italian white wines, is hardly ever found. If it doesn't settle after the bottle has been left standing several hours, it is a serious problem. The causes may be a blunder at the wine cellar or poor storage, but the result is almost always bad wine.

Dullness is usually the symptom of insufficient acid. A wine that looks dull will taste the same.

The first approach in looking at wine should be at eye level, with a bright, but not too close source of light behind the glass. Lift the glass to your eyes, holding it straight and about one foot or less away; examine the wine for clarity and brightness, and form a general impression of its color. Next, place the glass on a table with a plain white ground beneath, and look into it from above, directing your gaze toward the very center. This is the most effective method I've found for distinguishing hue, intensity, and nuances. Concentrate on the fine shades of color, particularly if it is a red wine. To end your inspection, pick up the glass, tilt it, and look through it against a white surface. Scrutinize the color. In a fully matured red wine it may become brick red or orange as it approaches the edge, and at the very rim it may fade to white. A large white rim in a young wine shows lack of pigmentation and may predict meager taste sensations.

ODORS

Wine begins as grape juice, an agreeable but far from memorable beverage. When fermentation, one of nature's most mysterious processes, has transformed it, the juice becomes an alcoholic complex that will in time contain over three hundred compounds. Many of these substances can be perceived as scents that are remarkably like those of many varieties of flowers, fruits, and other organic matter. That these odors of the fields, orchards, and woods really exist in the wine rather than in our fancy has been confirmed not only by the independent experiences of professional tasters, but by chemical analyses; the same odor-producing compounds that many organic substances contain have been found in wine.

Using one's nose is the most elusive exercise in tasting. To harness this impetuous organ we need to learn how to add mindfulness to instinct. One difficulty is that the words that describe the scents usually reach us with more force than the scents themselves. Such words as *rose*, *violet*, *pepper*, *coffee* rush to our brain, arousing imperious sensations that do not seem quite to match the ethereal fragrances in wine that go by the same name.

Another problem is our impoverished store of remembered smells. The fragrances of honestly ripened fruit, of wild berries and mushrooms, of field flowers, of wood have been edited out of everyday experience and replaced by those of plastic film, metal foil, polymers, and acetate.

For many of us it will be necessary to replenish the depleted stores of our olfactory memory, conducting our noses through produce markets, gardens, fields, woods, wherever they can assemble the most varied collection of well-identified impressions. Most of what a wine has to tell is spoken by its odors. Smelling is the most intimate contact we have with wine, when we draw close to, as it were, its very breath.

Simple wines have simple smells. The odor of most young wines of modest but respectable background and of many wines from southern Italy can be described as vinous. It is that winy smell of grape aromas and other primary substances dissolved in alcohol.

More distinctive odors are found in wines made from superior grapes, mainly in the cooler zones of northwest and northeast Italy. These can be separated in two main groups, the odors of youth and those of maturity.

In its youth wine will smell of flowers and fresh fruit. It has been noted that white wines recall the fragrances of pale and yellow flowers and fruits, such as honeysuckle, acacia, and field flowers, yellow apples, lemon, and pineapple. Violet, rose, cherry, red currant, grenadine, and raspberry are characteristic of some of the fragrances in red wines. There are exceptions. The odor of banana is present not only in some white wines, but in a young, fruity red wine like Valpolicella.

As wine evolves in the bottle, the light, fresh odors are replaced by concentrated, intense ones. The ethereal scent of faded roses is typical of a fine, fully matured Barolo. Tender impressions of fresh fruit make way for the heavier ones of jam and dried fruit. An example is the aroma of dried figs in Amarone or old Chianti and of strawberry jam in Barbaresco. Toasted almonds or hazelnuts appear in the bouquet of a few long-lived white wines.

In carefully matured red wines of exceptional caliber, an entirely new and spicy series of scents emerges: leather, tobacco, tea, pepper, tar, bruised bark, fur, musk. Vanilla will be detected in those wines that have spent time in wood.

In its appeal to the nose, wine not only declares its virtues, but exposes its defects.

The smell of vinegar, at the instant it becomes perceptible, is a defect. So is mustiness, which can be charged to excessive storage in wood or to contact with the insides of a less than impeccable barrel. When compounded by slovenly cellar practices, mustiness may call to mind the smell of a barnyard. This happens not as infrequently as one would hope to some of the lower-end Piedmontese reds dumped on the market at a bargain price.

A vegetal smell like that of crushed grass is a blemish, but it must not be confused with desirable herbal fragrances, such as fern, mint, sage, or fennel. The stale, decayed smell of oxidation is not tolerable in table wine. In red wines, the odors of caramel and cooked prunes are the indication of a vacant old age. Overpowering earthiness, which one sometimes meets in older Italian reds, is not a virtue. At best, it's a show of coarseness.

Sulfur, a disinfectant used universally and sometimes too liberally, should never leave noticeable traces in the odor of wine. It often does, however, particularly in young white wines. Although it sometimes escapes the notice of those whose noses have been brought up on the acrid smells of city traffic, it can be extremely disagreeable. In most cases it disappears with vigorous swirling of the wine in the glass. Corkiness is more frequently talked about than actually encountered. A corked wine does not smell of cork, but of the invisible mold that attacks cork. It can be perceived as a sharp, foreign odor. The only remedy for it is to open another bottle.

It is not a good idea when we begin smelling a wine to start by violently swishing it inside the glass. Some of the most ethereal odors, which are characteristic of fine mature wines, are so volatile that they may be propelled beyond reach. Raise the glass to the nostrils without moving the wine around and perform a few side-to-side passes with the nose, breathing in the faint, but not imperceptible vapors that arise.

Some tasters in Piedmont hold the glass at waist level and begin smelling from there.

Next, rotate the glass gently, moistening its sides. For beginners, and those with a less than steady hand, it is best to rotate the glass while its base rests on the table. Dip your nose into the glass, drawing in the new and fuller succession of smells. This is also a good occasion to observe how the wine flows down the sides of the glass. If its trails, which are called legs, are thick and viscous, it is probably a full-bodied wine, either sweet or high in alcohol, or both.

Finally, rotate the glass vigorously and repeatedly, thoroughly coating its sides with wine. This will loosen and lift the heaviest smells. It may be necessary to do this more than once if the bottle has just been opened. Do not overtax your nose, however, especially if you are tasting more than one wine; it can be easily fatigued and its alertness impaired.

STRUCTURE

Our communion with wine concludes in the mouth. Here the preliminary impressions of our eyes and nose are confirmed or revised, and the weight, shape, class of a wine, all its beauties and shortcomings are made plain.

On the tongue all tastes are sorted into four basic sensations: saltiness, bitterness, sourness, sweetness. These impressions are palpable ones; when they are produced by wine, they give us a feel of its anatomy, its texture, its force. (All other manifestations of flavor are actually odors that we perceive through the mouth's rear access to the organ of smell.)

We can ignore saltiness, which is perceived along the left and right sides of the tongue, inasmuch as it is virtually nonexistent in Italian wines.

The sensations of bitterness, sourness, and sweetness are the ones we rely on to appreciate a wine's structure.

Bitterness, which in this context is better described as astringency, is produced by the tannin in wine. An astringent sensation is one in which the tissues of the tongue, gums, and insides of our cheeks contract and feel wrinkled, and saliva dries up. Wine picks up tannin from grape skins and from the wood of the barrels in which it has been aged. White wines are not usually permitted to ferment in the presence of grape skins, and modern Italian winemakers have almost completely eliminated wood containers for storing white wines. We should therefore expect to experience tannic astringency primarily when tasting red wines.

Sourness, or acidity, is a pricking sensation that stimulates flow of saliva. Many people confuse astringency with acidity. It is absolutely necessary to be able to tell the difference; if one can distinguish between the taste of strong tea and that of lemon juice, there can be no problem. Astringency gives us a puckering, binding, dried-up feeling; acidity a tingling, lively one. We shrink from tannin, while we quicken to acidity.

Sweetness is detected by the tip of the tongue. In addition to the explicit sweetness of sugary wines, there is a kindred sensation produced by the various alcohols in completely dry wines, a sensation of viscosity, of softness. In warm-climate wines that are deficient in acid it is accentuated to the point of flabbiness, while in harmonious, very great wines from temperate zones it is felt as unctuousness, or what in Burgundy is called fat. Other sweet sensations that do not come from sugar are those that communicate an impression of fruit, and these as well are picked up on the tip of the tongue. Fruity sensations, like alcoholic ones, can be palpably soft, and for this reason a wine with substantial fruit is sometimes described as chewy or meaty.

The basic components of wine's anatomy detected by the mouth are tannin, acid, and alcohol. As their attributes become familiar, many inscrutable tasting terms begin to speak clearly.

Tannin is the muscle and sinew; acid the nerve, the vital force; alcohol the soft tissue, the body and warmth.

When sensations of tannin and acid are dominant, the terms unbending and hard are appropriate, as in describing young Barberas from Piedmont. A tilt toward tannin produces austerity; toward acid, angularity. When acid alone holds the field, the result may be called raw, sour, sharp. Lacking acid, wine will be dull, lifeless, empty.

In describing a wine whose alcohol is accompanied by adequate acid and tannin, the following terms can be used: velvety, supple, unctuous, round, generous, full. Their progression reflects a gradually increasing ascendancy of alcohol. If the balance tips decidedly toward alcohol, the wine may be vinous, heavy, hot; if combined with a deficiency of acid, it may become flabby or pasty. With insufficient alcohol, wine may become thin, short, feeble.

Big red wines will taste hard in their youth because impressions of tannin override all others. Ideally, most of the tannin should drop out in time and the fruit come forward, supported by the vigor of acid and the warmth of alcohol. In that happy event we would find the wine to be supple, round, opulent, profound, majestic. With more assertive tannin, it could be robust, sinewy, forceful. If the tannin outlasts fruit, the wine may be described as hard, harsh, astringent, woody, dry.

In a perfectly balanced red wine there is just enough tannin to confer firmness, but not roughness, and the warm, soft flow of alcohol is animated by sufficient acid. In Italian white wines, where there is rarely any tannin, we want enough acid for freshness and sprightliness and enough alcohol for suppleness.

Laboratory analysis may help winemakers to work toward, but never to determine, balance and harmony in wine. Wines with different proportions of alcohol and acid may taste equally well balanced. This is a matter for aesthetic judgment, an act that must take place entirely in the mouth.

STYLE

There is a stage beyond simple observation of acidity, body, astringency, and fruit. It's the stage when we become aware of wine's style. Style in wine, as in singing, writing, or personal deportment, rests not in its separate parts, but in how they are deployed. How does it deliver impressions of warmth, softness, flavor, vivacity? How do these play on each other? With what rhythm and emphasis do they alternate and connect?

Style is perceived as all of a wine's character unfolds and blooms in the mouth, a development French tasters call *épanouissement*. Words that describe style are necessarily less specific than those that describe taste, but if the concept of style is understood and experienced, they need not be any the less accurate. Some favorable terms are subtle, charming, graceful, straightforward, elegant, dynamic, assertive. Unfavorable ones: coarse, vulgar, sluggish, ordinary, blunt, dull, toneless, uncouth.

AFTERTASTE

Our final and perhaps most exquisite experience of wine comes when it is no longer there. As we swallow, volatile elements rise from the back of the throat into the upper nasal cavity, pervading it with renewed and intensified impressions of the wine's fragrances. Some taste sensations linger inside the mouth. Then comes the aftertaste, the moment in which all that we have smelled and tasted fits together and we understand the wine as a whole.

Aftertaste can be compared to what happens when a person we have been close to has just left. As the compelling stimulus of its presence is withdrawn, it is replaced in us by an inner awareness that is quiet, eloquent, and pervasive.

When, in a fine wine, aftertaste is consistent with all the taste sensations that preceded it, wine possesses finesse. The idea of finesse is charged with emotion and so are the words that describe it. Wine with finesse may be said to have breeding, refinement, grandeur, nobility. A wine that disappoints in the aftertaste may be labeled vulgar, crude, or clumsy.

WINE TYPE

We should not be disappointed if our first thoughtful efforts at tasting do not yield too much detailed information. Without a little practice, odors can be elusive and hard to put a name to; taste sensations are not as easy to sort out in the mouth as they are to set down on a page. And if the signals we pick up are very weak, it may just be because the wine doesn't have very much to say. But even meager and blurred impressions can provide us with a general awareness of the type of wine we are tasting or drinking. This is the most necessary and basic assessment we can make.

Before we attempt to discriminate between similar wines, and a long step before we decide whether we even like a wine or not, we should try to discover whether the wine before us runs true to type, whether it fulfills the expectations associated with its character. It does not increase our understanding to fault a young Chianti for prickliness, a Barolo for intensity and corpulence, an Asti Spumante for sweetness, a Trebbiano for tartness, a Bardolino for its lack of color and force. These are precisely the sensations we must expect from them. At this stage of evaluation it is more to our advantage to acknowledge a wine's claims to character, to recognize its essential traits, than to judge it arbitrarily by our likes and dislikes. It is after we know what to expect that we can make an informed choice and can pick the wine to suit our taste and grace the moment of consumption.

Terms and Usages
Employed in this Book

D.O.C. The abbreviation of *Denominazione di Origine Controllata,* Italy's version of France's *Appellation d'Origine Contrôlée* law. It controls the geographic origin, grape variety, yields per acre, methods of vinification, alcohol level, and aging requirements for qualifying wines.

D.O.C.G. A stricter version of D.O.C., which will begin to take effect in 1982 for Vino Nobile di Montepulciano, in 1984 for Barbaresco and Barolo, and in 1985 for Brunello di Montalcino.

VINO DA TAVOLA All the wines without a D.O.C. appellation. A rare few are as good as or better than most D.O.C. wines.

Below each wine name, in parentheses, appear its appellation status and the region of origin.

To avoid confusion between wine names and grape names, I have followed Italian practice, using capitals for the first and lower case for the second: for example, the wine, Barbera; the grape, barbera.

On pages 239-48 the reader will find a more complete explanation of the wine law and Italian wine terms.

[3]

THE RED WINES

OF ITALY

Almost every shade of experience one looks for in red wine can be found in Italian reds. They can be light and fresh or fruity and generous, powerful and full or supple and elegant, mellow or stern, racy or ethereal. There are wiry, dry wines and luscious, succulently sweet ones. Most are still, but they may also be slightly effervescent, frothy, or fully sparkling. There are wines to be consumed within six months of the vintage and others to be laid down for at least a decade.

The number of red grape varieties cultivated is enormous, more than two hundred, and providence has sown them with a prodigal hand over the Italian peninsula's full thousand-mile length and on its many islands. Vines grow luxuriantly everywhere, and there is hardly a plot that does not produce healthy fruit.

A few varieties are foreign transplants. Their names—cabernet sauvignon, cabernet franc, merlot, pinot noir—are already familiar to consumers of French and California wines. These are quite successful in Italy, principally in the Northeast, but they are not cultivated and are rarely vinified in the French tradition. Their style is usually suited to the simple requirements of everyday consumption; what an Italian Cabernet or Pinot Nero may lack in the subtle and elaborate sensations of the better bottlings of Bordeaux or Burgundy it makes up with an abundance of tender fruit and directness of flavor.

The great fascination of Italian reds is in the astonishingly varied achievements of the native grapes: nebbiolo, barbera, grignolino, dolcetto in Piedmont; schiava in Trentino–Alto Adige; Veneto's classic trio, corvina, molinara, and rondinella; sangiovese in central Italy; montepulciano and aglianico in the South, to cite only a few. The most important group of red wines are probably those from sangiovese and nebbiolo.

Sangiovese's reach and adaptability are without parallel. Its indelible presence, either as a 100 percent varietal or as a component of a blend, turns up in such different wines as the hearty and generous Sangiovese di Romagna; in all styles of Chianti, from the sprightly yearlings to the most stately Chianti Classico *riservas;* in the opulent Vino Nobile di Montepulciano; in the elegant Tignanello; in the stern Brunello di Montalcino; in some of the soft wines of Abruzzi, Apulia, and Calabria. To follow sangiovese in all its permutations is to discover how far and deep Italian red wines can range.

Of the two grapes, the scarcer and undoubtedly the more regal is nebbiolo. It is disinclined to enter into morganatic alliances outside the far North, where it reigns supreme and where, on occasion, it gives birth to those rarest of great wines, the ones that combine both power and finesse. In its native Piedmont the majesty of nebbiolo finds complete expression in such offspring as those princely twins, Barolo and Barbaresco, and a few of their siblings.

The notion that the best Italian reds are lesser wines than those of France or even California has enjoyed for too long more credit than it deserves. I am no stranger to the glories of Bordeaux, Burgundy, or the Napa Valley, yet I would not feel deprived if in their place I had to choose an equally fine-bred Barolo, or Amarone, or Taurasi, or one of the high-ranking sangiovese wines from central Italy.

That most Italian reds do not reach those heights cannot be disputed, but then neither do most red wines anywhere. On the other hand, in Italy it is a rare red wine indeed that tastes thin and mean, that fails to deliver a generous impression of fruit and ripeness.

That they are not even better than they are can be traced to several causes. For a long stretch of history wine has been an abundant, inexpensive, and casually consumed beverage, rather than the object of deliberate appreciation. It is only since the end of the Second World War that bottles bearing labels identifying the contents and provenance to a reasonable degree of reliability began to appear regularly on Italian tables. Wine, even of the most precious kind, was purchased in bulk and bottled at home. Crops are unquestionably too large. But the modest price that grapes bring and the loose standards of the cooperative cellars that buy most of them do not encourage farmers to curtail the easy yields that in a kind climate are so effortless to achieve. There has been too much emphasis on alcohol and too little on fragrance and balance. For many growers alcohol seems to be the equivalent of virility, and they will boast of grapes that produce 14 percent alcohol as they would of having fathered fourteen sons.

Many of these conditions still exist, most prevalently in the South and in the islands. A picture of quality in Italian red wines inevitably assumes a geographic shape. Southern and island reds deserve respect for the enormous improvement they have made in recent years. The better ones can be mouthfilling, juicy wines, and no one who has discovered and enjoyed them need be reluctant to admit it, for they are good standard fare. They cannot disappoint us as long as we limit our expectations to the frank flavor and vinousness they cleanly deliver.

For a broader range of sensations, however, we must raise our sights north of a line that can be drawn across the middle of the country, just south of Perugia, and principally to the products of vineyards on the slopes of Italy's central and northern hills. With few exceptions, it is there that we shall find red wines that command our attention for such qualities as charm, balance, length of flavor, lively character, complexity, or refinement. And it is mainly such wines that we shall proceed to examine in the pages that follow.

The Big Red Wines

The big reds are not mere heavyweights; they are wines whose best and most clearly articulated examples are characterized by complexity in odors and taste, by intensity and power, and are capable of delivering lasting impressions with elegance and authority. They are wines for attentive drinking, wines to be waited for, often raw in their youth, splendid in maturity.

FAMILIES OF BIG RED WINES

The Nebbiolo Family

If nebbiolo had not been such a stubborn homebody of a grape, it could have been more of a household word among wine drinkers. Unlike the French varietals of comparable class, cabernet sauvignon and pinot noir, nebbiolo has not taken root outside Italy, where it must share attention with a distracting multitude of other grapes. Even in Italy, it has not gone far beyond the borders of its native Piedmont. Yet nebbiolo is responsible for some of the world's most imposing reds, particularly those produced near Alba, long-lived wines of great depth, gracious style, and enveloping, elaborate taste.

Alba is also known for another sense-stirring product that has never flourished abroad, the potently aromatic white truffle. It makes one wonder whether it is through a sense of irony, or even mischief, that nature has bestowed on a region of long winters bracketed by weeks of fog and mist, whose people are stolid, matter-of-fact, and more likely to sin the sins of calculation than those of abandon, such unlikely and seductive gifts.

In Piedmont nebbiolo gives its best, fathering a majestic brood led by Barolo and Barbaresco. Other members of this family, the cadet branch so to speak, among whom one finds Ghemme, Carema, Donnaz, the reds of Valtellina, among others, all of which are lighter, less complex, or simply less grand than those about to be described here, have been grouped in the category of medium-range reds discussed on pages 90-8.

BAROLO AND BARBARESCO

Barolo and Barbaresco take their names from two small villages in the heart of their respective growing areas, Barolo lying a few miles southwest of Alba, the white truffle capital, and Barbaresco just north of the town. In both zones, the nebbiolo grape is grown on the upper portion of sunny slopes, while the lower part of the same slopes is given over to barbera or muscat. The hills of Barolo are distinctly steeper and more sharply humped, while those of Barbaresco are rounder, softer, and prettier, a difference of terrain that carries through into the character of the two wines.

The sensual and intellectual pleasures one can expect from the best examples of either wine can be intense, but they may not be immediately accessible to those just beginning to enjoy wine. These are large, prepossessing reds, whose multiple enticements are often enclosed by a firm, ungiving body. They are at the summit of wine experience and should be considered as the climax rather than the point of departure of one's exploration of wine.

❧ Barolo ❧

(D.O.C., TO BE D.O.C.G. IN 1984, PIEDMONT)

Barolo is in every way the senior of the two, and, alphabetical order notwithstanding, it will precede Barbaresco in this discussion. It was probably the first wine in Italy to have been bottled and labeled. It was indisputably the first to have been vinified completely dry, following the example of the French.

Although it has always been too scarce, too dear, too much of a mouthful to become anyone's everyday beverage, Barolo has always been the one red wine to turn to in Italy when one looked for grandeur, for a wine able to temper force with refinement. When its credentials are impeccable—a fortunate vintage year, a choice vineyard, thoughtful vinification, well-husbanded maturation—Barolo has few peers among the world's great wines.

Its first address to the nose and palate is undeniably powerful. The initial impression of alcohol, which makes one think of cognac, gives way to an intricate succession of odors. A heavy, dense, rubbery scent of tar muscles past the ethereal ones of faded rose, violet, and almond. The intriguing alternation of light and heavy aromas, flowery and tarry, is one through which we learn to identify not only Barolo, but most wines from the nebbiolo grape. In a fully mature Barolo it is accompanied by other sensations that may recall tree bark, leather, pepper, or tobacco.

The impact in the mouth is large, but not ponderous. The drama of Barolo's power is that it manages its great girth with supple and buoyant grace. The flavors bloom in the palate, conveying even in very advanced age an opulent and delectable impression of fruit. The aftertaste fades with haunting slowness, releasing as it retreats a seemingly indelible last emanation of flavor.

The controlled appellation requirements for Barolo are among the most stringent for any wine. It must be a 100 percent varietal: Only nebbiolo grapes grown in the restricted production zone may be used, without even minimal additions of other grapes or musts. It must be aged three years before it is released, with at least two of those years in wood. It must achieve a natural minimum alcohol level of 13 percent; the use of sugar to boost alcohol is not permitted in Italy.

D.O.C. standards are based on the original recommendations of producers, and those of Barolo reflect a traditional, late nineteenth-century approach about which there is today much controversy.

The two main schools of thought on how to make Barolo are derived from notions of winemaking and taste concepts that may be described as the old guard and the contemporary. Those who have had Barolo from a variety of producers are likely to have experienced examples of both.

The old guard emphasizes aging in wood. It is not uncommon for wine made in this style to spend seven or eight years in the barrel. Sometimes even longer. That some Barolos survive such long imprisonment and manage to be not only drinkable but interesting is a tribute less to the winemaker than to the extraordinary natural vigor of the wine. In many cases it is too long a sleep, during which oakiness, astringency, and earthiness overwhelm and replace other qualities.

The more forward-looking producers believe that an elegant and harmonious Barolo is one whose maturity is mainly achieved in the bottle. They point out that the endurance of the wine varies from vintage to vintage and from vineyard to vineyard and therefore claim a wine-maker's prerogative to decide when a wine needs more wood age and when less. The thin wine made in the 1973 vintage probably should have had little or no barrel aging and those of the 1975, 1976, and 1977 harvests less than the law required.

Vintage years are as uncertain in Piedmont as they are in Burgundy, Bordeaux, the Rhine, or any other temperate zone. It is the price growers must pay for the privilege of producing fine wines, and it can be a very steep price sometimes. In the grim year of 1972 the entire production of Barolo and Barbaresco was voluntarily declassified, and not a drop of wine was sold with either appellation. One will rarely find, in other areas, instances of such a collective sacrifice in defense of a wine's good name.

Barolo should not be thought of as a single wine issuing from a large communal plot. There are townships, and vineyard sites within each township, where differences of soil endow their wines with perceptible differences in character. With a great wine such as Barolo these differences are sufficiently interesting to make it worth our while to trace their source.

The entire production zone is of glacial origin with moderately loose, calcareous soil that in the best areas contains a high proportion of quartz-rich sand. Two valleys separate the huddled rows of hills bearing nebbiolo on the upper part of their sunniest sides. One is the valley of Serralunga; the other, the valley of Barolo.

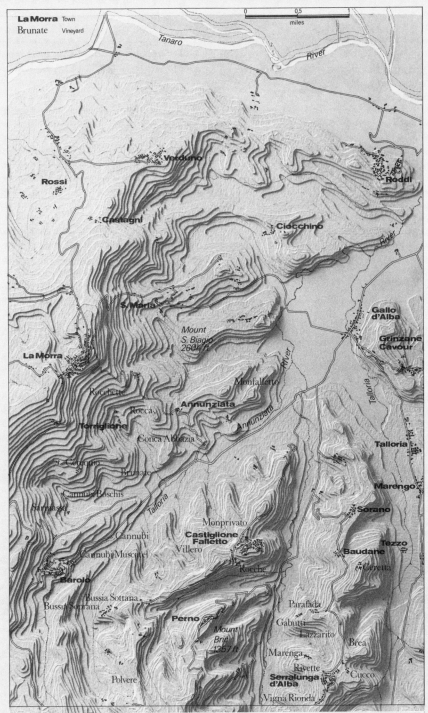

The slopes of the Barolo production zone, its townships and principal vineyard sites. See regional map of Piedmont, page 261.

Wines from the townships in the valley of Serralunga are the most muscular, exceptionally long-lived and full, with dense plummy flavors, great power, and persistent aftertaste. The most important towns in this valley are Serralunga, Castiglione Falletto, and Monforte, with the following great vineyards:

in Serralunga—Vigna Rionda, Gabutti-Parafada, Baudana, Marenga, Rivette, Cucco, Lazzarino, Ceretta, Brea

in Castiglione Falletto—Monprivato, Rocche, Villero

in Monforte—Bussia Soprana, Bussia Sottana, Pian della Polvere, Perno

Wines from the valley of Barolo are more soft-spoken; they are exceptionally velvety, fragrant, and slightly lower in alcohol than those of Serralunga. The most important towns are Barolo itself and La Morra. Their finest vineyards are

in Barolo—Cannubi, Cannubi Boschis, Cannubi Muscatel, Sarmassa, Brunate, Cerequio (The last two named overlap into the township of La Morra.)

in La Morra—Monfalletto, Rocchette, Rocche, Conca dell'Abbazia dell'Annunziata

Cannubi, although in the township of Barolo, stands geographically apart, between the valley of Serralunga and the valley of Barolo. It is a perfectly proportioned cone of a hill that has gently sloping sides and combines the finest characteristics of both valleys. Its wine has long been acknowledged to be the most harmonious and complete example of Barolo.

Although wine from Cannubi was labeled as such as far back as the 1750s and the merits of all the fine growths have been recognized locally for generations, it is only recently that a few producers and growers have begun to vinify, bottle, and label wines from single estates. Traditionally the production of Barolo has been in the hands of large shippers who buy grapes from farmers and vinify them or even buy finished wine in bulk, then age, assemble, and blend the different lots to suit their house style, and bottle the result under their own labels. This is not necessarily a less valid method of turning out great wine than estate-bottling, particularly when the palate guiding the operation is a gifted one. The substantial difference is that in the case of "assembled" wines one relies on the skills of the shipper, skills that are only as durable as the men who practice them. In estate-bottling the ability of the winemaker is not any less important, but it is backed up by the imperishable soil and microclimate of a specific plot.

Although the vineyard site on Barolo labels is not cited as often as one would like, it is still more common there than with any other wine in Italy. Most of the following recommended producers do note it, sometimes prefacing the vineyard with the word *bricco,* which is Piedmontese for the crown of a hill: Fratelli Barale, Cavallotto, Ceretto, Elvio Cogno, Aldo Conterno, Giacomo Conterno, Franco Fiorina, Fontanafredda, Bruno Giacosa, Cantina Mascarello, Mauro Mascarello (for Giuseppe Mascarello), Valentino Migliorini, Fratelli Oddero, Giovanni Pozzetti, Prunotto, Renato Ratti, Giuseppe Rinaldi, Bricco Rocche (a separate label used by Ceretto for its premium bottlings), Gigi Rosso, Paolo Scavino, Filippo Sobrero, Terre del Barolo, Accademia Torregiorgi, Vietti.

VINTAGES:
Acceptable Years: 1968, 1969, 1981
Good Years: 1964, 1965, 1967, 1970, 1974, 1979, 1980, 1983
Great Years: 1947, 1958, 1961, 1971, 1978, 1982

❧ *Barbaresco* ☙
(D.O.C., TO BE D.O.C.G. IN 1984, PIEDMONT)

Barbaresco was born into the nebbiolo clan in the 1890s as Barolo's lesser and somewhat delayed twin. For most of its short history, Barbaresco has lived in the shadow of its brother, but since the 1950s it has emerged, achieving the recognition and independent status that its distinct and ingratiating personality deserved.

The D.O.C. requirements for Barbaresco are similar to those of Barolo, except that Barbaresco can be released for sale after only two years, with only one year in wood, and with 12½ percent alcohol instead of Barolo's 13 percent.

When true to type, Barbaresco does not show the austerity, the muscle of Barolo. Its salient characteristic is richness of flavor delivered by a full, robust, yet velvety body. In a blind tasting of Barolos, drop in a Barbaresco and it will declare its presence by its ample and soft approach, its pronounced scent of violets, and, when fully mature, a

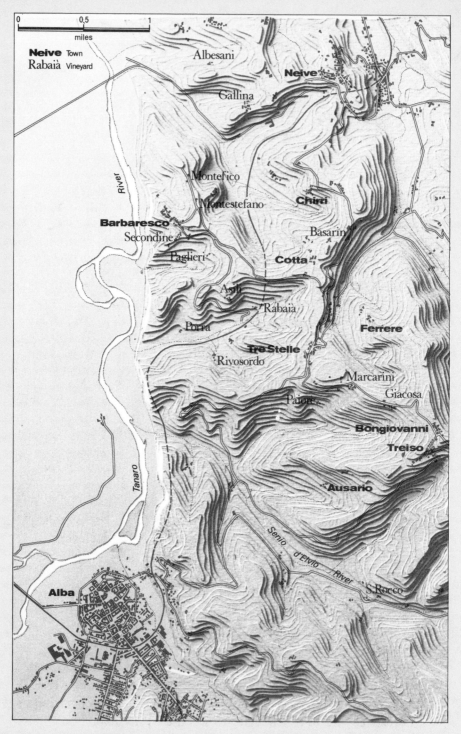

The principal towns of the Barbaresco production zone and its finest vineyards. See regional map of Piedmont, page 261.

suggestion of strawberry jam that hovers in the bouquet and is confirmed in the mouth and in the aftertaste. What Barbaresco lacks of Barolo's resonance and intensity, it makes up in warmth and charm. While it is a more amiable and less complex wine, it is by no means a slighter one.

The four townships where Barbaresco is produced are Alba, Neive, Barbaresco, and Treiso. Alba is of negligible interest, with very small acreage and no single notable vineyard. In the other three townships, the following vineyards stand out:

Neive—Gallina, Albesani, Basarin

Barbaresco—Rabajà, Asili, Paglieri, Montefico, Rivosordo, Porra, Secondine, Montestefano

Treiso—Pajorè, Marcarini, Giacosa (The last should not be confused with the producer of the same name.)

Some of the best producers of Barbaresco are Castello di Neive, Ceretto (who also bottle under a separate label, Bricco Asili, its choicest Barbaresco, made from grapes grown on the uppermost section of the Asili site), Marchesi di Gresy, Franco Fiorina, Bruno Giacosa, Cantina del Glicine, Giovannini Moresco, Fratelli Oddero, Parroco di Neive, Produttori del Barbaresco, Prunotto, Alfredo e Giovanni Roagna.

One cannot mention Barbaresco producers without bringing up Angelo Gaja, the largest and best known. His wines, especially the ones from single vineyards, Sorì Tildin and Sorì San Lorenzo, enjoy the most extravagant praise and prices. They are wines made with intense care and with the single-minded objective of making them as big and full and ripe as possible. I cannot deny that he succeeds, but, though mine may be the lone dissenting voice, I cannot bring myself to admire them wholeheartedly. Gaja's wine does not seem to me to give what one most looks for in Barbaresco. It attempts to outmuscle Barolo, but fails to achieve the gracefulness that makes Barbaresco's natural endowment of flavor and body stylish rather than pushy.

VINTAGES: Barbaresco matures and declines decidedly earlier than Barolo. Its optimum development comes between the fifth and eighth year, but it will keep up to a decade, with the usual adjustment upwards or downwards that should be made for an exceptionally good or weak year.
Acceptable Years: 1967, 1968, 1969, 1980, 1981
Good Years: 1970, 1974, 1979, 1983
Great Years: 1964, 1971, 1978, 1982

❧ *Gattinara* ☙
(D.O.C., PIEDMONT)

In writing about Gattinara, one risks doing an an injustice either to the reader or to the wine. To describe Gattinara as the wine it could be, and sometimes is, may excite expectations rarely fulfilled by the bottles on merchants' shelves. But if we reach only for what comes readily to hand, we shall have little to say of Gattinara's potential as a wine of world-class rank.

In Gattinara we have the one great red of Italy whose natural endowments could place it in a small company of wines that combine length of taste with charm and elegance, wines that are warm and full without being coarse, at once dramatic and refined.

The nebbiolo grape of which it is made is grown on the lean, porphyry- and quartz-freighted soil of hillside vineyards surrounding the village of Gattinara in northeastern Piedmont. No more than 195 acres of vineyards altogether have been registered as qualified to produce Gattinara, one of the smallest areas mapped out by the controlled origin wine statute. Many of these vineyards have been newly planted. For years the quantity of Gattinara from all producers did not exceed twenty thousand cases annually, but recently the figure has more than doubled. Here perhaps is one of the clues to the diluted quality of the wine.

At no time has the quantity of fine Gattinara ever been equal to the demand generated by its reputation. The natural, if short-sighted, response has been to concentrate on production rather than quality. Yields per acre strain the already too permissive limits of the D.O.C. laws. And another provision of the law that allows blending the noble nebbiolo with the plain but abundantly producing bonarda grape is, unfortunately, more fully observed than a strong concern for quality should permit. Moreover, the winemaking traditions in Gattinara appear not to have fostered that attention to grape quality and the vigilance in the cellar that have brought such closely related wines as Barolo and Barbaresco to lofty heights.

I do not want to question the taste of those who have been drinking Gattinara and have found it good. Much of it is indeed good, for the inherent class of the wine somehow shows through, however feebly. But it could be so much better; it could be exalted. My hope is that the tangible recognition that the marketplace is ready to award exceptional wines, wherever they may come from, will encourage producers to make a Gattinara as distinguished as its name.

There may, in fact, be such a wine forthcoming from a producer called Le Colline. Le Colline has recently resumed production of Monsecco, a legendary Gattinara made to exacting standards by Count Ravizza. Ravizza stopped making Monsecco in 1977, but his winemaker, Luigi Gerli, has taken over the cellars and vineyards and assures me the new edition of Monsecco will be as sumptuous as the old.

Another producer worth watching is Antoniolo, whose recent bottlings show strong promise.

VINTAGES: Gattinara is capable of long life, but one would have to specify which Gattinara. Past versions of Monsecco would qualify. So would a 1952 Gattinara I own, a few bottles of which I have been opening every year for the past four. Each was in stupendous good health, but unfortunately none carries the name of the producer. The Gattinara now commercially available is at the top of its form as early as its sixth year and should not be kept much longer than twelve.

Acceptable Years: 1967, 1975, 1978, 1980, 1981
Good Years: 1955, 1958, 1968, 1969, 1970, 1976, 1979, 1982, 1983
Great Years: 1952, 1964, 1974

Spanna
(VINO DA TAVOLA, PIEDMONT)

A great many people drink Spanna, but hardly anyone talks about it. Of all the proud offspring sired by the nebbiolo grape Spanna is the outcast child, the one that has never been officially acknowledged. The name *spanna* is itself a synonym of *nebbiolo,* a dialect word of uncertain origin used in Piedmont's northeast province of Novara. As a wine name it has never been recognized by the D.O.C. appellation of origin statute, and so it has had to make its way alone, without the support of its family connections. Nevertheless, when it is honestly made, it is capable of showing all the hereditary class of its nebbiolo parentage.

In good examples of Spanna, the characteristics associated with nebbiolo—earth aromas upheld by full and generous taste—are forcefully present. What it may lack of the suppleness of Barbaresco or the profundity of Barolo it replaces with expansive flavors, sustained by a robust and sinewy constitution, and a suitably rich aftertaste.

Very long barrel aging is standard practice in making Spanna. In 1974 I saw wine from the great 1964 vintage still in wood. In poorer years, of course, it is bottled earlier, but even so, dryness and astringency can be expected of this wine. In some of the less fastidiously aged examples, musty and oxidized odors are not as infrequent as one would like.

The production of Spanna is not regulated either by the D.O.C. laws or by clearly articulated local traditions, so that one must choose the maker with great care. One of the most consistent is the house of Antonio Vallana, whose wines often enough show well in blind tastings against Barolo or Barbaresco. It was Raimondo Vallana who showed me how to begin to inhale a wine's smells from a distance, holding the glass at waist level. It is not as taxing an exercise as might appear when the aromas are the emphatic ones of a good Spanna.

Vallana used to ship separate bottlings from single vineyards, but these are now blended and sold as one wine. Other good producers are Antoniolo, Dessilani, and Ermanno Rivetti.

VINTAGES: Spanna is not made to be enjoyed young. It has great lasting power, and I have had bottles from the 1930s and 1940s that had vigor to spare.
Acceptable Years: 1962, 1965, 1969, 1975, 1981
Good Years: 1958, 1967, 1968, 1970, 1976, 1978, 1979, 1980, 1982, 1983
Great Years: 1955, 1961, 1964, 1974

The Sangiovese Family

Sangiovese may not be a familiar name to wine drinkers outside Italy, yet it is the fundamental grape in the one wine that for generations was the best-known (and, in its straw-covered flask, the universal symbol for) Italian wine: Chianti.

Sangiovese is not just the basic grape of which Chianti is made; it is the only grape prescribed by the D.O.C. law as the main or sole component of all controlled appellation red wines in the central Italian regions of Tuscany and Umbria. I don't know whether any other single varietal in the world has uncontested dominion over such a vast production area. Furthermore, it is the principal grape of Romagna, whose Sangiovese di Romagna is described on page 106, and it is planted in more than half of Italy's ninety-five provinces, finding its way into the blends of dozens of wines, from north to south.

What it is that has made this blue-black grape so predominant is hard to say. It is a hardy vine, producing abundant quantities of good-size berries with high levels of sugar and acidity. When it is grown and vinified without special care, it makes a rough, inelegant wine, coarse in flavor, harsh in aftertaste. It is then the epitome of the crude, peasant's wine in whose very frankness lay its primitive appeal.

If one still finds evidence of that bruising, peasant taste in much Chianti and other central Italian reds—and it must be admitted that one does—it is a manifestation of the old sangiovese character coming through, the rough grain coming to the surface. And even in the most distinguished members of this family, particularly those subjected to excessive barrel age, one should be prepared to meet on occasion a certain unevenness, threads of coarse homespun within the silk.

Nevertheless, through much hard work some of Italy's most celebrated wines have issued from this grape, and specifically from the large-berried variety known as sangioveto grosso. However humble sangiovese's origin, by virtue of the remarkable wines it has fathered, its right to join the ranks of noble grapes cannot be denied.

As I have done with nebbiolo, I have distributed sangiovese wines among the the categories of Big and Medium-Range Reds, limiting the pages that follow to the nobler members of the family. Moreover, I have divided one wine, Chianti, into three: one, qualified as *riserva* and groomed to achieve complexity through slow development, is discussed here; another, a Chianti of middle weight, is with the sangiovese wines grouped in the Medium-Range category; the third Chianti, produced for early and uncontemplative consumption, is in the Light Red category. I hope that in organizing the material as I have done, differences that have been blurred in the past will now, through the space that has been placed between them, become more distinct.

❧ Chianti Classico Riserva ❧
(D.O.C., SLATED FOR D.O.C.G., TUSCANY)

What Is Chianti?

We have been accustomed to think of all that is Tuscan as the product of unshakable tradition, but there is no wine in Italy that has been so strongly buffeted by controversy as Chianti.

Chianti is a blend of grapes, and one of the controversies is about the composition of the blend. The D.O.C. law requires the planting of two varieties of red grapes—sangiovese and canaiolo—and of two varieties of white grapes—trebbiano and malvasia—in all Chianti vineyards. Red grapes account for more than 80 percent of the total. Of these the dominant one is sangiovese, to which one can attribute the flavor, the authority, the body, the overall impact, and much of the flowery fragrance that are characteristic of Chianti. The other red grape, canaiolo, is there to round off sangiovese's angularity, to soften some of its thrust.

The white grapes, trebbiano and malvasia, are added in hope that they will contribute brightness to the color, charm to the bouquet, freshness and vivacity to the taste.

This formula was supposedly developed in the nineteenth century by Baron Ricasoli at his castle in Brolio. Actually, Ricasoli had recommended adding just one white grape, malvasia, and then only for wines to be consumed young.

Many producers have lobbied for revisions in the law that would permit the vinification of Chianti with little or no white grapes or at least without trebbiano. They point out that trebbiano (known in France, where it is distilled for Cognac, as ugni blanc or st.-émilion) is an undistinguished varietal, that it makes Chianti sharp and hollow, that it drains Chianti of color and undermines its balance. These are defects that winemakers must then attempt to correct, within the limits prescribed by the D.O.C. law, through the addition of concentrated musts or deeply colored grapes from the South, which in turn dilute Chianti's character.

In practice, producers of the finest Chianti, backed by the recommendations of their own consortiums, are reshuffling the red grape/white grape proportions to suit their understanding of what Chianti should taste like. More sangiovese and less trebbiano are going into the fermentation tanks, and the improvement in color, constitution, and tasting qualities of their wines is notable. When the D.O.C.G. designation for Chianti becomes effective, producers will be permitted to reduce the proportion of white grapes to as little as 5 percent.

Another controversy is stirred up by a practice special to Chianti and known as *governo alla toscana. Governo,* an optional, but until recently a universally employed, technique, is used to revive the fermentation of the wine after the first tumultuous action of the yeasts has subsided. At harvest time a small quantity of choice, perfectly ripened grapes is set aside and spread on straw mats to dry. When they are partly shriveled, they are crushed; and as soon as they begin to ferment, they are added to the wine in the tank. It is a little like adding fresh, dry tinder to an ebbing fire.

Fermentation is not yet a completely unraveled mystery, and not all that happens inside the tank during *governo* is perfectly understood. What we know is that *governo* does produce a darker, softer, less acidic, more perfumed wine. It also accelerates its development. When the wine is bottled young, trapping some of the gas generated by *governo*, it is sprightly, fruity, and delicious. Known as Chianti *di pronta beva*, this style of Chianti is described on pages 133-4.

It is often stated, incorrectly, that *governo* is suitable only for producing the spritzy, fast-fading version of Chianti. I am acquainted with many producers who use *governo* even for *riservas*. And others who had abandoned the practice are resuming it, despite the added cost. Since *governo* does hasten Chianti's maturity, it should be omitted in light years. But well-born wines that have undergone *governo* seem to offer more in the way of fragrance and roundness than those produced without it.

Aging is one more subject on which there is no common agreement. The law does not make barrel aging mandatory, as it does for some other Italian red wines, and, theoretically, a producer who wanted to could bottle Chianti that never had been in wood. Mass-produced Chianti is handled just in this manner and is none the worse for it. A *riserva*, however, is not known to travel the road from fermentation tank to bottle without a stop in a barrel. In some wineries it may stay for as little as six months; in others, for years. How much wood age is desirable is a style concept that varies from producer to producer. It is a fact, however, that what Chianti needs most is to divest itself of astringency and to hold on to all the fruit it can, and neither of these objectives is compatible with prolonged aging in wood.

The Meaning of Riserva

I had long been aware of the difference in taste between a standard Chianti and a Chianti *riserva*, but until a few years ago I attributed it to the greater age of the *riserva*. That the two wines are different from birth became clear to me after a visit to the cellars of Fonterutoli.

Fonterutoli is a miniature and nearly intact example of the classic, small Tuscan hill town. One brief road that appears to materialize out of the fields, and soon disappears into them, curves along the brow of a hill. Lining both sides of it are the severe stone faces of Tuscan houses. At one end, the church. Just before it, a narrow branch of the main street lead to the great house, *la villa*. From the terrace one looks down past the hill tops, fields, vineyards, and olive trees to an animated reddish assemblage of roofs and towers in the far distance. It is Siena.

I was there to meet Lapo Mazzei, president of the Chianti Classico consortium, whose family has been making wine in Fonterutoli since the early 1400s.

When Mazzei came in, we briefly talked about consortium policies; then he set up the glasses and proceeded to pour Chianti from several vintages. Among them were two very young wines, not six months old, from separate lots of the same vintage. One was pale, thin, sharp, and not too far away from being ready for consumption as a fresh, carafe wine. The other was a deep, blackish red, with a penetrating aroma, and beneath the harsh, raw impression of astringency, dense and profound sensations of fruit came through. I asked Mazzei about the second wine and he replied, "It's my candidate for *riserva*."

Riserva is a term whose use is restricted by the Italian wine law to those wines that have had extra aging. For a Chianti, it means three years' minimum, either in wood or in bottle, at the discretion of the producer. A Chianti *riserva* is not merely a wine that has been hanging around longer. It is a special kind of Chianti. Unlike the standard version, it cannot be made every year. For a successful *riserva* one must set aside the choicest grapes picked during a better-than-average harvest. And even then one can't be sure. Sometimes the decision that a wine will make it as a *riserva* won't be taken until it has had one or two years to develop and show its potential.

A *riserva* is not, however, automatically a guarantee of quality; it cannot alone compensate for the variables in vineyard class and winemaking ability. But by and large, only those producers who have the raw material that will justify additional labor and tied-up capital, and will support the expectation of a premium selling price, will make a *riserva*.

What should we expect from a Chianti *riserva?* Let us make some large assumptions: that it comes from a fine vineyard, that it has been competently vinified and carefully aged, and that it is fully mature.

Its color will be a luminous garnet, more or less intense according to the vintage year and turning to orange at the edge. The immediately perceptible scents in its bouquet will be those of violet and iris, making way for oak, dried fruit, pepper, and such herbs as sage or fennel. It is one of the most flowery and seductively spiced bouquets in Italian red wine. The taste will be that of a firm, vigorous, assertive wine, sustained by adequate, if not overabundant, fruit. Very fine examples cushion their impact with a coat of velvet, but delicacy and reticence are not qualities one can expect of Chianti, even one of *riserva* class. While we look to Chianti for authoritative, powerful taste sensations, we must also set our palate for the energetic thrust with which they will be delivered.

The Chianti Classico Production Zone

Chianti Classico is a controlled geographic expression applied to the wine produced in a zone that begins immediately below Florence and stops just short of Siena.

Before it was a wine, Chianti was the name of a military league that bound the towns of Radda, Gaiole, and Castellina. The dust from their days of derring-do has long since settled between some of history's least-consulted pages, but the name of their league, with the qualification *classico* tacked on, has become the controlled appellation of a 430-square-mile territory.

Much of it is mountains, crags, brush, and woods, but below the forest line there are the olive groves, the cypresses, the castles, the stone farmhouses, composing still upon the ups and downs of bosomy slopes a fifteenth-century landscape. What has changed since then is the look of the vineyards: The vines are seldom strung now, as they were until a few decades ago, from tree trunk to tree trunk, but march along in close-set, regimented rows that engrave a new, linear geometry upon the ancient hills.

In Chianti they say you can make wine from rocks, sand, or clay. Chianti born in rocky soil is supposed to be the firmest, slowest to mature, while clay produces softer wine that is quicker to come round and quicker to expire. Sand is for wines of immediate appeal, to be consumed within the year following the harvest.

This may be true as far as it goes, but aside from the fact that one can't ask for a soil analysis before buying a bottle, it does not take into account that soil composition varies even within the same vineyard and that other factors contribute to wine character: exposure, altitude, microclimate, vintage year, and, ultimately, individual styles of winemaking.

A more manageable way to deal with the hundreds of Chianti Classico estates is to sort them out according to the nine townships where they are all located, just as in Bordeaux one traces a classified growth to the commune where it is produced. The township provides the context wherein we can comfortably place a Chianti Classico; once we are familiar with its basic identity, we can, with more assurance, go on to make relevant assessments of individual character.

Geographic origin tells us little, unfortunately, about the wine from large shippers and bottlers, who assemble their Chianti with the product of various zones. We are primarily interested, here, in estate-bottled Chianti Classico which identifies on the label the township, or even a specific locality within it, where the wine was made. A glossary on pages 246–8 lists terms that indicate estate-bottling.

The nine townships of Chianti Classico are listed below not in order of importance, nor alphabetically, but in geographic sequence as they appear on the map on page 39 going from north to south and west to east. The descriptions that follow are not based on an official classification, for, regrettably, there is none. They are derived from many conversations with growers and winemakers who are familiar with the characteristics of the nine townships and from blind tastings when examples from all the localities were compared.

The name of the township is given first. In parenthesis, next to it, are names of specific localities in the township that sometimes appear alone on the label.

S. Casciano Val di Pesa
(MERCATALE VAL DI PESA, MONTEFIRIDOLFI,
S. ANDREA IN PERCUSSINA)

S. Casciano is the northwesternmost township, part of whose territory is outside Chianti Classico. The part inside it, on the right bank of the river Pesa, produces a middle-of-the-road wine, one not likely to exhibit either the harshness or angularity to which Chianti is subject or the elaborate taste sensations of which it is capable. Rich in grape sugar and slow to mature, a representative S. Casciano is warm and full, but only moderately fragrant. Good producers are Castelli del Grevepesa (a cooperative), Castello di Gabbiano, Colle d'Agnola, Fattoria Il Poggiale, and Montepaldi.

At S. Casciano the house of Antinori has its cellars, where some of the best work in Chianti is done. Their Villa Antinori Riserva offers considerably more depth, body, and complexity than the standard of this township.

A portion of Chianti Classico illustrating the evenly graduated heights of hills and mountains characteristic of central Tuscany's harmonious landscape. See regional map of Tuscany, page 275.

❧ Greve ☙

In Italian, when used as an adjective, *greve* means weighty, heavy, or, if applied to manners, coarse. What the origin of Greve, the town name, may be, I don't know, but it is fascinating how appropriate *greve,* the adjective, can sometimes be in describing its wines. A young Greve embodies all the characteristics that can make Chianti such an awkward wine: It is hard, raw, sour, with nearly imperceptible fruit. Given time, the harshness does subside, the fruit blooms, and, on occasion, the texture may even turn to velvet. But an average Chianti from Greve can be expected to make predominantly blunt and assertive impressions. The most successful producers here are Castello di Uzzano, Fattoria Casenuove, Filetta, Riseccoli, Savignola Paolina, Vignamaggio, and Villa Cafaggio.

❧ Tavarnelle in Val di Pesa ☙

Much of this township lies outside Chianti Classico, and what lies within produces generally coarse wine with small *riserva* potential. An exception is the excellent Chianti from Poggio al Sole.

❧ Barberino Val d'Elsa ☙

Another of the townships straddling the Chianti Classico border. The production here is so uneven, even by Chianti standards, that it would be difficult to support a general characterization. Most notable are the wines of Isole e Olena and Monsanto. The latter is particularly warm and full-bodied, with depth and earthiness that are more frequent in Piedmontese wines than in Chianti. Monsanto is the producer Fabrizio Bianchi's label for his *riserva.* His standard Chianti is called Santa Caterina.

❧ Radda in Chianti ☙

Radda is Chianti Classico at its best and most complete. It is a profound, powerful wine whose forceful initial approach soon gives way to sumptuous, opulent flavor—a velvet fist in an iron glove. Although I do not agree with the belief that Chianti Classico *riserva* is a wine to lay down for a decade or more, if there is a Chianti capable of prolonged development in the bottle it is Radda's. Among its best producers are Castello di Volpaia, Monte Vertine, Pian d'Albola, and Vigna Vecchia.

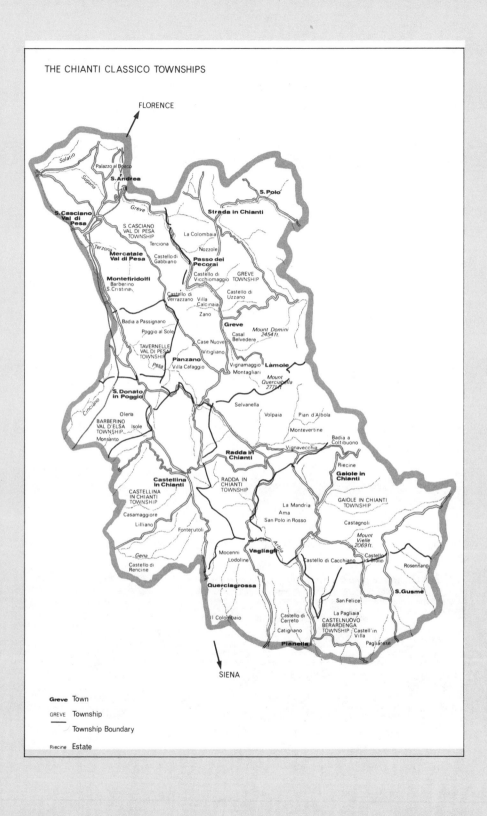

THE CHIANTI CLASSICO TOWNSHIPS

FLORENCE

Solatio

Palazzo al Bosco

S. Andrea

S. Polo

Sugana

Greve

Strada in Chianti

S. Casciano
Val di
Pesa

S CASCIANO
VAL DI PESA
TOWNSHIP

La Colombaia

Terzona

Terciona

Nozzole

Mercatale
Val di Pesa

Castello di
Gabbiano

Passo dei
Pecorai

Montefiridolfi

Barberino
S. Cristina

Castello di
Vicchiomaggio

GREVE
TOWNSHIP

Castello di
Verrazzano

Castello di
Uzzano

Villa
Calcinaia

Zano

Badia a Passignano

Greve

Mount Domini
2454 ft.

Poggio al Sole

Casal
Belvedere

TAVERNELLE
VAL DI PESA
TOWNSHIP

Case Nuove

Pesa

Panzano

Vitigliano

S. Donato
in Poggio

Villa Cafaggio

Vignamaggio

Lamole

Montagliari

Mount
Querciabella
2771 ft.

Cinciano

Olena

Selvanella

BARBERINO
VAL D'ELSA
TOWNSHIP

Isole

Volpaia

Pian d'Albola

Monsanto

Montevertine

Badia a
Coltibuono

Vignavecchia

Radda in
Chianti

Riecine

Gaiole in
Chianti

Castellina
in Chianti

RADDA IN
CHIANTI
TOWNSHIP

CASTELLINA
IN CHIANTI
TOWNSHIP

La Mandria
Ama
San Polo in Rosso

GAIOLE IN CHIANTI
TOWNSHIP

Castagnoli

Casamaggiore

Lilliano

Fonterutoli

Mount
Vielle
2069 ft.

Gena

Arbia

Mocenni

Vagliagi

Castello di
Rencine

Lodoline

Castello di Cacchiano

Castello
di Brolio

Rosennano

Querciagrossa

San Felice

S. Gusme

Il Colombaio

Castello di
Cerreto

La Pagliaia

CASTELNUOVO
BERARDENGA
TOWNSHIP

Castell'in
Villa

Catignano

Pianella

Pagliarese

SIENA

Greve Town

GREVE Township

—— Township Boundary

Riecine Estate

❧ Castellina in Chianti ❧

A Castellina is often one of the leanest and wiriest of Chianti Classicos, more generous with acid than with fruit. Its constitution is particularly subject to the fortunes of the vintage, in a poor year wizened, in an exceptional one austerely elegant. Some of the best examples of Castellina come from Castello di Fonterutoli, Fattoria Poggiarello, Lilliano Ruspoli, and Rencine (not to be mistaken for Gaiole's Riecine).

❧ Gaiole in Chianti ❧
(AMA IN CHIANTI)

Gaiole has a thin, hard frame, and in poor years, when shy of fruit, it can be despairingly lean and bony. But when filled out by the ripeness of a successful vintage, it is a glossy, suave, flowery, entrancing wine, delicate in flavor and aftertaste, one of the most appealing and graceful of Chianti Classicos.

John Dunkley, a transplanted Englishman, and his indefatigable wife Palmina have been bringing out of their miniature estate, Riecine, some of the outstanding wines of Gaiole. Riecine's 1978 *riserva* is a masterpiece, possessing all those qualities that Tuscans have always attributed to Chianti and most everyone else has struggled to find.

Other excellent Gaiole producers are Badia a Coltibuono, Capannelle, Castagnoli, and S. Polo in Rosso.

❧ Poggibonsi ❧

A very small part of this township is in Chianti Classico. What Poggibonsi wine has come to my notice so far has not encouraged a greater acquaintance with this area's production.

❧ Castelnuovo Berardenga ❧
(CERRETO, PIANELLA, QUERCEGROSSA, S. GUSMÈ, VAGLIAGLI)

Without question, the juiciest, plummiest of all Chianti Classicos. A Castelnuovo is flowing, silky, sumptuously fruity, palpably round and ample in the mouth. One could compare it to such Chianti townships as Radda and Greve as, in Bordeaux, one might compare the wines of Pomerol to those of Pauillac and Graves.

An estate that delivers, in good years, qualities that are representative of Castelnuovo is Pagliarese. Other excellent producers are Aiola, Catignano, Fattoria delle Lodoline, Felsina Berardenga, Fortilizio Il Colombaio, La Pagliaia, and S. Felice.

NOTE: Two of the most familiar names in Chianti, Brolio and Ruffino, are wines created to reflect the style of the house rather than the character of a particular locality. While neither expresses the more completely articulated personality of an estate-grown *riserva* from some of the smaller producers, both are, on the other hand, far less erratic from year to year than most Chianti tends to be. They both have a world-wide following which they have earned as much through their reliability as through their marketing skills.

BEYOND THE CLASSICO BORDERS, TWO GREAT CHIANTIS

More Chianti is made outside the Classico zone than within it. Most of it is thin, short-lived wine, poorly endowed for *riserva* stature. There are two areas, however, Montalbano and Rufina, where we find *riservas* that rank second to none in Chianti.

Montalbano and Rufina lie, respectively, to the west and east of the northern tip of the Chianti Classico territory. Florence is between them, little more than a ten-mile span away from each. The closeness of the city, once the seat of all power in Tuscany and the primary source of its splendors, has enriched these districts with some of the grandest houses to be found in any wine country. Poggio Reale, the serene, classic Spalletti villa in Rufina, is the work of Michelangelo. La Ferdinanda in Carmignano, the country retreat for Grand Duke Ferdinand I, rising like a colossus out of the surrounding farmland, owes its grave and noble proportions to Bernardo Buontalenti, the sixteenth century's most innovative theatrical designer.

Any wine coming out of estates like these, were it capable of self-awareness, would have to be uncommonly stout-hearted to look back and not feel overshadowed.

❧ *Chianti Montalbano Riserva* ☙
(D.O.C., SLATED FOR D.O.C.G., TUSCANY)

The Montalbano area begins west of Florence and moves north and west almost to the outskirts of Pistoia. The Pistoia end produces both the

Medium-Range and Light Reds described in their respective categories (pages 102 and 133). But in the eastern section, there is a small district between the villages of Carmignano and Poggio a Caiano whose Chianti *riserva* is a wine of uncommon quality, dominated by a flowery bouquet coupled with firm, vigorous, racy, mineral taste sensations.

The outstanding producer of Chianti Montalbano is Contini-Bonacossi, under the label Capezzana. Other good makers are Artimino (Riserva del Granduca label), Bacchereto, Bibbiani, and Il Poggiolo (since this is a common name in Tuscany, look for the proprietor's name, Cianchi Baldazzi.).

❦ Chianti Rufina Riserva ❧
(D.O.C., SLATED FOR D.O.C.G., TUSCANY)

This is a particularly fortunate area for making good wine, cornered by the banks of two rivers, the Arno and its tributary the Sieve, with sunny, well-ventilated vineyards planted in the hard, schistous soil of the foothills of one of the tallest mountain groups in Tuscany.

A choice Rufina can match in authority, and sometimes surpass, Chianti Classico at its finest. In character it is closest to a Chianti from Radda, page 38, making forceful first impressions that precede layer after layer of unfolding flavor.

The most celebrated producer in Rufina is Frescobaldi, who bottles three outstanding wines under that appellation. At the top of the line is their Montesodi, a small, single-vineyard bottling first produced in 1974 in an edition of less than five thousand bottles. Next is Nipozzano, nearly as fine, but much more accessible in price and quantity. The length and subtlety of taste of these two wines are largely due to the exceptional environment and highly accomplished winemaking; in part, they may also derive from the special blend of grapes, which includes some cabernet sauvignon and reduces the white grapes to a token presence. Frescobaldi's third Chianti Rufina wine is the softer, more charming Pomino, a perfumed, fast-maturing wine from high-altitude vineyards. Pomino, which contains some pinot noir as well as cabernet sauvignon, is awaiting its own separate D.O.C. appellation, which will permit it to omit white grapes entirely from its blend as it divests itself of the Chianti name.

Other noteworthy producers in Rufina are Fattoria di Bossi, Fattoria di Vetrice, Fattoria Selvapiana, I Busini, and Spalletti (Poggio Reale Riserva label).

NOTE: Rufina, with the accent on the first syllable, is the name of a production zone and should not be confused with Ruffino, accented on the second syllable, the well-known Chianti shipper.

VINTAGES: The essential imperfection of vintage charts reaches the state of almost total unreliability in Chianti. The territory is vast, the microclimates beyond count, the weather at harvest time subject to capriciously local storms, the number of growers in the hundreds. One would need to know, year by year, who picked too early, who waited too long and was caught by rain, who managed to bring in perfect grapes in the sunshine.

At the same time, in no wines like Chianti is the year so important. The lurking harshness of the breed needs but a small proportion of poorly ripened berries in order to surface and displace all other qualities. What would be an acceptable year elsewhere can be a disaster in Chianti.

I am suggesting therefore only the years to look for, on the double understanding that they are not equally valid for all producers and that some estates may have done quite well in the years unmentioned.

Good Years: 1975, 1977, 1978, 1979, 1982, 1983

Older *riservas* from 1967 through 1971 may be still good, but do not buy in quantity before trying one bottle.

OTHER D.O.C. RED WINES
FROM THE SANGIOVESE GRAPE

❧ *Brunello di Montalcino* ❧
(D.O.C., TO BE D.O.C.G. IN 1985, TUSCANY)

Brunello, made entirely from the sangiovese grape, comes from vineyards that slope away from the hill town of Montalcino, thirty miles south of Siena. For a visitor who has had no previous experience of the wine, the first intimation of its character comes from the landscape through which he travels on the way to the town: treeless spaces and scarred cliffs of tufa that give it a hard, unaccommodating look in vivid contrast with the affluent curves of the Chianti hills just to the north.

If one is in doubt about how the terms austere, big, and full are applied to wine, a mouthful of Brunello will give a forceful demonstration of their meaning.

In its youth, this must be the most unyielding of wines. It may take a decade or longer to loosen its reserve, but when ready, the powerful welcome of a thoroughbred Brunello is well worth the wait. The bouquet, an exciting mingling of floral essences, of tar, of spice, of fur, is a prelude to the palate-coating flavors that follow. These develop slowly in the mouth, as it is such a stiff-backed wine, but the successive, steadily expanding sensations of jam, of earth, of spice, the length of these impressions, and the suitably prolonged echo of the aftertaste are sufficient reward for the careful attention they demand.

The sangiovese grape used in Brunello is a darker, slightly larger variety of the one planted in Chianti, and it was first identified in Montalcino in the nineteenth century. The development of this variety and the special methods of vinification and aging all originate with the Biondi-Santi family, who created Brunello in the 1860s and eventually turned it into the one Italian wine with snob appeal.

Biondi-Santi's Brunello is made today as it has been from the first on the Il Greppo estate in Montalcino, now managed by the second- and third-generation Biondi-Santis, Franco and Jacopo. Whether or not it is the finest Brunello produced may be open to argument, but it cannot be disputed that the family created the wine and has always set the standards by which it is judged, thereby earning extended attention in any detailed description of Brunello.

The formula for high-quality wine is always the same, and all its parts are present in the making of Biondi-Santi's Brunello: good land, good grapes, good work in the cellar. The gently sloping vineyards at Il Greppo are rich in that rocky, schistous soil formation typical of Tuscany and known there as *galestro*. It is poor soil for the cultivation of most crops, excellent for producing grapes of intense flavor and color.

Vines at Il Greppo are pruned short to produce considerably fewer grapes than the legally permitted yield, and at harvest time the pickers make several selections. Three wines are made from Brunello grapes by Biondi-Santi. Grapes from vines less than ten years old produce a wine with slightly less body and alcohol that is labeled Greppo instead of Brunello. Vines that are twenty years old or older produce the grapes that go into the *riserva*, made only in excellent years. In those same years, grapes of intermediate quality are used to make a Brunello not qualified as *riserva*.

In good, but not outstanding, years only one type of Brunello is made, blending all the grapes save for those from vines less than ten years old. It is not a *riserva*. In poor years, and there have been three in the 1960s and 1970s, Biondi-Santi does not bottle any wine, but sells it in bulk as ordinary table wine.

All this explains in part, perhaps, how the Biondi-Santi name has acquired the luster that enables it to command prices for its *riserva* that equal those of a Bordeaux *premier cru*.

Brunello is subject to the longest mandatory aging in wood requirement of any Italian wine, four years. A *riserva* must be aged an additional year, but not necessarily in barrels. The exceptional aging requirement raises substantial questions about the Italian approach to aging in wood, both for Brunello in particular and for other big Italian red wines.

There is no denying that Brunello would be a different, possibly less complex, wine if it spent less time in wood, but it must also be admitted that the practice is responsible not only for some of the distinctive character of the wine, but for most of its flaws. And the flaws are not as infrequent as Brunello's reputation and steep price might lead us to expect.

For all living things, wine among them, aging is a process in which development is shadowed by decay. Gradually, as development slows down, decay accelerates its pace and closes the gap, eventually taking command. Wood barrels, and in particular the venerable barrels of Italian cellars, through the substances that become embedded in their inner walls and the infinitesimal but steady filtration of oxygen they permit, fuel decay's relentless advance.

Furthermore, long residence in wood imprisons wine into a tannic sheath that takes time for it to shed. Only a wine of exceptional endurance manages to divest itself of heavy tannin before the vital fruit beneath expires.

In Brunello, and I have experienced it even with some of Biondi-Santi's, one may occasionally encounter the sweet-sour smell and taste of decrepit fruit together with the raw astringency of still undissolved tannin. In lesser versions, there is sometimes only the tannin left, locking the mouth as in a vise.

Those perfectly constituted wines that survive barrel aging to achieve a healthy complexity of flavors are unquestionably among the most fascinating of wines. But for every one of these, there are several that have only tarriness and astringency to offer.

Moreover, even when successful, there are doubts that arise about the validity of extensive barrel aging for contemporary tastes. Do wines that have been long exposed to wood taste of themselves or of something foreign to their original character? Does not wood help to blur the differences in their natural constitution? And why should we want to add to wine flavors and odors that are not native to them? There may not be a single answer equally applicable to all wine. To a few—Brunello, Barolo, Taurasi among them—some wood age is undoubtedly beneficial. But the issue is acquiring increasing importance in Italy for producers who have to reconcile traditional concepts of winemaking that were written into law with modern notions of wine style.

In any event, Brunello's ability to bring the highest price of any Italian wine is likely to go unchallenged, an ability that has drawn to the ranks of its makers many new names, doubling their number in two decades and increasing the amount of wine produced tenfold.

No one has been able to come quite abreast of Biondi-Santi's prestige, at least as far as prestige is judged by price, but a few, some long established in Montalcino, can make wine that is as impressive and, on occasion, even more appealing.

Foremost among them is Emilio Costanti, whose family has owned land in Montalcino for half a millennium. Tenuta Caparzo makes a Brunello of extraordinary intensity and vitality. Col D'Orcia's version is most attractive, even if their grapes, grown on heavier soil, generate an earthy Brunello not wholly representative of the qualities one associates with the wine. Other outstanding producers are Nello Baricci, Castelgiocondo, Fattoria dei Barbi, La Meridiana, Lisini.

NOTE: Many Montalcino producers make a wine called Rosso dai Vigneti del Brunello. Although it is made from the same grape, it is not to be confused with Brunello. For a fuller explanation, see the Medium-Range Red category, pages 105–6, where it is described.

VINTAGES: Brunello from a top producer has exceptional staying power. If the vintage is a great one, it may not even begin to bloom until its first decade is well behind it. In poor to medium years, however, it simply never overcomes its astringency. Therefore, only good and great years are noted below.

Good Years: 1946, 1951, 1957, 1958, 1966, 1967, 1977, 1978, 1979, 1981, 1983

Great Years: 1945, 1955, 1961, 1964, 1970, 1975, 1982

✦ Carmignano Riserva ✦
(D.O.C., TUSCANY)

Although Carmignano is entitled to an individual D.O.C. appellation, it is produced within the Chianti Montalbano zone from a similar blend of red and white grapes wherein sangiovese predominates, and it is closely related to a Chianti in bouquet and flavor. But the tradition of a separate Carmignano wine has strong historical support. It may, in fact, have been one of the first wines in the world to have had its name and production legally protected when they were recognized by a regulatory edict issued by the Grand Duke of Tuscany in 1716.

There are a number of ways in which Carmignano technically differs from Chianti. There is less of the sangiovese grape in it, and there is cabernet sauvignon, up to 10 percent of it. No grapes or musts from other areas may be used. Aging in oak is mandatory, rather than left up to the discretion of the producer. A Carmignano *riserva,* which, like Chianti, must be three years old, must spend a minimum two of those years in wood. Except for the cabernet sauvignon, however, that is more or less how fine Chianti producers make their wine.

To place it in context, it helps to think of Carmignano as a particular kind of Chianti, one with a touch of refinement. Its bouquet is exceedingly pretty, marked by an intense floweriness together with sensations of nuts, resin, and black cherry: a beguiling introduction to the firm, but graceful, drawn-out flavors that follow and in turn build to a sustained, yet not overly frank aftertaste.

The preeminent producer is Contini-Bonacossi, the same responsible for the fine Villa di Capezzana Chianti Montalbano. They bottle two separate, single-vineyard Carmignanos, a Villa di Capezzana and a Villa di Trefiano. The latter is a newcomer to the Contini-Bonacossi line, made from wine that was formerly blended into Villa di Capezzana Carmignano. The first vintage, a 1979, is being released in 1982 and clearly promises well, although it is too early for a full evaluation.

Other excellent Carmignanos may be had from Artimino, Bacchereto, Fattoria Le Farnete (a very small producer), and Chianchi Baldazzi's Il Poggiolo.

VINTAGES: The discussion of Chianti vintages on pages 43 and 103 also applies to Carmignano.

❧ *Rubesco Riserva* ☙
(TORGIANO D.O.C., UMBRIA)

A definition of genius describes it as an infinite capacity for taking pains. The process of making exceptional wines could be similarly described. What puts Rubesco *riserva* high on any list of Italy's best red wines is its producer's willingness to take pains, fortunately combined with the means to execute that will and the raw materials that make it worthwhile.

Rubesco is grown on the low-sloping hills of central Umbria, south of Perugia, and within sight of the city's medieval skyline. It is entitled to a D.O.C. appellation, Torgiano *rosso,* which appears in very small print on the label because the man who owns or controls most of Torgiano's production, Giorgio Lungarotti, prefers to emphasize Rubesco, the proprietary name he has given the wine.

The D.O.C. statute recommends for Torgiano the same blend of red and white grapes used for Chianti. Lungarotti takes this as simply a suggestion and makes Rubesco from red grapes exclusively—sangiovese and canaiolo.

The soundest grapes from the choicest plots in the Torgiano territory —a minute fraction of the total crop—are selected to be crushed for the *riserva.* The rest go into standard Rubesco. The Lungarotti approach to fermentation and aging differs from that prevalent in Italy when making a major red wine. Fermentation takes place in stainless steel at controlled temperatures and the finished wine is kept in the barrel only one year. Barrel aging is followed by cellar storage of the bottles for two more years, a very rare practice in Italy, but one that contributes much to the sound development of fine wine.

When one appraises Rubesco *riserva*'s style, it is instructive to compare it with another central Italian red wine that contains no white grapes, Brunello, described on pages 43–6.

Rubesco *riserva* has a brighter, more transparent color; its bouquet has more lift and pure, fresh fragrance; there is less acerbity and bite in the taste, a more supple, open, delectable impression of fruit: qualities that can be traced to briefer maceration of the wine on its skins, to cooler fermentation, and most of all, to a shorter stay in wood, one-fourth that of Brunello.

It's a style that trades off slow development and an indefinite life span

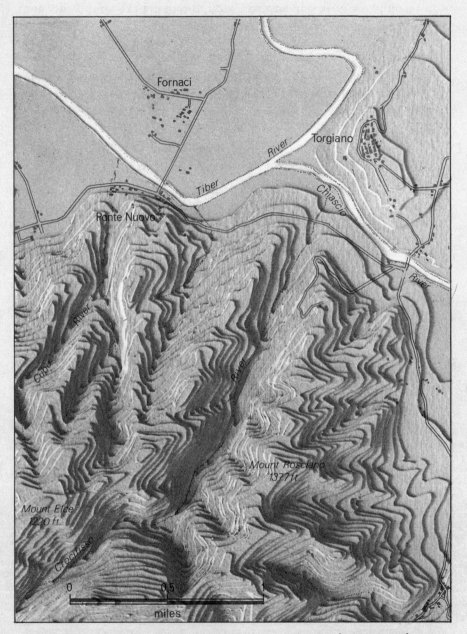

The gentle hills of the Torgiano zone southeast of Perugia, where
Rubesco Riserva and Torgiano Bianco are produced. See regional map
of Umbria, page 277.

for a more forward, spontaneous appeal, forgoing peaks of intensity and power in exchange for more level, buoyant taste.

VINTAGES: Rubesco *riserva* is usually ready within five years after the vintage, but it will improve further and is capable of staying at the top of its form for a surprisingly long period. A 1969 tasted in 1981 appeared to be as full of fruit and life as it was five years earlier, when I first became acquainted with it.
Good Years: 1967, 1973, 1974, 1977, 1978, 1980, 1983
Great Years: 1966, 1968, 1969, 1970, 1971, 1975, 1979, 1982

Vino Nobile di Montepulciano
(D.O.C., TO BE D.O.C.G. IN 1982, TUSCANY)

In my salad days I was very fond of beefsteak, and to this predilection I owe my first acquaintance with Vino Nobile. We were living in Rome at a time when the only good meat available was baby lamb. Delectable as this is, one tires of it; we therefore drove the hundred or so miles north to Montepulciano, where we had been told the best of the *fiorentine,* Tuscany's huge, savory T-bone steaks, could be bought. Along with a supply of meat for the freezer, we brought back several bottles of an inky, numbingly hard wine. The first bottle was so difficult to finish—it was so like the stony, somber, unengaging town it came from—that I put away the rest and forgot about them.

When I came across them again, a few years later, I was undecided whether to throw them out or give them to our surly doorman, but then, rather skeptically, I opened one. As I tasted it, skepticism gave way to astonished joy. The wine had shed its tannic armor; youthful pugnacity had been replaced by a robust, fleshy embrace. Thus I learned that an important thing to know about Vino Nobile is that one must give it time.

In its force, its weight, its overbearing style (one might say its arrogance), Vino Nobile is the quintessential Tuscan red wine. Like its kindred wines discussed in the immediately preceding pages, it derives its lineage from the sangiovese grape and carries with it the family graces and blemishes.

It is sangiovese and long wood age that are responsible for Vino Nobile's authoritative, strong attack on the palate. Its austerity is further marked by a sturdy vein of bitterness that extends from the initial development of flavors in the mouth well into the aftertaste. Those who enjoy forcefully vinous, solid, spiced sensations in a wine and are ready to forgo easier or more subtle tasting qualities will respond to the intensity of Vino Nobile.

The sangiovese in the blend, a dark-skinned variety locally known as prugnolo gentile, resembles the one used in Brunello di Montalcino. The other grapes prescribed by the D.O.C. law are, as in Chianti, a red grape, canaiolo, and the two white grapes, trebbiano and malvasia. Another white grape, grechetto, and a flowery red, mammolo, are permitted, but optional. Unlike Chianti, Vino Nobile cannot be subjected to *governo,* the Chianti practice of provoking a second fermentation by adding crushed, shriveled grapes to wine, described on pages 32–3. Also unlike Chianti, aging in wood is mandatory rather than optional, a minimum of two years. With an additional year it becomes a *riserva;* with two years, *riserva speciale.*

In recent years, many new vineyards have been planted for the production of Vino Nobile, an expansion that has caused much unevenness in quality. The one producer who makes a Vino Nobile deserving of the *nobile,* or "noble," in the name is De Ferrari-Corradi. Two others nearly as good are Fanetti and Fattoria di Gracciano. Fazi-Battaglia, the Verdicchio house, has taken a substantial position in Montepulciano, using the Fassati label.

VINTAGES: Vino Nobile is exceptionally long-lived, and a good thing it is, because its unforgiving hardness makes it almost unapproachable in its youth. Ten years is not too long to wait for a *riserva* from a great vintage, but lesser examples should be tried sooner.·
Good Years: 1964, 1968, 1969, 1973, 1977, 1979, 1980, 1981, 1983
Great Years: 1958, 1967, 1970, 1975, 1982

OTHER EMINENT, ALTHOUGH UNCLASSIFIED, RED WINES IN THE SANGIOVESE FAMILY

❧ *Tignanello* ☙
(VINO DA TAVOLA, TUSCANY)

In the preceding pages of this section on sangiovese wines, the problems of Chianti have been discussed: its sharpness, hollowness, lack of color, all problems connected to the occasionally excessive use of white grapes in the Chianti blend. While everyone talked about the kind of wine one could make if the white grapes were eliminated, Antinori, a major house in Chianti, did something about it. It's a wine called Tignanello, created in 1971. (The name was lifted from a Chianti that Antinori used to produce.)

In the making of Tignanello, the statutory Chianti formula—two red grapes (sangiovese, mainly, and canaiolo) plus two white grapes (trebbiano and malvasia)—has been ignored. The wine is made entirely of red grapes, principally sangiovese and up to 15 percent cabernet sauvignon. Canaiolo and red malvasia were included in the first two vintages, 1971 and 1975. With this drastic departure from controlled appellation requirements, Tignanello renounced its rights to call itself Chianti and came out without benefit of a recognized classification, as ordinary table wine, *vino da tavola*. But there is nothing ordinary about Tignanello.

The differences between it and any Chianti Classico *riserva,* even Antinori's own, are startling. The color is deeper by several shades, a blackish, intense, ruby red hue. Instead of the impetuous floweriness of good Chianti, Tignanello's bouquet is a dense, fascinating mixture of aromas that suggest vanilla, chocolate, herbs, and spices, together with the characteristic violet scent of Chianti, here more subtly expressed. The body is full, substantial, completely fleshed out, without the craggy edges and thinness in the middle of standard Chianti. In contrast with Chianti's immediacy, flavor impressions are austere and slow developing, emphasizing firmness rather than lushness, with length, depth, and a refined finish.

Antinori's master oenologist, Giacomo Tachis, ages Tignanello in a style that derives more from French than from Tuscan tradition; instead of the customary 1,200- to 1,500-gallon Yugoslav oak barrels he uses new, 60-gallon Limousin oak *barriques.* Barrel aging lasts about eighteen months, to which are added ten months or more in the bottle before the wine is released.

Tignanello should not be taken as the model along whose lines all good Chianti ought to be produced. One will always look to Chianti for warmer, less rigid, more immediate appeal. But the premise that led to its conception now has the force of demonstrated fact: In Chianti territory, out of its basic grape, better-constituted, more balanced wines can be produced.

VINTAGES: From what one can gather of its brief history, the aging potential of Tignanello is excellent. It may take a decade to reach full maturity, and possibly close to another before beginning to decline. Tignanello is made only in favorable years, so far only in 1971, 1975, 1977, 1978, 1979, 1980, 1982, 1983. The 1975 was the first exceptional vintage, and the 1978 and 1982 are expected to develop into the finest produced to date.

◄ Brusco dei Barbi ►
(VINO DA TAVOLA, TUSCANY)

A successful departure from the norm may take the road that leads to development of a new style of wine, as Tignanello, above, has done, or may reverse direction and return to practices fallen into disfavor. Brusco dei Barbi is an example of the latter.

It is made in the Brunello di Montalcino zone by one of Brunello's highest-ranking producers, Barbi Colombini. Like Brunello, it is made entirely from sangiovese. Unlike Brunello, it is produced using an old Tuscan vinification technique, *governo alla toscana*. In *governo*, discussed more amply on pages 32–3, partly dried grapes are added to wine, setting off a revived fermentation that transforms the wine's acids and accelerates its development. For Brunello it is not permitted, but it once used to be universal in Chianti. Most wine commentators look down upon it, and it has become fashionable to consider it suitable only for slight, guzzling wines. Since it is a costly and laborious procedure, many Tuscan producers have been happy to abandon it. In the passing up of *governo*, however, some of the most amiable qualities in Tuscan wine are being lost, and Barbi's Brusco is the best illustration of what these may be.

This brilliant garnet wine greets the nose with a bouquet of flowery and berrylike aromas that for vivacity and charm have few equals among the reds of central Italy. The flavors are supple, flowing, round, wholly enveloping, neither sluggish nor austere. Ampleness is a characteristic of Brusco, which easily exceeds 14 percent in alcohol, but it is balanced by a keen vitality. The sensation of freshness, remarkable for such a full wine, is nurtured by careful cellaring that keeps barrel aging to no more than one year.

VINTAGES: Like all wines that have undergone *governo*, Brusco is soon ready, but thanks to its native soundness of constitution and vigor, it possesses considerable endurance. The years for Brusco are the same as those for Brunello listed on page 46.

❧ *Castello di Monte Antico Riserva* ☙
(VINO DA TAVOLA, TUSCANY)

Giorgio Cabella, once a newspaper editor in Rome, then an industrialist in Milan, originally set out to make a Chianti-like wine on his beautiful Tuscan estate of Monte Antico, in the maritime province of Grosseto. He was using the conventional blend of red and white grapes until he realized that no more than a hundred yards away from his vineyards, on the other side of the Ombrone River, was Brunello di Montalcino territory, where striking—and high-priced—wines are made from the red sangiovese grape alone. Since then Cabella has been patterning his wine after Brunello, gradually reducing white grape proportions until, in the 1975 vintage, they nearly disappeared.

Castello di Monte Antico *riserva* is today one of the best balanced of the central Italian wines that emphasize the sangiovese grape and extended aging in wood. It is an intense, deep, but brilliant ruby red wine, whose bouquet presents a diversified but harmonious ensemble of aromas that suggest violets, vanilla, wild berries, musk, spice, and resin. The flavor is sturdy, but ripe, lithe, and velvety, disclosing a structure of exceptional distinction.

Monte Antico is good enough not to need the borrowed luster of Brunello. If there is a gap between it and its illustrious neighbor, it is mainly in the price and all to Monte Antico's advantage.

VINTAGES: Five to six years are sufficient to bring this wine around to agreeable drinking quality, but it is capable of developing further and, in great years, endures well past its first decade.
Good Years: 1973, 1975, 1978, 1982, 1983
Great Years: 1970, 1971, 1980

❧ *Le Pergole Torte* ☙
(VINO DA TAVOLA, TUSCANY)

Le Pergole Torte comes from a miniature, jewellike estate in the Chianti township of Radda, Monte Vertine. Here, Sergio Manetti has been bringing out in every favorable year one of the most consistently successful Chianti Classicos. He now has joined the still sparse ranks of producers making all-sangiovese wines, and he has come up with a gem.

In the glass, Le Pergole Torte is a deep yet bright ruby. To the nose it offers a profound bouquet, first leafy and tobaccolike, then followed by sensations of flowers, berries, vanilla, and white pepper. On the palate, it is large, palpably fruity, warm, and supple, but at the same time vigorous, extremely satisfying, and elegant. A faint and far from disagreeable echo of tannin and oak at the end brings the development of flavors to a firm and balanced close.

In the inescapable comparison with Tignanello, the trail-blazing sangiovese wine by Antinori described on pages 51–3, Le Pergole Torte shows a different but equally admirable personality, more flowing and accessible, perhaps less imposing, but closer to its Chianti origins.

Sergio Manetti and his cellar master, Bruno Bini, take advantage of Le Pergole Torte's uncontrolled, *vino da tavola* status to keep aging down to a minimum, one year in wood and another in the bottle. The wine's exquisite balance and liveliness may give additional support to those who are working to revise the practice of prolonged barrel age for some Italian reds.

VINTAGES: Le Pergole Torte was first produced in 1977 and is made only in good years. Happily, that has been true of every year since then through 1983.

INDEPENDENT BIG RED WINES

❧ *Amarone* ❧

(RECIOTO DELLA VALPOLICELLA AMARONE D.O.C., VENETO)

One of the rarely discussed, but nonetheless important, constituents of wine character is the ripeness of the grapes.

The notion of ripeness is a variable one. In cool growing areas of the North, one picks as late as one dares, hoping for as much sugar as the last warm days of autumn can produce. The same practice is unfortunately also followed by a few southern growers, whose dull, flat, neutral wines are rich in alcohol, color, and little else. But in the more advanced vineyards of the South, grapes are considered ripe for picking when they are still a little green, before most of their fresh, fragrant acids are baked away.

Another notion of ripeness is that which allows grapes to go beyond maturity into a partly shriveled state. Sauternes, and German wines of *beerenauslese* or *trockenbeerenauslese* class, are examples of sweet wines made from such grapes. In France and Germany the partial shriveling of the berries is accomplished while the fruit is still on the vine, assisted by the action of a skin-puncturing mold called botrytis. In Italy, when one makes Recioto or other wines from partly dried berries, the drying takes place after the grapes have been picked. The bunches are spread out, indoors, on straw or wire-bottomed pallets, to be crushed within one month or, sometimes, several months later.

One obvious consequence is that much of the berries' water content evaporates, concentrating the juice and increasing the proportion of sugar to pulp. But other, more complex transformations take place, during which some acids are lost, others created, and different sugar compounds formed. The end product is a more intense, aromatic, full-bodied wine, richer in alcohol, glycerine, and sugar.

Several Italian wines are made this way. Many are sweet, several of which are described in the section on sweet wines (pages 214-25). Other dry red wines from partly dried grapes are Sfurzàt (page 97) and Groppello Amarone (page 120). The practice is also employed in the *governo* method of making Chianti (pages 32–3). In the Veneto, when a Soave, a Gambellara, or a Valpolicella is produced from partly dried berries, the word *Recioto* precedes its name.

Recioto is a dialect word for ears, in this case the "ears," or protruding upper parts of the grape bunch, that are selected for this process because, having had the best exposure to the sun, they are the ripest. Recioto di Soave and Recioto di Gambellara are sweet, but a Valpolicella Recioto can be either sweet or dry. The sweet is called Recioto della Valpolicella. The dry adds the word *Amarone* to its name, which ends up being almost as large a mouthful as the wine itself. In standard usage this is abbreviated to Amarone.

Amarone is a dark, deep garnet wine, with odors of nuts and spice and dense, fruit jam flavors that call to mind dried figs and cherry preserve. The body is warm, unctuous, portlike, conveying a satiny impression of sweetness that comes not from sugar, but from glycerine. The bitter aftertaste of almonds, characteristic of Valpolicella and of many other wines of the Veneto, is here accentuated. The success or failure of Amarone depends on whether its vitality is sufficient to animate the weighty, dried-fruit flavors and the viscous body. When it is not, Amarone can be soupy, raisiny, ponderous stuff indeed.

A fine Amarone makes a luscious glass of wine, but at 15–16 percent alcohol one wonders how much more than one glass can be consumed during a meal. Those who are uncomfortable with so much alcohol and such density of flavor during the early stages of the meal may want to save Amarone for the end, to sip with walnuts and a firm, sapid cheese, such as Parmigiano-Reggiano.

Although it is one of the most expensive red wines of Italy, the price of a bottle of Amarone is still scarcely sufficient to justify the risk, the cost, the watchful labor that are required to produce it. The grapes must first be selected, bunch by bunch, in the vineyard, the "ears" snipped off, and inspected again before they are carefully spread out on their pallets; they must be checked every day while they are drying, and any bunch on which a spot of mold may have formed must be discarded before it infects the rest; when, at last, they are made into wine, their yield will be 50 percent or less what they would have given had they been crushed when they were fresh. Those who produce Amarone do it to follow a prestigious tradition, hoping that some of the glory will reflect on the commercial Valpolicella they also make.

Some of the best Amarones are produced by Allegrini, Bertani, Masi, Quintarelli, Speri, and Tedeschi. Masi has more than one Amarone in its line. The one under the traditional, gingerbready Veronese label is not particularly distinguished. The Masi labels to watch for are simple ones that look handwritten. These are two single-vineyard bottlings, one called Campolongo Torbe, the other Mazzano, from the choicest plots in Valpolicella. They take the Recioto concept as far as it can conceivably go, with alcohol levels as high as 17 percent, a voluptuous, but miraculously vigorous body, and massive concentrations of flavor.

VINTAGES: Amarone has a reputation for being extremely long-lived, but very old Amarones have always tasted dried out and prunelike to me. My impression is that they reach their peak at six or seven years of age and will maintain it for perhaps four years more before beginning a gradual decline. Some exceptional bottles, such as the special Masi Amarones mentioned above, have more staying power.

Acceptable Years: 1971, 1973, 1975, 1976, 1978, 1980, 1981

Good Years: 1969, 1974, 1977, 1979, 1983

Great Years: 1964, 1982

❧ *Chambave Rouge* ❧
(VINO DA TAVOLA, VAL D'AOSTA)

Like other wines of Val d'Aosta, the French-speaking region on Italy's northern frontier whose rocky vineyards are never far from glaciers and year-round snows, Chambave Rouge is produced in such small quantity that even in Italy few are aware of its existence, and fewer still have tasted it.

One might question the value of discussing the merits of an Italian wine so difficult to obtain. But we would be the losers if we restricted our curiosity about wine only to those that are commonly available Any bottle that exists will turn up somewhere, sometime, if there is enough interest in its contents and adequate reward for the seller. Provided it is pleasure to the senses that chiefly draws our interest to a wine, we are justified in spending words and time on this one.

Chambave Rouge is a blend of grapes wherein the principal one is the gros vien grape, known also as vien de nus; it is one of those varieties native to Val d'Aosta that flourish nowhere else. It is not uncommon elsewhere in the valley, but only when it grows on the slopes abutting the town of Chambave does it produce the depth of flavor and intense flowery fragrance that characterize Chambave Rouge. The other grapes usually present in the blend, dolcetto and barbera, are transplants from Piedmont, the great red wine region that adjoins Val d'Aosta at its southern end. Dolcetto contributes fruit and roundness; barbera gives color, wiry vitality, and backbone.

The color of a young Chambave Rouge is a brilliant deep crimson, which with age fades to brick red, then to orange. The bouquet is impetuous and ample in volume, filling out generous winy, grapy impressions with flowery and fruity sensations that may suggest crushed violets and raspberries. These promising scents are confirmed by rich flavors of fruit and grape skin, a warm, velvety constitution, and a harmonious aftertaste that lingers deeply.

Chambave Rouge improves dramatically with age, replacing some of the vigorous winyness with profounder, jamlike flavors. At its peak of development, Chambave Rouge is a deeply satisfying reds, irresistibly good with such Val d'Aosta specialties as roast venison or *carbonade,* a casserole of cubed, marinated beef tenderloin spiced with cinnamon and cloves.

VINTAGES: 1978–1980, and 1982–83 are good.

❧ *Sassicaia* ❧
(VINO DA TAVOLA, TUSCANY)

Comparisons between Italian wines and French are seldom instructive, but Sassicaia, a Cabernet, invites such reference. Nearly all Italian Cabernets, which are described on pages 71–81, aim at achieving sensations that —whether they emphasize charm, suppleness, or even intensity—express the more forward, less complex aspects of this varietal's character. The Sassicaia Cabernet is an exception, possibly the only one in Italy whose style would fit the expectations of those judging by the standards of Bordeaux reds or Napa Valley Cabernet Sauvignons.

The grapes in Sassicaia are 70 percent cabernet sauvignon and 30 percent cabernet franc. They are grown on flat or shallowly inclined land, composed of sandy and partly gravelly soil, close to the seacoast, and less than thirty miles south of the port of Leghorn. Cool sea breezes, lean soil, well-nurtured vineyards produce the kind of grapes that justify the maturation in small, new, French oak barrels and additional development in bottles to which the wine is subjected. Before release, Sassicaia is aged approximately three years, half in wood, half in the bottle.

The color is a deep, fat red, glowingly garnet in hue. The bouquet is a majestically measured refrain of lofty scents, led by odors that suggest pine, followed by those of truffle, of sage, and, in infinitesimal part, of tobacco leaves and peppermint. The flavor takes command of the palate with an unwavering development of taste sensations where rich fruit is supported by mineral impressions, smoothly integrated with grape skin texture, coming to a refined yet exciting finish in the subtly piquant and elaborate aftertaste.

Sassicaia is produced by Marchesi Incisa della Rocchetta and bottled and distributed by Antinori.

VINTAGES: The curve of Sassicaia's development arches upward for easily ten years. How long it will hold steady at its peak is hard to estimate, because the wine was first produced in 1968, and the oldest of the best vintages is 1972, still showing signs of improvement. It is bottled only in good years, fortunately not too infrequent in its ideally situated location.

Sassicaia was made in 1968, 1970–72, 1974–80, and 1982–1983. The great years are 1972, 1976, 1978, and 1982.

❧ *Schioppettino di Prapotto* ☙
(VINO DA TAVOLA, FRIULI-VENEZIA GIULIA)

The story of Schioppettino is as singular as the wine is rare and excellent. On the few acres surrounding a small village in the hills of Friuli's Colli Orientali zone, ribolla nera, a vine unknown to the rest of the world, had for centuries been producing a wine of exquisite flavor. Every attempt to grow it elsewhere and achieve the same results was unsuccessful; having failed everywhere but in its original, modest habitat, the variety, which had come to be known locally as schioppettino, disappeared from notice. When the official list of grape varieties was issued, as the Italian wine law took effect, schioppettino was missing. Since, officially, it didn't exist, its producers could not legally call their wine by its name.

The town's embattled few took on the bureaucrats and, miraculously managing to budge the immovable, obtained first from Rome, then from the Common Market headquarters in Brussels, recognition of schioppettino's existence. And so, although much of our old world may be disintegrating around us, one good wine at least has been rescued from oblivion.

Schioppettino is a scintillating ruby red, with an unflagging bouquet exuding subtly mingled earth and fruit aromas. In the mouth, superlative flavors develop graciously and firmly, delivering successive, overlapping sensations of fruit, minerals, and spice, lingering on with finesse into a slowly expiring aftertaste.

The producers of Schioppettino are Fratelli Rieppi, Ronchi di Cialla, Giuseppe Toti.

VINTAGES: Schioppettino is unusually fast blooming for such an elegant wine. It can best be appreciated at under six years of age. 1977–79 and 1982–83 were good years.

❧ *Taurasi* ☙
(D.O.C., CAMPANIA)

If Taurasi had been conceived within forty miles of the Alps instead of forty miles from Vesuvius, it would long ago have obtained broader recognition as one of the five or six greatest Italian red wines, which in fact it is. The lines on the map that indicate latitude are like the railroad tracks that used to separate the right and wrong side of town. It's on the right side of the line, the cool side, that we look for fine, vigorous, fruited wines; from the wrong side, the warm one, we expect only flaccid, stolid, flat ones. It is not an unreliable approach, but when followed inflexibly it will cause us to overlook those small enclaves in the South, favored by a cool microclimate and by particular conditions of soil, altitude, and exposure, where wines possessing all the attributes of their fine northern brethren can be produced. The province of Avellino, a thirty-minute drive from Naples, is such an enclave, and Taurasi is such a wine.

When the first snow of the year falls in the North, it also falls on the hills of Avellino. There, on vineyards 1,300 feet above sea level, beyond reach of the extreme heat that bakes the plains below each summer, grows the aglianico grape from which Taurasi is mainly derived. This may have been one of the first grapes cultivated on the peninsula for the production of wine. Its name, which is an Italian transformation of the Roman *vitis hellenica* (or "Greek vine"), reveals its provenance. In addition to aglianico, the law permits the addition in Taurasi of barbera, of sangiovese, and of piedirosso, a local red grape. But in the only Taurasi one is likely to find—and, fortunately, the only one worth looking for, that produced by Mastroberardino—there is nothing but pure aglianico.

Taurasi must be aged a minimum of three years, including at least one in wood, before it is released. To qualify as *riserva* it must be aged an additional year.

When young, Taurasi is a very dark, ruby red wine, dragging a heavy load of tannin that erases most other flavor impressions. From the moment it is bottled, it goes into a deep larval sleep that may last up to eight years or more, depending on the vintage, during which it gives few signs of life and no clues to the splendidly constituted wine that will emerge at maturity. The tightly closed nose of its infancy opens up then, scented with violet, wild cherry, and odors of earth, fur, and spice. The smooth, but stoutly fleshed body carries a rich succession of earth and mineral flavors into the mouth, nudged by subtle fruit sensations, all persisting with commanding style into the aftertaste.

VINTAGES:
Acceptable Years: 1965, 1969, 1972, 1974, 1976, 1978, 1983
Good Years: 1964, 1967, 1970, 1971, 1973, 1975, 1979, 1981
Great Years: 1961, 1968 (the Mastroberardino 1968 *riserva* is a wine of stunning power and opulence, perhaps one of the finest reds ever produced in Italy), 1977, 1980, 1982

The Medium-Range Red Wines

The group I call the Medium-Range Reds hangs together more through diversity than similarity. There are wiry, vigorous wines here and soft, round ones; some are precocious, and others slow-maturing. A few tend to edge over into the Big Reds category and several into the Light Reds. No one wine, however, is sufficiently complete for the first or slight enough for the second. They reach for tasting qualities in different directions, but within, as the title of the category suggests, an intermediate range.

Whether we are sharing a bottle with good friends or with the family, when we want neither to face a wine too compelling nor regularly to rely on one too narrow in scope, it is within this range that we do much of our drinking, and it is from this group of wines, with the immensely varied sensations they offer, that we may want most frequently to draw.

Vintage years are mentioned only when the longevity of the wine makes them relevant. In other instances it is to be assumed that the most desirable year is a good, recent one.

FAMILIES OF
MEDIUM-RANGE RED WINES

The Barbera Family

Although I had had a bottle of it now and then, I had never had much enthusiasm for Barbera, nor really understood the wine, until my first trip to Piedmont. I had arrived in the evening, late in November. It was foggy; the streets of Asti were dark and empty; I was cold. This was the hard, silent, impenetrable Piedmont I had always imagined and had long put off visiting.

It was nearly 10 P.M. and I asked to be directed to a *trattoria*. Only one was still open. I thought of balmy Rome, which I had left in the morning and where at that very moment restaurants would be just beginning to fill up. As I sat down, I was asked what I would be drinking. In small Italian restaurants one usually talks wine before talking food. Asti is Barbera country, so "Barbera," I told the man, "but bring me one of your best bottles."

The food was sturdy and extraordinarily good; *bagna caôda* to start with—a hot dip of olive oil, anchovies, and garlic for raw cardoons, finocchio, and other vegetables—and *bollito misto*—an assortment of boiled sausage, calf's head, and brisket of beef served with a sauce of parsley, capers, and olive oil. But the star of the evening was the Barbera, a five-year-old from the village of Rocchetta Tanaro. The color was flashing garnet; the fragrance intense, of crushed flowers and concentrated fruit. It was a mouthfilling, chewy wine, brawny, but without any hard edges. The sense of comfort was immediate, chasing the chill, the loneliness, the oppressive awareness of the fog waiting at the door. That is what Barbera is about.

The difference between a young, newly minted Barbera and a mature one can be dramatic. In its youth, substantial alcohol, tannin, and acid give it a hard bite. With age, however, Barbera can become warm, expansive, even tender. A full-blooded Piedmontese Barberas can rarely be expected to extend its full welcome until it has spent several years developing in the bottle.

PIEDMONT'S BARBERA

❧ Barbera d'Alba ❧

(D.O.C., PIEDMONT)

Its territory largely coincides with that of the two greatest Piedmontese reds, Barolo and Barbaresco. To use a local term, Barbera d'Alba can be *baroleggiante*, Barolo-like, a not surprising comparison given the similarity of terrain and the fact that custom dictates and the law permits correction with up to 15 percent nebbiolo, the grape of Barolo. It is the most long-lived of Barberas, in some cases capable of entering well into its second decade without signs of fatigue.

Good producers of Barbera d'Alba are often those already known for their Barolo or Barbaresco. Among them are Ceretto, Aldo Conterno, Fontanafredda, Franco Fiorina, Gaja, Giacosa, Mauro Mascarello (for Giuseppe Mascarello), Oddero, Pio Cesare, Prunotto, and Vietti. Of the many small producers, Cantina del Glicine is outstanding.

VINTAGES:
Acceptable Years: 1969, 1970, 1979, 1981
Good Years: 1961, 1964, 1967, 1971, 1974, 1978, 1980, 1982, 1983

❧ Barbera d'Asti ❧
(D.O.C., PIEDMONT)

Barbera d'Asti, produced in a much larger territory than Alba's, can be made with no other grape but barbera. It is perhaps the truest-to-type Barbera, full-bodied but not too tannic, with vigorous aroma and flavor.

Much of the soil it is grown on is heavier, more clayey, moister than Barbera d'Alba's; and Asti's wine is generally not so long-lived.

The producers in this densely cultivated, vast zone are almost beyond count. Among the ones known to me, I would recommend Antiche Terre dei Galleani, Balestrino, Giacomo Bologna, Carlo Brema, Ca' Tesi della Pianca, Amilcare Gaudio, Luigi Pia, Pinbologna, Rabezzana, Ravetto, and Scarpa.

Both Barbera d'Alba and Barbera d'Asti must be aged in wood a minimum of one year. The minimum alcohol required of Alba is 12 percent and of Asti 12½ percent. When either is aged an additional year and reaches a minimum of 13 percent alcohol, it may carry the qualification *superiore*.

Each wine has supporters that claim it as preeminent. Since the differences that exist between them are of kind rather than degree, switching from one to the other to decide the issue might become an unending, but agreeable project.

VINTAGES:
Acceptable Years: 1969, 1970, 1971, 1973, 1979, 1981
Good Years: 1964, 1974, 1978, 1980, 1983
Great Years: 1958, 1961, 1982

❧ Barbera dei Colli Tortonesi ❧
(D.O.C., PIEDMONT)

❧ Barbera del Monferrato ❧
(D.O.C., PIEDMONT)

In contrast with the Barberas from Alba and Asti, both these appellations permit greater yields per acre and blending with a variety of other grapes.

In the Colli Tortonesi up to 15 percent freisa, bonarda, and/or dolcetto may be added. It has a frankly vinous nose and a plain but brisk flavor to match. Some choice, but not common, examples are full and round, improving gracefully with two to three years of bottle age.

The Monferrato Barbera may contain as much as 25 percent other grapes: dolcetto, freisa, or grignolino. It's a formula that allows substantial variability, and Barbera del Monferrato is indeed exceptionally variable. On the whole it is lighter in body and a faster maturing than the preceding three, and it is probably the most approachable for those beginning to cut their teeth on Barbera.

VINTAGES: Barbera dei Colli Tortonesi had great years in 1978 and 1982 and a good one in 1983. For the Monferrato the same years were also good, although each was a notch below that of the Tortonesi.

The traditional, robust style of Barbera is so closely linked to one's image of Piedmontese wine that it is startling to find it is losing support from consumers and producers, naturally in that order. The old Barbera drinkers are being replaced by a new generation that is switching from Barbera's sturdy virtues to the paler, flimsier wines of the Veneto. In recognition of this, the D.O.C. statute for Barbera d'Alba and d'Asti has been amended to reduce the aging-in-wood requirement from two years to one. Winemakers are keeping the must in briefer contact with the dark skins, blending in less of the austere nebbiolo grape in Barbera d'Alba, more of the soft bonarda in the Colli Tortonesi and of the light grignolino in the Monferrato. Growers are planting new vines for Barbera d'Alba in looser, drier soil. No doubt, in time, a remodeled, meeker Barbera will become commonplace. I, for one, will have no objections, provided that alongside it there will always be a supply of the dark, rich, brawny kind, the true Barbera.

❧ Rubino di Cantavenna ❧
(D.O.C., PIEDMONT)

The four major controlled origin appellations for Barbera in Piedmont were described above. A fifth and minor one is Rubino, which was devised in 1949 by the cooperative cellar of Cantavenna, a tiny area on the right bank of the Po River. They make it with about 75 percent barbera and the rest a combination of grignolino and freisa. Its name comes from the bright ruby color, rather light for a Barbera. It is correspondingly light in flavor, a pleasant, small-scale wine, similar to some of the Monferrato Barberas.

OTHER WINES FROM THE BARBERA GRAPE

There are several hundred wines made in whole or in part from the barbera grape—how many, exactly, I would just as soon not know. Although it is cultivated from the North to the South and on the islands, it is in the North where it is most solidly entrenched. More than half of Piedmont's red wine production is from barbera, of which the D.O.C. appellations discussed above account for only a portion, about 30 percent. The others are unclassified wines, and among them one can find pink Barbera, white Barbera, Barbera *di pronta beva* (a light, acidulous wine made for immediate consumption), effervescent Barbera, and even sweet Barbera, about which the less said, the better.

Outside Piedmont, the most successful and extensive use of the grape is made in neighboring Lombardy. Next in importance, and geographically, comes Emilia-Romagna, with a much smaller but nonetheless interesting production.

LOMBARDY'S BARBERA

Barbera dell'Oltrepò Pavese
(D.O.C., LOMBARDY)

Oltrepò ("beyond the Po") designates an area of mainly sloping vineyards, some rather steep, south of Milan and, more precisely, south of the Po River and of the city of Pavia, in whose province they lie.

Oltrepò's Barbera is a true-to-type varietal, deep red, hearty, winy, frank in aroma, flavor, and aftertaste. Quite sharp at first, it soon develops into a round, satisfying wine, which, while it may not match the elegance of Alba's or the intensity of Asti's, has an appreciative and justified following among devotees of Barbera.

Its best producer is Carlo Boatti. Other good makers are Cella di Montalto, Membretti Balestreri, Orlandi, Piccolo Bacco dei Quaroni, 4 Castagni, and Edmondo Tronconi.

VINTAGES:
Acceptable Years: 1970, 1973, 1981
Good Years: 1971, 1974, 1978, 1979, 1980, 1983
Great Years: 1964, 1982

❧ *Botticino* ☙
(D.O.C., LOMBARDY)

Made in Brescia province, west of Lake Garda, from a blend of grapes in which barbera has the largest share. The others, in order of importance, are schiava, marzemino, and sangiovese. It is somewhat less acidic than most wines from barbera and at the same time richer in glycerine, consequently softer, rounder, more velvety, with suggestions of glycerine's sweetness. A good producer is Giacomo Giossi.

VINTAGES:
Acceptable Years: 1971, 1972, 1973, 1974, 1976, 1978, 1980, 1981, 1983
Good Years: 1979, 1980, 1982

❧ *Buttafuoco* ☙
(D.O.C., LOMBARDY)

It is a blend of 60 percent barbera plus a mixture of local red grapes: croatina, tinturino, vespolina, uva rara. Buttafuoco was first produced in the cellars of one of the oldest families in the Oltrepò zone, the Albericis. Although other makers are now permitted to use the name, the most worthwhile example is still the handiwork of an Alberici, Bianchina. Despite its name, which means fire thrower, and Alberici's scarlet label depicting a musketeer in the act of firing his gun, Buttafuoco is a gentle, ingratiating wine. The aroma is softly vinous, the flavor ample, deeply fruity, on a rounded, well-filled body. It has fairly good endurance, although it drinks smoothly within four years of the vintage.

VINTAGES:
Acceptable Years: 1976, 1977, 1978, 1981
Good Years: 1974, 1979, 1980, 1982, 1983

❧ *Rosso dell'Oltrepò Pavese* ☙
(D.O.C., LOMBARDY)

The Oltrepò designation, without any grape or wine name except for the simple term *rosso,* applies to a wine blended from barbera and from the local grapes croatina, uva rara, and vespolina. Barbera accounts for up to 65 percent of the total. This is the classic Oltrepò formula for enhancing the aroma and lowering the acidity of barbera. It is so prevalent in the area that the wine has been given the name of the production zone itself. The substantial amount of unclassified red wine made in the Oltrepò Pavese is also composed of the same grapes.

This is a wine intense in color—a deep ruby with flashes of garnet —and in smell—predominantly vinous, with the sweetish perfume of flowers and strawberries. In the mouth the sensation of size is supported by some tannic astringency. Brief aging, two to three years, polishes off the inital roughness, uncovering deep reserves of flavor.

Out of the crowded ranks of its producers, I would single out Lino Maga with his Ronchetto di Maga. Among the many others, some of the best are Ca' Longa, Frecciarossa, Il Frater, La Madonna Isabella, Le Fracce, Nazzano, Angelo Paroni, and Castagni.

VINTAGES: The same as Barbera dell'Oltrepò (page 66).

EMILIA-ROMAGNA'S BARBERA

❧ Barbera dei Colli Bolognesi di Monte San Pietro ❧
(D.O.C., EMILIA-ROMAGNA)

One of the most appealing manifestations of Barbera's earthy charms takes place in the Colli Bolognesi, the hills southwest of Bologna, where they make excellent red wines whose renown has yet to catch up with their undeniable merits.

Here Barbera sheds most of the sharpness common to the Piedmontese version and some of the weight characteristic of the Oltrepò. It matures quickly, exuding vinous and berrylike odors, developing in the mouth smooth, warm, fleshy impressions of deliciously ripe fruit.

Good producers are Aldo Conti, Fattoria Montebudello, and Bruno Negroni.

VINTAGES: 1975 and 1982 were great years, and except for 1981, 1976 through 1983 were good.

❧ Barbera dei Colli Piacentini ❧
(VINO DA TAVOLA, EMILIA-ROMAGNA)

Near Piacenza, just south of Lombardy's Oltrepò zone, on the sloping vineyards that spread out from the town of Ziano, the barbera grape is widely cultivated and vinified in a youthful style. It is a purplish red wine, tart, but sound, suitable for early and local consumption.

❧ *Gutturnio dei Colli Piacentini* ❧
(D.O.C., EMILIA-ROMAGNA)

I have been told again and again by its enthusiasts that this is Emilia's greatest red, but as hard as I've tried, I cannot summon any admiration for Gutturnio. It may be the jarring, guttural sound of its name, but I think it's more than that: It's the taste.

Gutturnio is made in three separate areas west and south of Piacenza from a blend of 60 percent barbera and 40 percent bonarda. The color is dark red, the aroma pungently vinous, the flavor coarse and lean. To me it is a bleak and melancholy wine.

When consumed in local *trattorie,* one may find Gutturnio slightly spritzy and, on occasion, even faintly sweet.

The Bonarda Family

❧ *Bonarda dell'Oltrepò* ❧
(D.O.C., LOMBARDY)

This is the only Bonarda listed by the D.O.C. statutes, but it owes its name to mistaken identity, since it is made not from the bonarda grape, but from the croatina, to which is added a small amount of barbera. The misnomer has been made irreversible by long-established usage, and it does not matter all that much except as one more illustration that to master the unpredictable game of Italian wine names requires resilience and, sometimes, forbearance.

What is important to those who want to try the wine is that there is a marked difference between Oltrepò's Bonarda and true Bonarda from Piedmont. Like much of the wine from the conical hills of this densely cultivated zone south of Milan, Bonarda dell'Oltrepò emphasizes robustness and frankness. It is usually higher in alcohol than Bonarda del Piemonte, more tannic, decidedly firmer, bringing its straightforward taste impressions to a short and slightly bitter close. It is best served slightly cool, without ceremony and, for that matter, without apologies, for it is a worthy red in its plain, sturdy way.

Producers include Giovanni Agnes, Orlandi, Tenuta di Nazzano, Edmondo Tronconi. Possibly the best of all Bonardas is one sold as *vino da tavola,* under the proprietary name Gaggiarone.

VINTAGES: Bonarda from good makers and exceptional years may last seven or eight years or more. The average bottle reaches its peak in under five years.
Acceptable Years: 1975, 1976, 1977, 1981, 1983
Good Years: 1974, 1978, 1979, 1980, 1982

OTHER BONARDA WINES

❧ *Barbacarlo* ❧
(D.O.C., LOMBARDY)

Another Oltrepò red made from croatina, barbera, and other red grapes. One of the most distinctive wines produced in this zone, with pronounced grape aromas, delicious flavor, and deft suggestions of almond-like bitterness in the aftertaste. Barbacarlo pours with a lively foam that settles quickly to a subdued sparkle, and it ages well. Although the D.O.C. appellation permits several producers to make it, a steeply sloping hillside long known as Barbacarlo and celebrated for its wine has for generations been the exclusive property of the Maga family. Lino Maga's Barbacarlo, D.O.C. laws notwithstanding, is not only the finest wine of this name, but the only one that deserves to bear it.

❧ *Bonarda Novarese* ❧
(VINO DA TAVOLA, PIEDMONT)

Produced in Piedmont's Novara province again not from bonarda, but from croatina, discussed on page 69. It is closely related to the neighboring Bonarda dell'Oltrepò, but it is a little fuller wine, rounder and softer.

❧ *Bonarda del Piemonte* ❧
(VINO DA TAVOLA, PIEDMONT)

This is the one Bonarda actually made from the grape whose name it bears. At one time bonarda accounted for 30 percent of all red grapes grown in Piedmont. When the phyloxera louse destroyed European vines in the late nineteenth century, and these were replaced with immune American root stocks, most of the growers of bonarda switched to barbera and freisa, which satisfied the then current preference for sharper, sturdier wines. Now that taste is again changing course, turning to softer, gentler qualities in wine, bonarda is enjoying a small revival.

Bonarda makes a light-bodied wine of rustic, homey charm. Its appeal is immediately manifested by the aroma, a simple, straightforward mixture of flowery and winy odors. It is followed in the mouth by tender taste sensations, low in tannin and acid, flowing easy and agreeable. If one tailors one's expectations to the modest but pleasing dimensions of Bonarda, it can be a reliable source of casual enjoyment. It should be consumed young and served cool, but not iced.

In addition to dry *(secco)* Bonarda, there is a semisweet *(abboccato)* version, about which the most encouraging thing that can be said is that it is very difficult to find outside the local taverns of the production zone.

The Cabernet Family

Several years ago, when I had brought back from the States a bottle of California Cabernet Sauvignon for an Italian friend, his response was "Cabernet and sauvignon? How interesting. I was not aware Americans had produced such a hybrid." Bordeaux's noblest grape is no longer that unfamiliar to Italians, but still, when the label says simply Cabernet, the wine in the bottle is likely to be made either exclusively or predominantly from the lesser cabernet franc grape. Although plantings of cabernet sauvignon are steadily increasing, and some of the remarkably fine wines now being made from it (see Sassicaia, in the Big Reds category, page 59) are calling attention to its merits and will eventually lead the way to greater expansion, it is cabernet franc that commands the field.

There are two equally strong reasons for its preeminence, one being economics, the other being taste. Cabernet franc's vigorous growth, heavier bunches, and larger berries make it a more abundant producer. In a country whose wine business is characterized by high labor costs at one end and relatively moderate prices at the other, generous yields cannot be wholly ignored by those who are in the trade to make a living. But even if it brought in less bountiful crops, the tasting qualities of cabernet franc would continue to assure it a large measure of popularity.

The circumstances that first placed cabernet franc in the hills outside

Padua early in the nineteenth century may have been fortuitous, but the way it has spread since throughout the Veneto and then to its neighbors in northeastern Italy—Friuli, Trentino, Alto Adige—owes more to choice than to chance. There is no clearer example available than the predilection for Cabernet Franc to illustrate what the people of these regions most want from a wine. It can be summed up as liveliness, fragrance, immediate attraction, and generous, unctuous flavor sharpened by a light, acidic bite. They are qualities that may not seduce those whose only loves are the classic clarets of the Médoc or the thick-textured reds of the Napa Valley, but they are nonetheless valid and appealing ones. This is a concept of wine style to which barrel age, oakiness, astringency, austerity are foreign, as they are indeed to most of the winemaking in the Northeast.

Such a blanket appraisal is no doubt too loosely woven to cover the large body of Italian wine known as Cabernet. But in approaching any related group of wines, or of anything else for that matter—paintings, literary works, or even people—an awareness of similarities is the necessary foundation for an evaluation of differences.

THE VENETO'S CABERNET

Of all the Cabernets of the Northeast, we find the broadest range of expression in those of the Veneto, where they are produced in the provinces of Vicenza, Padua, Venice, and Treviso, both on slopes and in the plains.

❧ *Breganze Cabernet* ☙
(D.O.C., VENETO)

The Breganze zone, a tranquil composition of flourishing little plains and modest hills, lies in the province of Vicenza, north of the city and well out of the way of the main motor arteries and the traffic that surges without respite through the eastern and southern sections of the Veneto. Most of its red wine is Merlot, which goes into a blend called Breganze Rosso, an indifferent wine, stirring neither enthusiasm nor disdain. Far better is its Cabernet, although, unfortunately, far less abundant. It is a dark ruby with garnet flashes, exuding a true, intensely herbaceous cabernet aroma and delivering full flavor to match—warm, velvety, with a touch of earthiness, a winning fusion of genteel and rustic charms. Most of Breganze's production is channeled through the local cooperative cellar. A good individual producer is Maculan, who indicates on the labels of his excellent Cabernets the vineyards where they were grown.

⤳ Colli Berici Cabernet ⤲
(D.O.C., VENETO)

Also in Vicenza province, but just south of the city, is the Colli Berici zone. The strong bouquet of its Cabernet is characterized by both berry-like scents and a sharp, spicy, bell-pepper aroma. Flavors are full, with a tendency to softness. Good producers here are Alfredo Lazzarini, whose Cabernet bears the name Le Rive Rosse, and Castello di Belvedere. Also from this area comes Count Da Schio's Costozza Cabernet Franc. Although he is entitled to a D.O.C. designation, Da Schio prefers to go his own way and markets his wine as an unclassified *vino da tavola*. Costozza enjoys an excellent reputation in Italy, one I am unable entirely to reconcile with the wine. Its color, while exceptionally deep, is dull, a presage of the slack, heavy taste impressions that follow.

VINTAGES:
Acceptable Years: 1977, 1978, 1981
Good Years: 1976, 1979, 1980, 1983
Great Year: 1982

⤳ Montello e Colli Asolani Cabernet ⤲
(D.O.C., VENETO)

Although Montello was only recently ennobled by a D.O.C. designation, it can claim paternity of a Cabernet whose pedigree is second to none in Italy and which, for a long while, may have been the single most admired red of the Veneto: Venegazzù. Until its recent sale, Venegazzù was the property of the Loredan family, whose ancestors ruled Venice when it was not just a city, but the most glorious nation in the Western world.

The Loredans were among the first in Italy to produce a wine modeled after the reds of Bordeaux, blending cabernet sauvignon, cabernet franc, merlot, and malbec and calling it Riserva della Casa. To compare it with claret, however, as many of its admirers insist on doing, distracts attention from its own gracefully Venetian virtues. Venegazzù does not have the color or the elaborate structure and intensity of flavor of the very best wines of Bordeaux. It is a more delicate breed of

Cabernet, with a subtle, gently penetrating bouquet, followed by a silken flow of understated flavor, lightly but firmly sustained into the keen aftertaste. Riserva della Casa is aged four years before release, three of them in traditional, used, large Yugoslav oak barrels.

Since 1978, Venegazzù has also produced a D.O.C. Cabernet Sauvignon, a strong, well-balanced wine with explicit herbaceous aromas and deep, intensely fruity flavor, a firmer, more vigorous, if slightly less elegant wine than the Riserva della Casa. The Cabernet Sauvignon is aged two years before release, one in wood, and, with proper storage, will improve with an additional two or three years' aging.

VINTAGES:
Acceptable Years: 1974, 1975, 1978, 1981
Good Years: 1976, 1977, 1979, 1980, 1983
Great Years: 1964, 1968, 1971, 1972, 1982

❦ *Piave Cabernet* ❧
(D.O.C., VENETO)

❦ *Pramaggiore Cabernet* ❧
(D.O.C., VENETO)

Both these adjacent areas are flat. The first is divided almost exactly in two by the Piave River and extends from the base of the hills of Montello and Conegliano at the west to just short of the Adriatic shore at the east. The Pramaggiore district is hemmed in by water on three sides, on the west and east by two rivers, the Livenza and Tagliamento, and on the south by the Adriatic Sea.

The soil of both is composed of the deposits from ancient floods and of much clay. The Pramaggiore zone, the smaller of the two, has looser, drier soil, richer in mineral content.

D.O.C. regulations require that Cabernet from either Piave or Pramaggiore be made entirely from cabernet sauvignon or cabernet franc or a combination of both. In practice, it is nearly all cabernet franc.

Cabernet from Pramaggiore is usually more interesting than the Piave, with a lengthier, better-sustained development of flavor; it is less coarsely fruity and not so blunt in its address to nose and palate.

Cabernet from these districts is rarely aged for long in wood, when at all, and a good thing that is. But it is also shipped promptly after it has been bottled, not so good a thing.

Pramaggiore's potential ability to turn out finer wines than it does has long been recognized. With less generous yields, more emphasis on cabernet sauvignon than on franc, more patient bottle aging in good cellars, it could equal—even surpass—the quality of the hill-grown cabernets.

In Piave some of the good producers are Collalto, Marcello del Majno, Stepski Doliwa, and Tenuta Mercante. (Possibly the finest Cabernet made in the Piave area is an unclassified red called Villa Giustinian, a blend of the two cabernet varieties, plus merlot, malbec, and petit verdot.) In Pramaggiore: Castello di Porcia, Paolo De Lorenzi, Fattoria di Summaga, La Frassinella, and Club Produttori Associati di Pradipozzo.

VINTAGES:
Acceptable Years: 1977, 1978, 1980
Good Years: 1979, 1983
Great Year: 1982

FRIULI'S CABERNET

Veneto's neighboring region to the east has six controlled appellation zones for Cabernet, two of them hilly, four on riverine or low, rolling land. The customary expectations in Italy of finer wine from slope-grown grapes assert themselves here with full justification.

Cabernet delle Grave del Friuli
(D.O.C., FRIULI-VENEZIA GIULIA)

Cabernet dell'Isonzo
(D.O.C., FRIULI-VENEZIA GIULIA)

Cabernet di Aquileia
(D.O.C., FRIULI-VENEZIA GIULIA)

Cabernet di Latisana
(D.O.C., FRIULI-VENEZIA GIULIA)

The above four are the flat, controlled appellation districts of Friuli. Their Cabernets are sound and satisfying, but generally present less finely modulated bouquets, blunter flavor, and more rustic texture than the wines from the higher-altitude vineyards. Of the four, those from Isonzo and from the gravelly soil of Grave seem to me to be the most successful, in that order. The least appealing is Aquileia's Cabernet.

Good producers in these zones are in Grave: Antonutti, Il Castello di Gianfranco Fantinel, Giacomelli, Kechler, Pighin, and Vinicola Udinese; in Isonzo: Angoris, Cantina Produttori Vini del Collio e dell'Isonzo, Cappelletti, Luisa Eddi, Il Gallo, Prandi d'Ulmhort, and Tenuta Villanova; in Latisana: Isola Augusta, and Volderie.

VINTAGES:
Acceptable Years: 1975, 1978, 1980
Good Years: 1979, 1982, 1983
Great Year: 1962

❧ Cabernet del Collio ❧
(D.O.C., FRIULI-VENEZIA GIULIA)

❧ Cabernet dei Colli Orientali del Friuli ❧
(D.O.C., FRIULI-VENEZIA GIULIA)

Collio and Colli Orientali are Friuli's two hilly D.O.C. zones. In the Colli Orientali both cabernet franc and cabernet sauvignon are permitted, either alone or blended, whereas Collio's Cabernet may be made only from the franc.

In both areas, Cabernets are characterized by the full, ripe flavor, the roundness, the fleshiness, the warmth that are representative of the numerous reds and whites produced here. Their aromas develop into bouquets that may not be complex, but are clean and pretty. The most notable feature of these wines is their ample constitution, which declares itself with the first firm impact on the palate.

Out of a great many good producers, some of the most consistent in the Collio are Attems, Paolo Caccese, Cantina Produttori del Collio e dell'Isonzo, Enofriulia, Formentini, Jermann, Komjanc, Princic, Schiopetto, and Villa Russiz. Drufovka also makes a fine blend of cabernet and merlot called Dragarska, sold as unclassified *vino da tavola*. In the Colli Orientali, good names to look for are Valentino Butussi, d'Attimis, Girolamo Dorigo, Livio Felluga, Lesizza, Pascolini, Paolo Rodaro, Ronchi di Manzano, Villa Belvedere, and Volpe Pasini.

VINTAGES:
Acceptable Years: 1978, 1980
Good Years: 1977, 1979, 1982, 1983

TRENTINO–ALTO ADIGE'S CABERNET

These Siamese twins of a region, the Trentino half speaking Italian, the Alto Adige/Südtirol half using mainly German, are two distinct yet inseparable entities, endowed with similar physical resources but producing from the same grapes sharply different wines. The "Italian-speaking" ones are rather thin and inexpressive, while the Tyrolean ones are exuberantly fragrant and packed with flavor.

❧ *Cabernet del Trentino* ❧
(D.O.C., TRENTINO–ALTO ADIGE)

Trentino's Cabernets are Italy's lightest, barely whispering the varietal's aromas and tendering flavor with a gossamer touch. Accepting as perfectly valid the objective of making light-bodied, soft-spoken wines from cabernet franc, some of these must be judged successful, but many are simply flimsy. Trentino's wines can be discouragingly variable in quality, and one must choose carefully to choose well. The Istituto Agrario Provinciale, which is one of the country's major oenological schools at San Michele all'Adige, makes a good example of Trentino Cabernet. Other good producers are Bossi Fedrigotti, Castel Segonzano, De Tarczal, Fratelli Endrizzi, Pedrotti, Pisoni, Carlo Rossi, and Tenuta San Leonardo.

The choicest Trentino wines containing cabernet are blends of both cabernet franc and merlot, sometimes with the addition of cabernet sauvignon. Since their composition does not coincide with D.O.C. specifications, they are sold as *vino da tavola* under proprietary names. The best of these are the oenological school's own Castel S. Michele, Bossi Fedrigotti's Foianeghe Rosso, Letrari's Maso Ledron, Salvetta's Rauten, and Tenuta San Leonardo's San Leonardo.

VINTAGES: The best years of the 1970s are 1971 and 1975, but are now past their prime. 1980 was good; 1982 and 1983, excellent.

❧ Cabernet dell'Alto Adige/Südtiroler Cabernet ❧
(D.O.C., TRENTINO–ALTO ADIGE)

Alto Adige, the northern half of the Trentino–Alto Adige region, is the ex-Austrian Tyrol, turned over to Italy after World War I as its reward for having chosen, then, the right side to fight on. The Südtirol, as its inhabitants prefer to call it, makes what are possibly Italy's most enticing Cabernets. While they are often considerably lighter than their counterparts from Veneto and Friuli, they have the effusively perfumed scents, the clarity of flavor, the remarkable freshness, and the perfect balance that earn the better wines of the Alto Adige enduring allegiance from those fortunate enough to be acquainted with them.

Production is regrettably very small, but Cabernet from the Südtirol is not exactly a rarity and well repays what effort may be required to find it.

The cooperative cellars that dominate production in Alto Adige work to a standard of quality that seems to be beyond the reach of most cooperatives elsewhere. Two of the best ones are Kellereigenossenschaft Girlan with its Baron Kurtatsch Cabernet and Kellereigenossenschaft Terlan with its Cabernet Riserva. Among the individual producers, I would recommend Hirschprunn, Josef Hofstätter, Alois Lageder, Laimburg, Schloss Schwanburg, and Soini.

NOTE: The most exquisitely made wines of Alto Adige, those of Giorgio Grai, are wrapped in mystery. Part of the mystery is how Giorgio can, in good years and bad, outstrip all others in producing reds of depth and refinement and whites of seemingly imperishable delicacy. The larger part of the mystery is how to get them, because their maker, like many artists, appears to feel that creating his masterpieces is the beginning and end of the process and whether anyone buys them is inconsequential. Despite rumors to the contrary, I can confirm that they do exist, for I have had them at the Grai home and occasionally even found them in Italian wine shops and restaurants. The labels Giorgio Grai uses are Herrnhofer and Bellendorf. His own name does not appear. Grai's 1971 Cabernet is as beautiful a red wine as I have ever tasted and for its extraordinary range of odors and flavors would deserve a place in the preceding category of Big Reds, or perhaps, in a category of its own.

Vintages:
Acceptable Years: 1978, 1979, 1981
Good Years: 1968, 1971, 1974, 1975, 1976, 1980, 1982, 1983
Great Year: 1969

LOMBARDY'S CABERNET

❧ *Franciacorta Rosso* ☙
(D.O.C., LOMBARDY)

Franciacorta is produced about fifty miles northeast of Milan, on the slopes of a hilly district near Lake Iseo. It is a curious blend of cabernet franc, barbera, nebbiolo, and merlot, the cabernet accounting for about 50 percent of the total. The result is a wine that resembles no other in the cabernet family, bright ruby in color, with a pleasing, uncomplicated vinous nose, and frank but gracious flavor. It combines some of the gracefulness of Veneto's wines with the body and impact one expects in a Lombard red.

Some of the good producers of Franciacorta are Barboglio de' Gaioncelli, Cà del Bosco, Castello di Bornato, Della Croce, Fratelli Berlucchi, and Monte Rossa.

Vintages: About three to five years is the average life span for Franciacorta. Save for 1977 and 1981, all the years from 1974 through 1983 are good.

OTHER WINES FROM CABERNET GRAPES

❧ *Cabernet Sauvignon Terre Rosse* ☙
(VINO DA TAVOLA, EMILIA-ROMAGNA)

Terre Rosse is the property of Enrico Vallania, a Bologna physician who created a mild stir a few years ago when he cleared away from his cellar the entire stock of wood barrels. In agreement with the newest Italian approach to making red wine (which maintains that flavors developed in wood are foreign to wine character) Vallania makes a fresh, fragrant, clean-tasting Cabernet Sauvignon. The attention he has got is possibly in excess of the allurement of the wine, but within its modest range, Terre Rosse is a most attractive Cabernet, firm in flavor and graceful in body.

Cabernet Sauvignon di Miralduolo

(VINO DA TAVOLA, UMBRIA)

Lungarotti, the same man responsible for the marvelous Rubesco Riserva described on page 48, began a small production of Cabernet Sauvignon in 1974. It is a powerful example of the breed, loaded with fruit, with that depth of flavor the French call *fond.* It may become one of Italy's great reds some day, but at the moment it lacks balance; it is a bit too blunt, lacking the gracious development on the palate that would bring refinement to the intensity of its taste impressions. It is also marred by the presence of CO_2, just a slight prickliness, a defect of which the producer is aware and which he is working to eliminate.

Ghiaie della Furba

(VINO DA TAVOLA, TUSCANY)

This blend of cabernet sauvignon and merlot is the work of Contini-Bonacossi, the producers of the fine Montalbano Chianti and of Carmignano already discussed on pages 41-2 and 47. It is an exceptionally successful wine, clearly stamped with cabernet character. The color is a deep, flashing ruby; the bouquet a sustained emanation of herbaceous, fruited, and resinous aromas; the flavor supple, but not overmuch so, for it rests on a firm structure that brings the wine to a vigorous finish. The only vintages I have news of are 1978, 1979, and 1980, which appear to be good, particularly the 1978.

Fiorano

(VINO DA TAVOLA, LATIUM)

From vineyards just ten miles outside Rome, laid out beside the ancient Appian Way, comes this silky blend of cabernet franc and merlot. Fiorano has a heady, ripe bouquet that is confirmed by supple and warm taste sensations. Its charms bloom early and should not be savored much later than five or six years after the vintage.

❦ *Torre Ercolana* ❧
(VINO DA TAVOLA, LATIUM)

Created by Luigi Colacicchi, the late director of Rome's Philharmonic Orchestra, Torre Ercolana is both one of the rarest and one of the most highly esteemed Italian reds. In Italy rarity and esteem sometimes grow at the same pace, but quality does not always stay abreast of them. This blend of cabernet franc and merlot, which includes Rome's native cesanese grape, is an excellent wine, but if a few more people had an opportunity to taste it, it might be ranked as just a little less than exalted. The color is a garnet to ruby red. The bouquet is keen, but pinched, and far short of elaborate. It shows well on the palate, very round and full, with exceptionally good flavor, if a touch too supple and warm. Its vintages from 1968 through 1971 have all been rated good, as are 1975 and 1977 through 1982.

❦ *Favonio* ❧
(VINO DA TAVOLA, APULIA)

The southernmost outpost, the Key West as it were, of cabernet production in Italy is Foggia, inland of the spur on the eastern coast of the Italian boot. Here Attilio Simonini makes a 100 percent Cabernet Franc varietal he calls Favonio, after the local name for a westerly wind that blows from Africa. It has not the suavity of Rome's Fiorano, but stresses instead the generous vinosity, the forthright flavor, the juiciness of a well-made Cabernet Franc. It is closest to some of the wines from Piave or Pramaggiore in the Veneto described above on pages 74–5. Favonio develops with time nothing so attractive as the vigor and fruit it possesses in its youth and should be consumed not older than three or four years.

The Merlot Family

In talking about wine, one is drawn by necessity, if often with reluctance, into discussions of climate, soil, grapes, and cellar techniques. But, as I have suggested elsewhere, an equally illuminating approach to Italian wine could be to view it as an expression of the character of those who make it and drink it.

If merlot has become the most widely cultivated red grape of the Veneto, it is because the wine's sweetly perfumed aromas, its prompt charm, its youthful, easy, softly fruited flavors so neatly coincide with the tastes of the gentle-mannered people of this most ingratiating of Italy's regions.

THE VENETO'S MERLOT

The bulk of Veneto's Merlot is produced and consumed without the benefit of controlled appellation status, but there is nonetheless a substantial amount that carries one of the following D.O.C. designations.

❧ *Breganze Rosso* ☙
(D.O.C., VENETO)

It is composed of at least 85 percent merlot, with the remainder left to the producer's choice of any of six other red grapes, alone or combined. This is perhaps the feeblest rendition of Merlot character, a wine of mainly local interest, most of whose production issues from a cooperative cellar. The best individual producer of it is Maculan.

❧ *Colli Berici Merlot* ☙
(D.O.C., VENETO)

On this small group of tenderly rounded hills south of Vicenza the eternal cover of Mediterranean vegetation—oak woods, olive trees, flourishing vines—is torn now and then by crags and rocks where the earth's bones have broken through its velvety green skin. It is a striking setting for wines, both red and white, that sometimes reach notable peaks of distinction. Among the Colli Berici Merlots, one is outstanding, Lazzarini's Campo del Lago. An exquisitely composed bouquet of fresh floral scents is followed in the mouth by warm, fleshy sensations of fruit, coming prettily to a close in a stylish, gently tapering finish. Of Lazzarini's fine red wines—his Cabernet is discussed on page 73 and his Pinot Nero on page 100—this is the most remarkable, perhaps the most appealing of Italy's Merlots. Another good producer in Colli Berici, although not quite a match for Lazzarini, is Castello di Belvedere.

VINTAGES: Colli Berici Merlot should be enjoyed in its youth. The best recent vintage is 1982. Also good was 1983.

❧ Colli Euganei Rosso ❧
(D.O.C., VENETO)

Just south of the Berici hills, and into the province of Padua, is a large group of steep, volcanic hills, more forbidding than the Colli Berici and known as Colli Euganei. The turbulence of their volcanic past still seethes in the steaming waters of underground streams that have been tapped to feed the therapeutic baths of Abano and other spas clustered at the hills' feet.

At present, there is no D.O.C. designation for a Colli Euganei Merlot as such, but there is a Colli Euganei Rosso that must contain up to 80 percent merlot grapes, plus some cabernet franc, cabernet sauvignon, barbera and/or raboso. It is a soft, full, meaty wine whose most distinctive characteristic is a powerfully vinous odor. Production is controlled mainly by a cooperative cellar.

VINTAGES: The same as Colli Berici (page 82).

❧ Merlot del Piave ❧
(D.O.C., VENETO)

❧ Merlot di Pramaggiore ❧
(D.O.C., VENETO)

Piave and Pramaggiore, two adjacent, flat zones northeast of Venice, are the principal sources of Veneto's Merlot. Piave is by far the larger, producing four times as much as Pramaggiore. Both their Merlots are at least 90 percent varietals, to which up to 10 percent cabernet may be added, particularly in less sturdy vintages. They are fully representative of the soft, easy-drinking, vinous qualities one expects from Merlot in the Veneto. The wine from Pramaggiore often has the edge in character, with a perceptibly herbaceous keenness to the nose and more animated, berrylike sensations in the mouth. Good producers in Piave are Bertoja di Ceneda, Bianchi Kunkler, Marcello Del Majno, Stepski-Doliwa, and Verga Falzacappa. In Pramaggiore it is Paolo De Lorenzi, Fattoria di Summaga, and the producers' association known as Produttori Associati di Pradipozzo. (For a fuller description of the Piave and Pramaggiore zones, turn to Cabernet, page 74.)

VINTAGES: There is nothing to be gained in looking for old vintages of Piave or Pramaggiore wines. The years from 1976 through 1979 and 1982–83 were good. 1982 is the best of recent vintages.

❧ *Montello e Colli Asolani Merlot* ❧
(D.O.C., VENETO)

The Montello zone, recently elevated to D.O.C. status, is better known for its wild mushrooms and the imperishably romantic town of Asolo than for its production of Merlot, which is small. What there is tends to be firmer and fuller than that of other zones and penetratingly vinous in smell. No individual bottler of Merlot worth noting has yet emerged here.

FRIULI'S MERLOT

❧ *Merlot dei Colli Orientali del Friuli* ❧
(D.O.C., FRIULI–VENEZIA GIULIA)

❧ *Merlot del Collio* ❧
(D.O.C., FRIULI–VENEZIA GIULIA)

❧ *Merlot delle Grave del Friuli* ❧
(D.O.C., FRIULI–VENEZIA GIULIA)

❧ *Merlot dell'Isonzo* ❧
(D.O.C., FRIULI–VENEZIA GIULIA)

❧ *Merlot di Aquileia* ❧
(D.O.C., FRIULI–VENEZIA GIULIA)

❧ *Merlot di Latisana* ❧
(D.O.C., FRIULI–VENEZIA GIULIA)

In the six controlled appellation zones of Friuli, the northeastern region squeezed in between Veneto and Yugoslavia, merlot is grown side by side with cabernet. Although Friuli's Merlot is, on the whole, a less flimsy and more interesting wine than the Veneto's, it is still less fascinating than the Cabernet. Since the observations that were put forward on the relative merits of the six Friuli appellations with respect to Cabernet are equally applicable to Merlot, the reader interested in the particulars should refer to that section (pages 75–6). To sum them up briefly here, the slope-grown wines from the Colli Orientali and Collio zones have a refined and complete bouquet, together with intensity and length of flavor, that the products of the plains (Grave, Isonzo, Aquileia, Latisana) rarely approach.

In all six zones, the producers mentioned in the Cabernet chapter are similarly valid sources of Merlot. In addition, Humar's Merlot from the Collio, De Rossi's in Grave, and that of I Mori from Colli Orientali are highly recommended.

VINTAGES: All the years from 1969 through 1979 and 1982–83 were good to excellent, with the exception of the very uneven 1976 vintage. If a perfectly stored bottle of the great 1962 vintage should miraculously turn up, it just may be worth trying. Otherwise, it will be a rare bottle of Merlot older than five years that has not begun its descent into decrepitude.

TRENTINO–ALTO ADIGE'S MERLOT

❧ Merlot del Trentino ❧
(D.O.C., TRENTINO–ALTO ADIGE)

Here, on the Italian-speaking half of the region that incorporates the ex-Austrian Tyrol, both Merlot and Cabernet are popular. Perhaps because one's expectations of Merlot are smaller in scale, it is frequently more satisfactory than the Trentino's thin Cabernets and develops quickly into tender, graceful, appealingly fragrant wine.

The most successful Merlots and Cabernets from the Trentino are often blends of both varieties, usually sold as unclassified *vino da tavola*. Several producers do bottle varietal Merlot, and among the best of these are Bossi Fedrigotti, De Cles, De Tarczal, Istituto Agrario Provinciale, Mandelli, Pedrotti, Soardi, and Tenuta San Leonardo.

VINTAGES: Until the excellent 1982 harvest, there were only two good vintages in the last decade, 1975 and 1980. Both of these are well past their prime now, and we can turn happily to the 1982 and the nearly as good 1983.

❧ Merlot dell'Alto Adige/Südtiroler Merlot ❧
(D.O.C., TRENTINO–ALTO ADIGE)

In the northern half of the Trentino–Alto Adige region, the German-speaking Südtirol, not much Merlot is made, but what there is stands out from all other versions for its ebullient bouquet of flowers and berries and for the delicacy and balance of its flavors. The finest is produced by Josef Hofstätter; it contains a small percentage of petit verdot, a firm, vigorous grape whose sturdy frame supports merlot's fruity softness, giving it backbone and depth, which are rare in Italian merlots. Another good producer is Hirschprunn.

VINTAGES: The 1982 and 1983 vintages were excellent and, at present, are the only ones to look for.

OTHER MERLOTS

❧ Colli Morenici Mantovani del Garda Rosso ❧
(D.O.C., LOMBARDY)

A large name for a small wine. A minimum of 20–40 percent merlot grapes are blended with several other red varietals in this pale ruby, fresh, light wine, hill-grown near the southern tip of Lake Garda, on soil composed of rocky, glacial debris.

❧ Merlot delle Tre Valli Bergamasche ❧
(VINO DA TAVOLA, LOMBARDY)

A very dark, winy, soft, fast-maturing example of pure Merlot, produced near Bergamo. Like the Colli Morenici Rosso mentioned above, it is a wine whose availability is restricted to its zone of production.

❧ Merlot Montelio ❧
(VINO DA TAVOLA, LOMBARDY)

Very full, chewy, grainy, high-alcohol Merlot from Lombardy's Oltrepò Pavese zone, where wines from this grape are not entitled to a D.O.C. designation.

❧ Merlot dei Colli Bolognesi di Monte San Pietro ❧
(D.O.C., EMILIA-ROMAGNA)

It is produced in the fertile hills southwest of Bologna. Its full and sometimes overripe flavors, its warmth in the mouth and softness give away the origin in rich soil and sun-baked slopes. What it lacks in delicacy and freshness it makes up in substantial and prolonged taste impressions. The best-known producer is Aldo Conti.

❧ Merlot di Aprilia ❧
(D.O.C., LATIUM)

Produced near Rome, a decent, but dull, leaden wine, in whose coarseness it is hard to recognize the presence of the grape responsible for the scented charms and spryness of Merlot in the northeastern regions.

The Montepulciano Family

❧ Montepulciano d'Abruzzo ❧
(D.O.C., ABRUZZI)

The sturdiest feature of Montepulciano d'Abruzzo is the second half of its name, taken from the central Italian region where it is produced. Rugged mountains, difficult roads, isolated towns, niggardly soil have made Abruzzi a tough, inward-looking land. Civilization after civilization has slid around it, stopping elsewhere to deposit its glories. Only recently has Abruzzi begun to be pried open by fast highways and promoters of winter sports. One might expect the principal red wine of this rough-cast region to be strong, heavy, long-lived, and deep in flavor. Anyone who does will be disappointed.

This is a purplish wine with a simple, straightforward aroma, clean, vinous, and agreeable. Its tasting impressions are warm and generously fruited, punctuated by a slight tannic astringency. A broad development of flavors, however, and lingering aftertaste are not Montepulciano's distinguishing characteristics. It is a wine for easygoing drinking, satisfying a thirst for simple, honestly winy flavor, demanding no more than a casual response from either the palate or one's critical faculties.

Montepulciano d'Abruzzo is often confused with Vino Nobile di Montepulciano, the dark Tuscan wine made in the Chianti style which is described on page 50. The similarity is only in the names, for no two red wines could be more different. While Vino Nobile is a hard, slow-maturing wine of complex flavors and seemingly never-flagging power, the pleasure of drinking Montepulciano d'Abruzzo, which can be considerable when it is young, declines after its third or fourth year. What the two wines share is the name of the town where it was believed the grape had originally come from. There is no montepulciano in Vino Nobile, however, which is made almost exclusively from sangiovese. On the other hand, there is a little sangiovese in Montepulciano.

My evaluation of this wine must be qualified by pointing out that within its vast D.O.C.-designated zone, which embraces the entire Abruzzi region, there are pockets of production, particularly in the north, near Teramo, that are capable of giving rise to wine of sturdier structure. Nevertheless, it would not accurately portray the character of a wine produced in such abundance to judge it other than by those examples that are most representative of its general standard.

A producer whose wine's longevity and depth are so extraordinary as to be anomalous for Montepulciano is Emidio Pepe. Other makers producing better-than-average wine, although not at Pepe's level, are Lucio Di Giulio, Illuminati, and Valentini.

VINTAGES:
Acceptable Years: 1982, 1983
Good Years: 1977, 1979, 1980

OTHER WINES
FROM MONTEPULCIANO GRAPES

❧ *Rosso Conero* ❧
(D.O.C., MARCHES)

Rosso Conero is similar to Montepulciano d'Abruzzo and with good reason, since it is made from the same proportion of montepulciano and sangiovese grapes, although the current tendency is to reduce or eliminate sangiovese. Rosso Conero is made immediately north of Abruzzi, in the region called Marches, better known for its popular white wine, Verdicchio. The name Conero is that of the landscape's most prominent feature, a hulk of a mountain that rests on the Adriatic shore, looking like the upended stern of a colossal ship. Rosso Conero has the same frank, vinous appeal in aroma and flavor of Montepulciano d'Abruzzo, with a dry, astringent finish. It should be drunk young.

The montepulciano grape is grown extensively in the Marches, where it is made into such non-D.O.C. wines as Montepulciano del Piceno, Montepulciano del Nevola, Montepulciano dei Colli Pesaresi. They may vary in intensity of flavor and fragrance from Rosso del Conero, but not enough to matter. Of them all, one may expect more alcohol, a heavier impact, and greater longevity from the Colli Pesaresi Montepulciano.

Good producers of Rosso Conero are Garofoli, Fratelli Torelli, and Umani Ronchi.

VINTAGES: 1980 and 1982 were good years; 1979, a great one.

◄ *Rosso Piceno* ►
(D.O.C., MARCHES)

The wine produced in greatest abundance in the Marches is not the universally known Verdicchio, but this red made from sangiovese and montepulciano. Although it contains more of the sangiovese, it looks and tastes more like a thin Montepulciano. Purplish in color, it is a simple, fresh, lightly fruited wine. It can be charming, but usually has little to promise after its second year. A heavier version of it from a more restricted area is entitled to the qualification *superiore*.

Good producers of Rosso Piceno are Boccabianca, La Torraccia, and Villamagna; of the *superiore,* Picenum.

VINTAGES: The currently most desirable years are 1982 and 1983.

◄ *Rosso della Bissera* ►
(VINO DA TAVOLA, EMILIA-ROMAGNA)

One of the most attractive wines made from the montepulciano grape, produced southwest of Bologna in the hilly zone known as Monte San Pietro. Its fruited appeal is native to the grape, but the warm, dense, juicy flavor is something it shares with other reds made in the same area. The producer is Bruno Negroni.

❧ *Riserva Il Falcone* ❧
(CASTEL DEL MONTE D.O.C., APULIA)

A special edition of Castel del Monte Rosso produced by the house of
Rivera. Whereas standard Castel del Monte Rosso is primarily composed
of the native Apulian varieties—nero di troia and bombino nero—with
minor quantities of montepulciano, Rivera allows the montepulciano
grape to dominate the blend in its *riserva*.

Riserva Il Falcone is a dark, ruby-garnet wine, with a thickly scented
bouquet and a warm, velvety, sinuous body. It undergoes several years
of barrel aging and is exceptionally long-lived. It is perhaps the most
distinguished wine made from the montepulciano variety.

VINTAGES: The best current vintages are 1975, 1977, and 1978.

❧ *Cori Rosso* ❧
(D.O.C., LATIUM)

A blend of two local Roman red grapes—nero buono and cesanese—
with montepulciano, the latter's presence being the most commanding.
A spicily perfumed, soft, mild-flavored red. Like nearly all wines from
the montepulciano grape, it is best consumed young.

The Nebbiolo Family
of Medium-Range Red Wines

The wines discussed here are all descended from the same fine grape that
fathers Barolo and other noble reds described in the Big Reds category
on pages 19–30). They have been grouped separately from the others not
because they are insignificant wines, as indeed they are not, but because
their reach falls short of that aristocratic finesse, that complete expression
of nebbiolo character, which distinguishes the loftier branch of the
family.

◀ *Nebbiolo d'Alba* ▶
(D.O.C., PIEDMONT)

The banks of a slow, yellow river separate Nebbiolo d'Alba from Barolo and Barbaresco, the two majestic reds made from the same grape.

On the slopes of the hills on the right bank of the Tanaro River, exposed full south, are the vineyards of Barolo and Barbaresco; on the ones on the left bank, turned more to the east, those of Nebbiolo d'Alba. The grape, nebbiolo, is the same. The wines are not. Left-bank Nebbiolo is lighter, less alcoholic, livelier, as are other wines from grapes grown largely by the cooler, brighter light of morning. Nebbiolo d'Alba is not subjected to prolonged barrel aging and becomes ready for consumption early. It does not possess the heavier, tarlike odors of the fuller wines made from the grape, but it exceeds them in delivering to a marked degree that fruited scent that recalls raspberries. Moderate tannin and next to imperceptible oakiness allow for more emphasis on freshness, which, combined with firm, palpable flavor, make a two- to three-year-old Nebbiolo d'Alba more appealing than most of its related Piedmontese reds at the same stage of development.

The most graceful examples of the wine are produced in the western section of the controlled territory, a zone called Roeri, particularly within the townships of Monteu Roero and Vezza d'Alba. A small portion of the Nebbiolo d'Alba designated area overruns the right bank of the Tanaro, encroaching on Barolo and Barbaresco territory, where, not surprisingly, it sometimes yields a more robust, even complex wine.

A large quantity of Nebbiolo is produced in Piedmont without any D.O.C. designation, bearing simply the grape name, either alone or combined with such generic geographic qualifications as Nebbiolo del Piemonte, Nebbiolo delle Langhe, Nebbiolo di Tortona, and so on. It is exceedingly variable: some of it quite interesting, most of it simple carafe wine.

The names of good producers of Nebbiolo d'Alba are often the same as those of Barolo and Barbaresco. Among them are Accademia Torregiorgi, Ceretto, Franco Fiorina, Angelo Gaja, Bruno Giacosa, Mauro Mascarello (for Giuseppe Mascarello), Oddero, Prunotto, Renato Ratti, Scarpa, Serafino, and Terre del Barolo.

VINTAGES: Nebbiolo d'Alba has a short life span. 1982 and 1983 are the best of recent vintages.

SIX NEBBIOLO WINES
FROM NORTHEASTERN PIEDMONT

❧ *Boca* ☙
(D.O.C., PIEDMONT)

A common feature of Boca and the five wines that follow is that while they are composed predominantly of nebbiolo, they also contain varying quantities of lesser grapes, mainly bonarda and vespolina.

Boca is a deep red wine produced in vineyards not far from those of Gattinara. The characteristic flowery scent of the nebbiolo grape is in the nose, but on the palate the texture is more rustic and the aftertaste strong. A good producer is Bertolo.

❧ *Bramaterra* ☙
(D.O.C., PIEDMONT)

Produced on a single hill by the same name, just west of Gattinara. In its youth it is a brilliant garnet, tough, off-putting wine. It develops with time; and in great vintages, which may take close to a decade, a fine, protracted bouquet, with the customary nebbiolo floweriness and earthiness, is succeeded by firm, mineral taste impressions with a bitter undertow. It has perhaps the most sharply articulated personality of the entire group of wines discussed here. The producers of Bramaterra are Luigi Perazzi and Tenuta Agricola Sella.

❧ *Fara* ☙
(D.O.C., PIEDMONT)

Grown in moraine-rich soil south of Gattinara, it is one of the most immediately pleasing, least austere of these wines, with a small, but flowery nose and tenderly fruity taste sensations quickened by notable acidity.

❧ *Ghemme* ☙
(D.O.C., PIEDMONT)

The town of Ghemme is just south of Gattinara, and its wine displays tasting qualities that are close to the finer breed of nebbiolos, although decidedly blunter. In Ghemme one meets explicit and intense sensations of earth and tar in the nose, combined with the penetrating odor of faded flowers. Impressions on the palate are ample, enveloping, and, at times, velvety; they may not unfold with the complex development of a first-rank Gattinara, but they are substantial and solidly satisfying. At the modest price it usually bears, a good bottle of Ghemme can be one of the best values in Italian red wine.

Some of its good bottlers are Bertolo, Ponti, and Sebastiani.

❧ Lessona ☙
(D.O.C., PIEDMONT)

The vineyards of Lessona, well west of Gattinara, have long been the fief of the Sella family, who began production of this wine. Lessona can be nearly as fine as a good Barbaresco, combining both the earthy and the ethereal, flowery qualities of nebbiolo. To the mouth its solid, fleshy structure brings deep, smooth flavor. It is moderately tannic for a nebbiolo wine and can be quite palatable rather early in its development, but good acid levels give it considerable endurance, and in particularly successful vintages it can sail with full force well into its tenth year. Lessona's producers are Azienda Agricola Sella and Ormezzano.

❧ Sizzano ☙
(D.O.C., PIEDMONT)

A minor, fast-maturing wine, of basically local appeal, whose muted expression of nebbiolo character confirms the substantial presence of other and lesser grapes in its blend.

VINTAGES: Of the wines described above, the most long-lived is Bramaterra, followed by Ghemme, Boca, Lessona, Fara, and Sizzano, in that order.
Boca, Bramaterra, and Lessona
Acceptable Years: 1976, 1981
Good Years: 1964, 1969, 1970, 1971, 1974, 1978, 1979, 1980, 1983
Great Year: 1982

Fara
Good Years: 1978, 1979, 1980, 1983
Great Year: 1982

Ghemme
Acceptable Years: 1975, 1976, 1981
Good Years: 1964, 1970, 1971, 1973, 1979, 1980, 1983
Great Years: 1974, 1978, 1982

Sizzano
Good Years: 1974, 1978, 1979, 1980, 1982, 1983

TWO MOUNTAIN WINES
FROM THE NEBBIOLO GRAPE

❧ *Carema* ❧
(D.O.C., PIEDMONT)

You are on the highway taking you into Italy from France through the Mont Blanc tunnel. When the border is about eighty miles behind you, move into the slow lane, ease the pressure on the accelerator, and look up to the right. You will see what appear to be the ruined stumps of a sprawling, hill-climbing temple, now roofed over by vines. They are the vineyards of Carema, whose vines are supported, like no others in the world, by a forest of broad, stately, stone pillars rooted in the hillside.

It is a strange and wonderful place, well worth unhurried acquaintance, and so is the rare and good wine it produces.

Carema, like Barolo and Barbaresco, is a full-blooded offspring of the nebbiolo grape, with no other grape permitted, not even in minimum percentages. Before the wine is released, it must be aged no less than four years, including at least two in wood. The lime-rich soil it comes from is composed of rocks and sand left behind a million years ago by the glaciers that scooped out the valley. The vineyards climb steeply above the valley, to a height of two thousand feet and more, fully exposed to the sun, while the force of the winds blowing down from the Alps is spent against the mountainside at their back.

In these conditions a somewhat different wine is made from that produced with the same nebbiolo grape in the lower, mistier, more compact hills of Barolo and Barbaresco. Some describe it as being lighter, but Carema is not really a light wine, even though it is a trifle paler. What distinguishes it from other Piedmontese wines of the nebbiolo family is a purer, more elevated fragrance, stripped of much of the earthiness and weighty aroma one expects of this varietal. Round fruit flavors expand in the mouth with silkiness and elegance; they may lack Barolo's commanding intensity, but they develop nonetheless to a remarkable depth.

The total acreage of Carema is minuscule, about one hundred acres altogether, fragmented among many small growers who do not have facilities for aging and bottling wine. The only two labels to look for are Luigi Ferrando and Cantina Produttori Nebbiolo di Carema. The latter is a cooperative cellar that ages and bottles wine made by its members. In favorable years it bottles a special selection called Carema dei Carema. If you say it quickly it sounds like *crème de la crème,* and that is exactly what it is.

VINTAGES: Carema is a wine of moderate longevity, one that reaches its peak within five to six years and, in a sturdy vintage year, may maintain it another three or four years before losing its vigor.
Good Years: 1974, 1978, 1979, 1980, 1982, 1983

⋗ *Donnaz* ⋖
(D.O.C., VAL D'AOSTA)

In fixing Donnaz's place within the family of medium-range red wines from the nebbiolo grape, it helps to take into account its close relationship to Piedmont's Carema. Although a regional border separates them, their vineyards are less than five miles apart, and the two wines are grown in environments that are substantially similar: high altitudes, steep slopes, soil composed of the lean, loose mixture of gravel and sand left behind by the prehistoric migration of glaciers.

Like Carema, Donnaz has the bright, transparent color of mountain-grown wines and the winning freshness, the airy lightness of their bouquet. A violet-scented, faintly tarlike nose discloses the nebbiolo lineage, to which Donnaz brings a whiff of almonds that is its own. It is a more slender, more buoyant, less palate-gripping wine than the more robust examples of the breed from Alba or Novara, but none surpasses it in graceful delivery of flavor.

Donnaz must be made from no less than 85 percent nebbiolo and has to be aged three years before release, two of them in wood. Its life span is relatively brief, usually reaching a peak of development by its fifth year.

Production is always small, and what bottles are commercially available carry the labels either of the Caves Cooperatives de Donnaz or of Luigi Ferrando.

VINTAGES: The oldest vintage that may still have enough vitality to make it interesting is 1974. Other good years are 1978–80, and 1982–83.

THE NEBBIOLO GRAPE IN LOMBARDY

❧ *Valtellina Superiore* ☙
(D.O.C., LOMBARDY)

Grumello, Inferno, Sassella, Valgella

The circumstances that encourage the breeding of fine wines—lean soil, abundant light, warm days, cool nights, well-ventilated, sloping vineyards, a noble grape—all come together in Valtellina. Its vineyards face south toward the sun's day-long warmth. Below their terraced ranks, more light bounds up, tossed off the broad back of the river Adda as it canters west toward the lake of Como. Behind them, sheltering the vines from stunting winds, is the alpine barrier that separates northern Italy from Switzerland.

The grape for Valtellina is nebbiolo, although here it is known by a local name, chiavennasca. However it is called, the brilliant, garnet color, the alcohol nose trailing scents of violet and tar, the depth of flavor, the slow tapering off of the aftertaste leave no doubt as to the true nebbiolo character of Valtellina wines.

It is only the wine from the upper slopes—Valtellina Superiore—that is made almost entirely of nebbiolo. Wine from the valley bottom is labeled simply Valtellina, and it contains up to 30 percent of other grapes. The minimum aging requirement for Valtellina is one year, while for Valtellina Superiore it is two, of which one must be in wood. Valtellina Superiore may be further qualified—and usually is—as Grumello, Inferno, Sassella, or Valgella. These are geographic subzones.

Their differences are less apparent than their similarities, except to those regularly exposed to them. Sassella has the largest number of enthusiasts and appears to be the amplest, most long-lived wine of the four. Valgella is the freshest and liveliest. Inferno can be beautifully balanced, delivering deep flavor with grace and even charm. Grumello, sturdy and warm, closely resembles Sassella. All of them are characterized by berrylike flavors that give them a more immediate and simpler appeal than the more elaborate and austere Piedmontese wines from nebbiolo.

The wines of Valtellina have a long history of success, and among the testimonials to their quality are references in the writings of Pliny, Virgil, and Leonardo. The promise of this exceptional growing area, however, is not always completely fulfilled. The major obstacle is the very success that Valtellina has traditionally enjoyed with its neighbor on the northern side of the mountains. Much of Valtellina's production goes to Switzerland, where a thirsty and uncritical market makes the struggle for excellence superfluous.

A recent blow has been the death of Nino Negri, who for many decades was the most knowledgeable and dedicated of Valtellina's producers, a tireless bearer of the burdensome standard of quality. The mass-produced wines now distributed under the Negri labels are sound and offer good value, but more character may perhaps be found in the excellent bottlings of Enologica Valtellinese. Other good producers are Nera, Rainoldi, Tona, and Fratelli Triacca.

❧ Sfurzàt or Sforzato ❧

(D.O.C., PRECEDED BY THE DESIGNATION
VALTELLINA, LOMBARDY)

Sfurzàt is Valtellina produced from grapes that have been allowed to shrivel after the harvest and before the crush. (For a fuller description of this technique, see Amarone, pages 55–6.)

Its deep garnet color is tinged early on with orange. The high alcohol content is apparent at the first sniff, together with odors of sun-dried fruit. It is full and warm on the palate with thick, resinous flavors edged by astringency that lingers on even in wines of considerable age.

A fascinating and robust wine, Sfurzàt is, however, more heavy-handed than Veneto's Amarone, never quite attaining the seductive texture and exquisite balance of the similarly produced wine from Valpolicella. For those just beginning to make an acquaintance with nebbiolo, it may be best to try first those wines that are products of conventional vinification and more closely representative of the breed.

VINTAGES: Like most wines from the nebbiolo grape, Valtellina tends to take the slow road to maturity. Wines from fine vintages may take five or six years to come around, and special selections, such as the *riservas,* may hang back even longer. Sfurzàt has particularly long endurance, but even a choice Sassella from an outstanding year is capable of striding into its second decade without flagging.

Acceptable Years: 1973, 1975, 1979, 1980
Good Years: 1959, 1961, 1969, 1970, 1971, 1978, 1983
Great Years: 1947, 1952, 1964, 1982

The Pinot Noir Family

The pinot noir is a much-courted but skittish and reluctant grape. Sometimes it produces incomparably delicious wines from a few plots in Burgundy (but not quite as often as wine mythology would have us believe). Elsewhere in the world it plays a less showy role. Although popular in California, it is not one of that state's most successful wines. Outside Burgundy one of the places where pinot noir can be coaxed into giving a better-than-routine performance is in Italy, in the Northeast and particularly in the bilingual but largely German-speaking province of Bolzano, in Alto Adige.

TRENTINO-ALTO ADIGE'S PINOT NOIR

Pinot Nero dell'Alto Adige/ Südtiroler Blauburgunder

(D.O.C., TRENTINO–ALTO ADIGE)

The high standards of viticulture and winemaking that have earned for the wines of Alto Adige unqualified admiration from connoisseurs in Italy, Switzerland, and Germany are evident in its Pinot Nero, more frequently known as Blauburgunder.

The color, which elsewhere is sometimes light enough to be taken for a rosé, is here a bright, decided ruby. The expansively perfumed bouquet that distinguishes all Alto Adige wines brings to Blauburgunder emphatic suggestions of fresh berries. The flavor is vivaciously fruity, but reined in by a firm, yet subtle sensation of bitterness that lingers into the aftertaste. The overall impression of harmony developing evenly and steadily from the bouquet into sensations on the palate and in the aftertaste makes a good Blauburgunder uniquely graceful for an Italian wine from this grape.

Among the good producers are Kellereigenossenschaft Girlan, Josef Hofstätter, Alois Lageder, Laimburg, and Kellereigenossenschaft Terlan. Josef Brigl makes a fine Pinot Nero marketed as *vino da tavola* under the proprietary name Kreuzbichler.

VINTAGES: Blauburgunder is for drinking early, although some bottles from good years may still have considerable vigor after five years.
Acceptable Years: 1978
Good Years: 1980, 1982, 1983

Pinot Nero del Trentino
(D.O.C., TRENTINO-ALTO ADIGE)

In Trentino, Pinot Nero has yet to develop the affirmative character of its counterpart in the northern, Bolzano half of the same region. The potential, represented by ideally exposed sloping vineyards and lean, well-drained soil, undoubtedly exists for making less vapid wine than heretofore. The slowly but steadily increasing pressure to meet higher expectations of quality is bound to make Trentino a more reliable source of fine wine before too long. At present less than a handful of producers are showing the way. Outstanding among them is Pojer & Sandri, who, paradoxically, do not market the wine with a Trentino D.O.C. designation, but as Pinot Nero di Faedo, *vino da tavola*. The others are Castel Segonzano, Foradori, and Gaierhof.

VINTAGES: Pinot Nero del Trentino should be consumed very early. The good vintages of 1982 and 1983 are the ones to look for at present.

THE VENETO'S PINOT NOIR

Breganze Pinot Nero
(D.O.C., VENETO)

It is the only D.O.C. designation for Pinot Nero in the Veneto is Breganze. D.O.C. status notwithstanding, one cannot yet look to Breganze (compare Breganze Cabernet, page 72) to set the standard for Pinot Nero in its region. It is a light, unremarkable wine, thinner than most.

Several Veneto Pinot Neros sold as *vino da tavola* are more worthwhile. One is Falzacappa's, produced near Conegliano, at the northern end of the region; another is Count Da Schio's Costozza from the Colli Berici, near Vicenza. Neither is particularly generous with bouquet, but both compensate with warm, ripe flavor developed on a smooth, silky body. Even finer is Alfredo Lazzarini's Rosso del Rocolo from the Colli Berici, with a positive and engaging earthy, fruity bouquet.

FRIULI'S PINOT NOIR

❧ *Pinot Nero del Collio* ☙
(D.O.C., FRIULI–VENEZIA GIULIA)

❧ *Pinot Nero dei Colli Orientali del Friuli* ☙
(D.O.C., FRIULI–VENEZIA GIULIA)

Of Friuli's six controlled appellation districts, which are more amply described under Cabernet, page 75, only the two hilly zones, Collio and Colli Orientali, are permitted to make Pinot Nero with a D.O.C. designation. Their wine closely rivals Alto Adige's Blauburgunder in quality, although it is substantially more robust and at the same time decidedly less perfumed. One looks to this area primarily for its fine white wines, but the same favorable environment and skills are evident in its attractive Pinot Nero. It is a less fragrant wine than the buoyantly scented Friuli whites, but the deep color, the strongly sustained development of flavors, the sturdy frame identify it as one of this region's well-endowed breed.

In the Collio some of the better producers are Gradnik, Komjanc, Scolaris, and Villa Russiz. Jermann, one of the zone's finer makers, bottles his Pinot Nero without D.O.C. designation as *vino da tavola* under the proprietary name Engelrose. It is a charming pink version of the wine, very fresh and light.

In the Colli Orientali, some of the names to look for are Valentino Butussi, Livio Felluga, Ronchi di Manzano, and Volpe Pasini.

VINTAGES: Please refer to those recommended for Friuli's Cabernet, page 76.

PINOT NOIR IN OTHER REGIONS

❧ *Pinot Nero dell'Oltrepò Pavese* ☙
(D.O.C., LOMBARDY)

A fair amount of pinot noir is grown on the slopes of this hilly appellation south of Milan, but much of it is lost to the sparkling wine houses, who vinify it white, off the skins. A pity, for the little that makes it on its own is above the average level of Pinot Nero in Italy.

Its color is a flashing ruby red; the bouquet is an engaging mixture of mushroom, earthy, and fruity aromas; and the flavor is satisfyingly frank and robust.

Wineries here concentrate on reds from barbera, croatina, and bonarda grapes, but one house that makes a specialty of its Pinot Nero is Piccolo Bacco dei Quaroni.

VINTAGES: The 1982 and 1983 harvests were good. None older is recommended.

❧ *Favonio Pinot Nero* ☙
(VINO DA TAVOLA, APULIA)

It is another of the brood of wines from French varietals that Attilio Simonini has successfully established in the southeastern region of Apulia (also see Cabernet and Pinot Bianco, pages 81 and 181).

Like the Favonio Cabernet Franc, this is a soft, pleasing, simple wine, prevalently vinous in smell, with light but penetrating berrylike aromas. Warm, round, full in the mouth, it delivers an ample load of satisfying fruit flavor. Also like the same house's Cabernet, it is a fast-maturing wine.

The Sangiovese Family
of Medium-Range Red Wines

The sangiovese grape plays roles of varying importance, from walk-on part to one-man show, in more than eighty Italian red wines, some charming and short-lived, others of nearly inexhaustible power. The more aristocratic members of the family are described on pages 30–55 of the preceding category, Big Reds. Here we shall look at some of the sangiovese wines of smaller or at least less complex constitution, of which the most important are medium-bodied Chianti and Sangiovese di Romagna.

❦ *Chianti and Chianti Classico* ❧
(D.O.C., SLATED FOR D.O.C.G., TUSCANY)

Earlier in these pages, the notion was put forward that Chianti is not one wine but several, and therefore discussion of its various styles has been distributed among all three categories in which Italian red wine is classified in this book. The more profound, slow-maturing Chiantis of *riserva* class were described in the category preceding this one. The lightest Chianti, produced for immediate consumption, comes up in the last group, that of the Light Reds. Here we are concerned with Chianti of intermediate age and constitution.

While it is the least fascinating of the three, of all bottled Chiantis this is the most abundant. It is the one we are most likely to find on merchants' shelves, usually released by its maker two years after the vintage, although in this group one might also include some of the three-year-old *riservas* from most of the lighter-producing areas outside Chianti Classico.

The sharply varying nature of the soil, elevation, microclimate of the vast territory where Chianti is produced, the differences in the intentions and capabilities of hundreds of producers—from artisan winemaker to huge shipper—make this one of the most disparate and uneven groups of wines. What they have in common is the Chianti formula of red and white grapes in which the red sangiovese grape predominates. It is a blend to which can be traced some of the virtues and most of the defects they share, and which I have discussed more fully in the section on Chianti Classico Riserva on pages 31-5.

In Chianti of this middle range, which has advanced beyond youthful freshness but will never reach the deep flavor of slow-paced maturity, the negative aspects are the most prominent. The less exacting standards of grape selection that are inevitable with a more modest and sometimes mass-produced wine favor the emergence of the rough, aggressive traits latent in sangiovese and of the sharpness and thinness that can be attributed to the presence of white grapes.

It is largely through the performance of this middle-weight style that angularity, coarseness, and bluntness have become associated with Chianti in general. It would be a disservice, however, both to hard-working producers and to consumers looking for moderately priced bottles not to point out that, while much of this kind of Chianti is ordinary, some of it is commendable wine indeed.

In Chianti Classico, out of the nine townships that constitute the Classico zone, three of them are fairly consistent in producing a reasonably well-balanced intermediate Chianti. They are Castelnuovo Berardenga, Radda, and Gaiole. An evaluation of the wines of each township, and a list of recommended producers, will be found in the section on Chianti Classico Riserva, pages 31–6.

Immediately to the south of Chianti Classico, the Colli Senesi zone is a reliable source of easy-drinking, agreeable wine. Some of the good producers here are Chigi Saracini, Fattoria di Monte Oliveto, La Foce Castelluccio, Montenidoli, Poderi Boscarelli, and Tenuta La Lellera.

North of Chianti Classico another choice section is Colli Fiorentini, in the province of Florence. An outstanding producer here is La Querce, in Impruneta township. *Querce,* Italian for oak, is a name used by other producers, so it is important to note also the name of the proprietors, Marchi Montorselli. Two other worthy producers in Colli Fiorentini are Fattoria di Sammontana and Torre a Decima.

VINTAGES: Mature vintages are unlikely to be rewarding in this style of Chianti. The most worthwhile years to look for are 1980, 1982, and 1983.

OTHER CENTRAL ITALIAN REDS
FROM THE SANGIOVESE GRAPE

❦ *Elba Rosso* ❧
(D.O.C., TUSCANY)

A robust red from the island of Elba, made almost exclusively from sangiovese, sometimes blended with minimal quantities of local trebbiano and other island grapes. It is a dark ruby red, grapy, strong-flavored wine from iron-rich soil. Astringent at first, it ages well, developing into one of the most attractive wines of its class. The most expressive version of it is the work of a woman winemaker, Giuliana Foresi, who bottles under the label Tenuta La Chiusa.

❧ *Montescudaio* ❧
(D.O.C., TUSCANY)

A fruity, lively red made in the province of Pisa from the basic Chianti blend of red and white grapes, sangiovese alone accounting for up to 85 percent of the total.

❧ *Rosso delle Colline Lucchesi* ❧
(D.O.C., TUSCANY)

A light-bodied wine of exclusively local interest, produced near Lucca. In addition to sangiovese it may contain small quantities of six other grapes, three of them white.

❧ *Montefalco Rosso* ❧
(D.O.C., UMBRIA)

One of Umbria's newest D.O.C. appellations, Montefalco Rosso follows substantially the formula for nearly all red wines in Tuscany and Umbria, primarily sangiovese, with a little trebbiano and malvasia. Small percentages of other red grapes are permitted. In color, nose, and taste it is much like one of the less assertive, lighter Chiantis, a simple, straightforward pasta wine.

❧ *Morellino di Scansano* ❧
(D.O.C., TUSCANY)

Morellino is a synonym of sangiovese, of which this wine from southern Tuscany is made almost entirely. Some of its producers blend in a little malvasia. It is deep ruby in color, with that scent in between strawberry and raspberry characteristic of some sangiovese wines. In the mouth it is broad and firm, a hearty representative of the sangiovese breed. A well-known producer is Sellari-Franceschini.

❧ *Parrina Rosso* ❧
(D.O.C., TUSCANY)

A blend of only red grapes, but predominantly sangiovese, made close to the Tyrrhenian Sea in southernmost Tuscany. It is a particularly full-bodied wine, with the fruity nose and punchy flavor characteristic of its principal grape. The best example of it is made by Fattoria La Parrina.

❧ Rosso dai Vigneti di Brunello ☙
(VINO DA TAVOLA, TUSCANY)

The controversy over the name, which obviously trades on the prestige of the far more expensive Brunello di Montalcino, described at length on pages 43–6, distracts attention from the substantial merits of this wine.

Rosso dai Vigneti di Brunello can be translated as Red from Brunello Vineyards. It is made from the same special variety of sangiovese used to make Brunello di Montalcino, but unlike its close namesake it is not subject to the mandatory requirement of four years in wood.

The growers of the Brunello variety of sangiovese who are either unwilling to immobilize their capital by keeping their entire production so many years in wood, or lack the aging facilities that would permit them to do so, cull only the choicest portion of their harvest for Brunello and bottle the rest as the unclassified Rosso. They had originally asked permission to call this wine Vino Rosso di Montalcino. The authorities chose instead the name currently being used, a decision that has caused confusion for consumers and animosity among producers.

Franco Biondi-Santi, whose family created Brunello di Montalcino and who was slated to become president of the consortium of Brunello producers, withdrew his candidacy and resigned his membership in protest over what he and some of his fellow producers considered unfair exploitation of the regal Brunello name.

In turning one's attention to the wine itself, one finds it to be one of the best products of the sangiovese grape, with a light, flowery bouquet, sturdy, well-balanced, deep flavor, both smooth and sinuous. In comparing Vino Rosso with Brunello itself, one finds it indubitably less complex, but also less tarlike and astringent. On most occasions one may well be willing to trade off complexity in exchange for less austere and fresher tasting qualities. Not to mention the advantage of buying up to a case of Vino Rosso for the price of a bottle of Brunello.

The growers of Montalcino are now pressing for a D.O.C. designation for Vino Rosso, which it well deserves, but if and when it comes, there is no doubt that it will be accompanied by a less ambiguous name.

Among the many producers bottling this wine, one seems to me to achieve consistently greater heights of quality than the others. It is Altesino.

The vintage recommendations for Vino Rosso dai Vigneti di Brunello are the same as those for Brunello listed on page 46.

THE SANGIOVESE GRAPE IN ROMAGNA

❧ *Sangiovese di Romagna* ☙
(D.O.C., EMILIA-ROMAGNA)

My acquaintance with Romagna's 100 percent varietal Sangiovese goes back further than with any other Italian wine, and my feelings toward it are perhaps affected by the happy memories with which it is associated.

While still a very young man, I courted a beautiful, amber-eyed girl whose father made Sangiovese. I knew nothing about wine then, nor for that matter much more about women. My recollections of that period are not primarily of food or drink, but I remember being puzzled when my beloved's father described his wine as generous. At that time the most frequently used words in my wine vocabulary were *red* and *white* and expressions such as *nice* or *not so nice*. In rare moments of self-assurance I might even have ventured *smooth* or *rough*. But generous? I ended, I am afraid, by having to draw amply on the generosity of the house before I finally appreciated that of the wine.

Generous. It is the word that most aptly describes Sangiovese di Romagna. A generous wine is one that fills the mouth with forthright, abundant flavor. It lacks the complexity that might challenge the keenness of our perceptions; it doesn't bear down on them with overwhelming power; it doesn't need any puzzling out. All it wants is a ready, open welcome to match its own.

If it is possible to hazard a single general observation about the taste of a nation, and especially of one that makes a greater variety of wine than any other, I would say that generosity is the one quality that most Italians respond to spontaneously in wine. The paramount popularity of the sangiovese grape gives some support to this statement. And of the dozens of wines from this grape none delivers that quality more straightforwardly than the Sangiovese made in Romagna.

Romagna is the reluctantly hyphenated eastern half of the region called Emilia-Romagna, in northern Italy. It is mostly flat land, with a low ruffle of hills at its back; at its feet lies the surfless Adriatic Sea, still as a carpet. The two provincial capitals are Forlì and Ravenna, each with several townships, all of whom produce Sangiovese.

In Romagna people start drinking it in April of the year immediately following the harvest, when it is rough, but bracing and exuberantly fruity. Huge quantities are put away by the Adriatic's summer visitors, who soon discover it is not an ill-chosen accompaniment to the local, savory seafood.

Some producers do age their best Sangiovese a year or two and make a *riserva,* sometimes with remarkable results. The most successful ones, usually those produced on the slopes near the town of Cesena, develop lovely, flowery scents and a fluid, satiny texture in three to four years. But on the whole, one should look to other reds for the burnished graces of maturity and enjoy Sangiovese di Romagna for the brashness of its youthful flavor.

The best producer is Spalletti. Other excellent ones are Guarini, Matteucci, Pasolini dall'Onda, Tenuta del Monsignore, Tesini, Vallunga, Zanetti, and Zerbina.

VINTAGES:
Acceptable Years: 1976, 1980
Good Years: 1978, 1979, 1983
Great Years: 1977, 1982

MORE SANGIOVESE WINES
❦ Sangiovese dei Colli Pesaresi ❧
(D.O.C., MARCHES)

Produced in the province of Pesaro, a sea town in the Adriatic region of Marches, bordering Romagna on the south. Unlike Sangiovese di Romagna, a small percentage of other red grapes may be added here. While a trifle heavier and flabbier than the Romagna version, it is not a substantially different wine.

❦ Sangiovese di Aprilia ❧
(D.O.C., LATIUM)

The provenance is largely volcanic soil south of Rome. It's a light, pale wine of little substance and no memorable characteristics, of which the best one can say is that it can be refreshing when slightly chilled.

Sangiovese dei Colli Vastesi
(VINO DA TAVOLA, ABRUZZI)

A thin, pale wine with feeble aroma but pleasant tartness.

Sangiovese di Arborea
(VINO DA TAVOLA, SARDINIA)

A very full, high-alcohol (13 percent) Sangiovese, far closer in its soft, heavy, baked style to other reds of the island than to its kin on the mainland.

Solopaca Rosso
(D.O.C., CAMPANIA)

Sangiovese is the predominant grape in this blend produced in a mountainous area in the northeastern tip of the region of Campania. It is excitingly vinous and fruity to the nose, warm and soft in the mouth. Of moderate longevity, but best when young and lively.

NOTE: A recent addition to the D.O.C. roster is Capriano del Colle, produced in Lombardy, near Brescia, mainly from sangiovese plus some marzemino. I have not yet tasted it and can submit no evaluation.

INDEPENDENT MEDIUM-RANGE WINES

Cannonau
(D.O.C. WHEN FOLLOWED BY THE DESIGNATION DI SARDEGNA OR WITH THE DISTRICT APPELLATION OLIENA OR CAPO FERRATO; OTHERWISE VINO DA TAVOLA, SARDINIA)

There are two ways to approach Cannonau: as an inseparable element of the folk culture of Sardinia or simply as a wine. The first opens up a distinctly more fascinating view.

Call up if you will images of an early evening campfire in the ancient mountains of central Sardinia, of sheepskin-mantled shepherds roasting baby pigs in a pit lined with scalding stones, of sharp, fresh cheeses grilled over charcoal, of coarse-textured breads, of pitchers making the rounds, filling tumblers with a bright red liquid, bringing soft, welcome heat with each deep swallow. It is a scene that has been described to me by nearly every Sardinian I have spoken to and that turns up in most accounts of Cannonau I have read. Someday I propose to experience it for myself. In the meantime, my report on the wine must be based on what I have tasted in more workaday circumstances.

The grape known in Sardinia as cannonau was brought to the island from Spain, where it is called garnacha. It is the same varietal as France's and California's grenache. If you have ever had a Tavel rosé or a California pink Grenache or one of the commercial bottlings of Châteauneuf du Pape made prevalently from grenache, you are already acquainted with some of the wines that are made from this grape.

In Sardinia, cannonau is grown in every part of the island, and even though, from district to district, there are differences in the wine that are not negligible, it's not impossible to pull together enough of its common features to produce a representative portrait.

The color is a vivid, transparent, crimson hue that early on acquires a deep orange cast. The bouquet is its most entrancing feature, thickly perfumed in a way that suggests the aromas of a subtropical flower garden. The flavor is unctuous, dense, slightly almondy and bitter, rarely achieving sustained development on the palate, communicating nothing more memorable than an impression of mellow but motionless warmth.

Although the D.O.C. statute's minimum alcohol requirements for Cannonau di Sardegna are exceptionally high—13½ percent for the standard version, 15 percent for the *superiore*—some Cannonaus exceed them, reaching natural alcohol levels of 16 to 17 percent. But the Sardinian tradition that stresses superripe fruit producing high alcohol and listlessly low acid levels is reluctantly yielding to contemporary demands for balance and vitality. Growers are being persuaded to anticipate their harvests, and the island's original *alberello* vines—dwarflike bushes trained close to the hot soil—are steadily being replaced by vines made to climb high off the ground, where grapes are exposed to better ventilation.

In addition to the D.O.C. Cannonau di Sardegna appellation, which embraces Cannonau production wherever it takes place on the island, there are two smaller, district designations: Oliena, also known as Nepente di Oliena, and Capo Ferrato.

Oliena is in the heart of the mountainous province of Nuoro in central Sardinia. The Nepente half of its name is borrowed from the drink the ancients believed could banish all sorrows. It was affixed to this

Cannonau by Gabriele D'Annunzio, a grandiloquent figure of the turn-of-the-century and early Fascist years. D'Annunzio, a teetotaler, was inebriated solely by the wine's smell, an intense, ardent fragrance that is, indeed, Oliena's most distinctive feature.

The other D.O.C. district, Capo Ferrato, faces the sea at the south-easternmost tip of Sardinia. Cannonau from this prevalently sandy territory is one of the best balanced, with characteristically supple grenache flavor displaying more vigor than one usually meets in this wine.

No other zones are singled out by the controlled appellation statute, but some are equally as important as Oliena and Capo Ferrato. The most noteworthy are Ogliastra in the East and Romangia in the Northwest.

Ogliastra, between the mountains of Gennargentu and the seacoast, is named after the wild olive trees scattered through it. The soil of Ogliastra is primarily composed of lime, sand, and potassium, and the wine produced on it—dark, strong, and exuberant—is regarded by Sardinians as the richest, most classic of their Cannonaus. The archetypal example of an Ogliastra Cannonau is the one produced at the village of Jerzu.

My own preference is for Romangia's Cannonau di Sorso, the only one in which strength of flavor is moderated by small subtleties in fragrance and aftertaste to a degree that nearly approaches elegance.

Most Cannonau produced on the island is sold and bottled without the official di Sardegna appellation. To Sardinians, Cannonau is so much *their* wine that D.O.C. recognition is superfluous, and most growers have not bothered with registering their vineyards to earn controlled appellation status. The Cannonau that travelers to Sardinia are most likely to find will therefore be an unclassified one, labeled *vino da tavola*.

In addition to the basic dry red Cannonau described here, there exists a pink—*rosato*—version as well as fortified or naturally sweet Cannonaus that at their best remind one of port, such as Anghelu Ruju, page 219.

Cannonau rarely improves with age. It is ready to drink as soon as it is released, and it begins to decline within two to three years after that.

Like most Sardinian wines, the most reliable bottlings are produced by cooperative cellars. Some of the best are Cantina Sociale Castiadas, Cantina Sociale di Dorgali, Cantina Sociale di Jerzu, Cantina Sociale di Mamoiada, Cantina Sociale di Oliena, Cantina Sociale di Sorso-Sennori, and Cantina Sociale di Tortoli.

Among the private producers there is Mario Mereu, who bottles a highly esteemed Cannonau called Perda·Rubia and wrapped in a beautiful label depicting an antique Sardinian rug from his collection. Another private winery, Sella & Mosca, the largest estate in Sardinia, makes a Cannonau that, like all its other wines, is substantially lower in alcohol and lighter in body than the average for the island.

❧ *Dolcetto* ☙

(D.O.C. WHEN FOLLOWED BY ONE OF SEVEN DISTRICT NAMES, PIEDMONT)

Those who recognize in Dolcetto's name the Latin root it shares with Italian, Spanish, French, and English words for sweet—*dolce, dulce, douce, dulcet*—may be puzzled to find it is a totally dry wine. Sweetness, however, is an appropriate term to describe the character, if not the taste, of Dolcetto. It is an intensely fruity, soft-bodied wine, low in acid, high in charm, one whose easy drinking qualities make it the most instantly attractive of Piedmont's red wines.

Dolcetto is produced from the grape of the same name over a large area in Piedmont subdivided by the D.O.C. statute into seven appellations: Dolcetto delle Langhe Monregalesi, Dolcetto d'Acqui, Dolcetto d'Alba, Dolcetto di Asti, Dolcetto di Diano d'Alba, Dolcetto di Dogliani, Dolcetto d'Ovada.

In a territory that sprawls over so many townships one can obviously expect to find immense variety. For that matter, as long as there are two vineyard plots, though they be side by side, and two winemakers, though they work with the same grape, there are likely to be two different wines. But unless one wants to make it his life work to classify the fine shades of difference in Dolcetto, it is sufficient to be aware of two basic styles.

One is round, full, velvety, warm in the mouth, having rich fruit flavors in which, in very good years, one may recognize the taste of quince. This style is prevalent in Dolcetto delle Langhe Monregalesi, Dolcetto d'Alba, and particularly Dolcetto di Diano d'Alba, product of a very small area in the very center of Alba's territory.

The second fundamental style is characterized by a coarser, more rugged constitution, some astringency, and pronounced vinous odors. The slightly bitter, nutty aftertaste of almonds that to some extent is present in virtually all Dolcetto becomes here more explicit. It is a style usually associated with Dolcetto d'Acqui, Dolcetto di Asti, and Dolcetto d'Ovada.

Like many of Italy's wines that have yet to make their mark abroad, only a small part of Dolcetto's production is bottled and labeled. Most of it is sold in bulk and likewise consumed. The locals say that if you analyze a sample of their blood, half of it will turn out to be Dolcetto. Parts of Dolcetto country are also in Barolo country, but when you sit down to eat with the family of a man who makes both wines, if you are more a friend than guest, it will be Dolcetto rather than Barolo that you'll find on the table.

That Dolcetto should be paramount in the affections of people whose region produces Italy's most important red wines is testimony to its substantial charms. It is reasonable to expect that steadily increasing quantities of it will be diverted from demijohns for local consumption to fifths for the general market. Even now, a bottle of Dolcetto is far from being a rarity, and some of the best examples are shipped by the same houses that bottle the finest Barolo and Barbaresco.

The outstanding name in Dolcetto is Renato Ratti, whose accomplishments as historian, administrator, oenologist, and producer make him the Renaissance man in the world of Piedmontese wines. Among the scores of good producers are Accademia Torregiorgi, Cantina del Glicine, Castello di Neive, Ceretto, Elvio Cogno, Aldo Conterno, Einaudi, Fontanafredda, Angelo Gaja, Gemma, Bruno Giacosa, Oddero, Giuseppe Poggio, Prunotto, Giuseppe Ratto, Gigi Rosso, Terre del Barolo, Giovanni Veglio, and Vietti.

VINTAGES: Maturity is not a virtue in Dolcetto, and any evaluation of vintage years, save the most recent, has little usefulness. A bottle of the 1978 vintage, if it should still turn up, or the 1982, may have something to offer even after a decade. But those were both years of untypical intensity. What one looks for in Dolcetto will most likely be found in its first two or three years of life.

❧ Enfer d'Arvier ❧
(D.O.C., VAL D'AOSTA)

The steep and barely accessible vineyards of French-speaking Val d'Aosta produce small quantities of little-known but extraordinary wines.

Val d'Aosta is set thigh-high on the left side of the Italian boot, with France at its north, on the other side of the Alps, and Piedmont at its southern end. It is crossed by a matriarchy of rivers several of which bear as their first name Dora. The queen of the tribe is Dora Baltea, whose length creases the valley in two, flowing side by side with the super-highway that hastens travelers into Piedmont. On either side of Dora Baltea are the high-altitude vineyards of Val d'Aosta. Alpine peaks, capped with year-round snows, look down on the sheltered slopes upon whose rocky soil the sun of long Mediterranean summers spills unremitting warmth.

Grape varieties are cultivated here that are found nowhere else in Italy. One of the most popular is the dark, small-berried petit rouge, from which Enfer d'Arvier is made. The name *Enfer* ("hell") is attribut-ed to the intense heat reflected by the stone-faced valley at Arvier, on Dora Baltea's right bank. This is a deep garnet wine, with subtle per-fumes in its aroma that suggest wildflowers. It is nimble and silky in the mouth, with a quick, clean, dry finish. The alcohol content is moderate, usually exceeding only slightly the minimum 11½ percent required by law.

Age is not a virtue with Enfer. It is good to drink as soon as it is released, about one and one-half years after the vintage and for not much later than another two to three years.

❧ Torrette de St. Pierre
and Other Wines from the Petit Rouge Grape ☙
(VINO DA TAVOLA, VAL D'AOSTA)

A short distance south of Arvier, on the opposite bank of the river, a fine but, alas, rarer wine than Enfer is made from the same grape. It is Torrette de St. Pierre, a lustrous, purplish ruby wine. With age—and unlike Enfer, Torrette can last a decade, sometimes two—it acquires an intensely scented bouquet, in which some are able to distinguish wild berries, faded roses, and almonds. Flavors are firm and deep with a body whose warmth discloses the high alcohol, rarely less than 13 percent, sometimes surpass-ing 14 percent.

Other wines from the petit rouge group, all of lesser stature and impact than Torrette, are Aymaville, Côte de Quart, Colline d'Aosta, Gressan, Introd, and Villeneuve. Some simply bear the varietal name Petit Rouge.

Producing either Enfer or other petit rouge wines are Co-Enfer Arvier, Antoine Charrère (his wine, perhaps the best of all, is sold as *vino da tavola* under the proprietary name Le Sabla), Ecole d'Agriculture Aoste, and Joseph Gerbore.

❧ *Lagrein Dunkel* ❧

(D.O.C., TRENTINO–ALTO ADIGE)

When you are in the ex-Austrian province of Bolzano, now known as Alto Adige/Südtirol, and ask for a full-bodied red, you are likely to be served Lagrein Dunkel. Most of the other red wines here are made from the pale, thin juices of the schiava grape, discussed on page 128; and compared with them, Lagrein Dunkel is indeed deeper in color and more substantial. To those, however, whose notions of sturdiness have been formed by drinking Chianti or Barbera, not to speak of Barolo or Barbaresco, Lagrein Dunkel's impact will seem not so weighty.

The most appealing feature of this wine is its ebullient bouquet, typical of Südtirol's style, a powerful evocation of berries and flowers, with a faint, sweet scent of vanilla. Tasting impressions do not quite carry out the promise made to the nose; they are agreeably fruity, even silky, but slight, fading quickly on the palate save for a brisk, bitter finish. It is one of those wines whose personality, seemingly so elusive, emerges forcibly with food. When taken alongside some of Südtirol's specialties —such as *leberknoedelsuppe,* liver dumpling soup, or *schnurbraten,* braised beef—or with roast lamb, it responds with remarkable firmness.

Although it is by no means rare, fine Lagrein Dunkel is no longer so abundant as it used to be. The land that produces the choicest lagrein grapes is adjacent to, and much of it is within the perimeter of, the prosperous city of Bolzano. To accommodate the city's expansion, thousands of vines have been cut, the soil beneath them has been excavated, and where their roots used to burrow, concrete has been poured for the foundations of neo-Tyrolean villas and apartment blocks. The competition between vineyards and real estate developments is a mismatch. Vineyards always lose.

Of the grapes that are produced, a substantial number is diverted into making Lagrein Kretzer, a popular rosé that is likeable enough, if you like rosé. More lagrein grapes go into strengthening St. Magdalener, Lago di Caldaro, and other wines of the schiava family. The moderate amount left for Lagrein Dunkel is consumed almost entirely at its origin, but some strays abroad and is worth looking for.

The best producer of Lagrein Dunkel is Klosterkellerei Muri Gries; others are Herrnhofer, Josef Hofstätter, Kellereigenossenschaft Girlan, and Soini.

TRENTINO–ALTO ADIGE'S OTHER LAGREIN

❦ *Lagrein del Trentino* ❧
(D.O.C., TRENTINO–ALTO ADIGE)

A dark Lagrein produced in the province of Trento, the southern half of the region. While it resembles Bolzano's Lagrein Dunkel in flavor and suppleness, Trento's wine rarely matches the intense fragrance that is Lagrein Dunkel's most stirring quality.

Good producers of Lagrein Trentino are Conti Martini and De Cles.

VINTAGES: Lagrein holds up reasonably well, but nothing older than five or six years is likely to be worth trying. 1978–80 were good; 1982–83, much better.

❦ *Teroldego Rotaliano* ❧
(D.O.C., TRENTINO–ALTO ADIGE)

There are one or two things about Teroldego that set it apart from other Italian wines of comparable standing. Many wines of Italy are like the traditional Italian households of the past. They are part of large family groups, with several full-blooded relations and numerous other siblings of varying closeness, some running out their lives side by side, others scattered abroad. The Barbera, Nebbiolo, and Sangiovese families are good examples.

Teroldego, on the other hand, is a loner. It is the most important red in the Trentino half of the northeastern region of Trentino–Alto Adige, but it is virtually unknown elsewhere, nor, except for a minor appearance in Sorni red, described on page 132, has it branched off into related wines.

Other Italian wines are spread over several townships, often sharing plains, slopes, even single plots with different varieties of reds and whites. Teroldego is exclusively concentrated on and dominates a single broad plain, the Campo Rotaliano, an expanse crossed by one river, skirted by another, the large sky above it scored at the edges by dog-toothed mountain peaks. It is strange to find, on the largely hill-encrusted Italian mainland, such a landscape, so much uninterrupted flatness so thickly spread with a single variety of vine.

The thick-skinned, blue black Teroldego grape produces a wine that when young has a very dark, purple color, intensely vinous odors, and a racy, tart, slightly bitter taste. Most of it is produced for a market that does not object to a somewhat grating address to the palate. But careful selection of the grapes, judicious blending with a small proportion of gentler varietals, and one to two years' aging can beget a wine of highly polished quality, subtle in aroma, fluid and supple in the mouth with persistent length of flavor.

Fine Teroldego accounts for a very small proportion of total production, but it does exist. Some of its producers are Barone de Cles, Foradori, Gaierhof, and Roberto Zeni.

VINTAGES: Teroldego is not a late-blooming wine. It is probably at its peak between three and five years of age, although a choice bottle from an exceptional year may last close to a decade.
Acceptable Years: 1977, 1978, 1979
Good Years: 1975, 1976, 1980, 1982, 1983

Some Other Medium-Range Red Wines

❧ *Aglianico del Vulture* ☙
(D.O.C., BASILICATA)

Produced on Mount Vulture's volcanic slopes from the ancient aglianico grape, which also sires a far greater red, Taurasi, described earlier on pages 60–1. Aglianico del Vulture has smooth, fleshy, abundant flavor, but is short on vitality. After three years' aging, it is designated *vecchio;* after five, *riserva.* Presumably long-lived, but I can't say since I've never had an old bottle.

❧ *Aglianico dei Colli Lucani* ☙
(VINO DA TAVOLA, BASILICATA) ☙

❧ *Aglianico di Matera* ☙
(VINO DA TAVOLA, BASILICATA)

Dull, heavy reds from the aglianico grape.

❧ Cacce'e Mmitte ❧
(D.O.C., APULIA)

Ordinary carafe-quality wine made from varying combinations of red and white grapes. A free translation of its name would be "keep downing it," possibly to achieve forgetfulness, a prerequisite to the appreciation of this wine.

❧ Campidano di Terralba ❧
(D.O.C., SARDINIA)

A faded, ruby red wine made in southern Sardinia from a local grape called bovale. Simple, straightforwardly vinous, with frank, soft flavor, it is lighter in body than most Sardinian reds.

❧ Campo Fiorin ❧
(VINO DA TAVOLA, VENETO)

Made from the same blend of grapes used for Valpolicella: corvina, molinara, and rondinella. Although it could qualify for a Valpolicella designation, the producers, Masi, prefer to market it under its coined name as unclassified *vino da tavola*. Very dark in color, with deep, elegant flavor, it is much fuller and longer-lived than regular Valpolicella because it is partially fermented on the skins of shriveled grapes after they have been used to make Amarone, described on pages 55-7.

❧ Capitel San Rocco Rosso ❧
(VINO DA TAVOLA, VENETO)

Similar to Campo Fiorin (see above). Made by Tedeschi, one of Valpolicella's best wineries.

❧ Carignano del Sulcis ❧
(D.O.C., SARDINIA)

Medium-bodied but juicy, winy red made from the Spanish carignane grape popular also in southern France. The best is made by the Cantina Sociale (cooperative cellar) of Sant'Antioco, an island off the southwestern tip of Sardinia.

❧ Castel del Monte ❧
(D.O.C., APULIA)

A sound, well-balanced, easy-flowing wine made from two Apulian grapes, uva di troia and bombino nero, plus a little montepulciano. Produced by Rivera, known for their widely distributed rosé. (For a superior version of Castel del Monte, see Riserva Il Falcone, page 90.)

❧ Cesanese di Affile ❧
(D.O.C., LATIUM)

❧ Cesanese del Piglio ❧
(D.O.C., LATIUM)

❧ Cesanese di Olevano ❧
(D.O.C., LATIUM)

Cesanese—the grape and the wine—enjoy the highest prestige among D.O.C. Roman reds. This is perhaps because there isn't much else to measure them against. The wine is a respectable, occasionally well-structured wine, with a modestly flowery, vinous bouquet and smooth texture supported by a slightly astringent body. Of the three zones, Piglio is probably the best.

❧ Ciro' ❧
(D.O.C., CALABRIA)

A better-than-average southern wine, long-lived, dark ruby in color. It has intensely vinous aromas that develop into a penetratingly peppery bouquet when fully mature, plushy texture, and strong, if somewhat parched, flavor. When made in the inner, traditional production zone, it is qualified as *classico*. Ciro' claims descent from the wine served to the athletes of the first Olympic games.

❧ Copertino ❧
(D.O.C., APULIA)

One of a group of five similar D.O.C. wines from the Salento peninsula, the heel of the Italian boot. (See Leverano, Martina Franca, Salice Salentino, Squinzano.) They are plump, fruity wines, a touch too warm in the mouth, perhaps. Made primarily from negroamaro, a local varietal.

❧ Corvo Rosso ☙
(VINO DA TAVOLA, SICILY)

Produced from a blend of local grape varieties by the same house responsible for the better-known white Corvo described on page 175. Ruby red with warm flashes of deep orange, it has a penetrating, fine bouquet that promises more flavor than it delivers. Smooth and supple, even if not profoundly satisfying.

❧ Creme du Vien de Nus ☙
(VINO DA TAVOLA, VAL D'AOSTA)

An exceedingly rare and lovely wine, strikingly dark, with an outspread, flowery bouquet and flavor that is both vigorous and intense. Made from native valdostan grapes, mainly vien de nus, and a little petit rouge.

❧ Donnici ☙
(D.O.C., CALABRIA)

Soft, berrylike flavor, not too persistent, but surprisingly fresh, despite high alcohol. From a blend of both red and white grapes in which the most important of Calabria's red grapes, gaglioppo, predominates.

❧ Etna Rosso ☙
(D.O.C., SICILY)

Sicily's most appealing red; violet scents in the nose and warm, chewy flavor in the mouth. Ages moderately well. Best producer is Vignaioli Etnei. The grape variety is nerello mascalese, the most prevalent in Catania province, of which Etna is a part.

❧ Faro ☙
(D.O.C., SICILY)

Another good wine from nerello mascalese. *Faro* is Italian for beacon, referring in this case to the one in the lighthouse above the Strait of Messina, also overlooking the vineyards. A perfumed, firm, ample red, produced in minute quantities.

❧ *Faustus Rosso* ❧
(VINO DA TAVOLA, SICILY)

Unusually graceful and lively for a Sicilian red. The bouquet is terse and piquant; the taste impressions satiny, sleek, and, while not profound, firmly sustained.

❧ *Groppello Amarone* ❧
(VINO DA TAVOLA, LOMBARDY)

Resembles, in the impressions of concentrated fruit it conveys, Valpolicella's Amarone, described on pages 55-7, but all the deeply resonant sensations of the opulent wine from the Veneto are here much abridged. Made from partly shriveled groppello grapes.

❧ *Lamezia* ❧
(D.O.C., CALABRIA)

Faded ruby in color, it is starkly vinous in aroma and flavor. Made from a blend of grapes in which greco nero predominates.

❧ *Leverano* ❧
(D.O.C., APULIA)

Same general provenance, composition, and characteristics as Copertino, described on pages 118-19.

❧ *Maccarese* ❧
(VINO DA TAVOLA, LATIUM)

A blend of the native Roman red grape, cesanese, with montepulciano, carignano, and merlot. Strong, soft flavor. The large Maccarese winery, just inland of the beaches north of Rome's Fiumicino airport, produces some of the most consistently satisfying Roman wines. Also see Maccarese Bianco, page 202.

◆ẻ *Malbec* ᴤ◆
(VINO DA TAVOLA, VENETO AND FRIULI-VENEZIA GIULIA)

A round, chewy, sappy, herbaceous wine, appealingly straightforward. In France, the malbec grape is sometimes added to the basic cabernet/merlot blend of the wines of the Médoc, but one must come to Italy to find it in its pure, varietal state.

◆ẻ *Martina Franca* ᴤ◆
(D.O.C., APULIA)

Another red from the Salento peninsula. Similar to Copertino, described on pages 118-19.

◆ẻ *Melissa* ᴤ◆
(D.O.C., CALABRIA)

Similar to Ciro', described on page 118.

◆ẻ *Monica di Sardegna* ᴤ◆
(D.O.C., SARDINIA)

A lackluster, thin wine made in various parts of the island, largely from the grape of the same name. A more interesting version is Monica di Cagliari, a sweet wine discussed on page 221.

◆ẻ *Per 'e Palummo* ᴤ◆
(VINO DA TAVOLA, CAMPANIA)

An intense ruby red, flowery, vivaciously fruity, full-bodied wine. One of the most attractive wines of the south, made by Casa D'Ambra on the island of Ischia in the Gulf of Naples. The grape is called *piedirosso,* Italian for red foot, and *per 'e palummo* is Neapolitan dialect for dove's foot. It is an important grape in the provinces of Avellino and Naples, particularly in the vineyards around Vesuvius, where it is used to improve the blends of other wines.

Pollino
(D.O.C., CALABRIA)

From a blend of mountain-grown red and white grapes. Light in color, it has the fragrance of high-altitude wines and the strong flavor of its native South.

Primitivo di Manduria
(D.O.C., APULIA)

A forward, meaty wine from the native Apulian grape, primitivo, believed to be the ancestor of California's Zinfandel.

Raboso
(VINO DA TAVOLA, VENETO)

A blackish ruby wine, sharply vinous in odor and flavor, it is tart and brutish in youth but can develop with a few years' aging into a balanced, if always austere red. It is produced from the grape of the same name, on either side of the Piave River flats in the provinces of Treviso and Venice.

Refosco
(D.O.C., FRIULI-VENEZIA GIULIA)

A late-maturing and sometimes not fully ripening grape, refosco makes a purplish wine, grassy in aroma, with hard and even sour-tasting qualities. It may come around with age, but there must be better things to wait around for than Refosco.

Regaleali
(VINO DA TAVOLA, SICILY)

One of Sicily's most highly regarded reds, yet dull and flat when compared with Faustus or Corvo, discussed earlier. Produced by Count Tasca D'Almerita, who also makes a premium red he calls Riserva del Conte. It is a wine subjected to overextended barrel aging, with slack, overripe, raisiny flavor that does not justify the high price tag.

❧ Rossese di Dolceacqua ☙
(D.O.C., LIGURIA)

It is the only D.O.C. red in Liguria, and a winner. The bouquet is exceedingly lovely, harboring scents of wild berries and crushed flowers. The taste impressions are soft and flowing, low in acid and moderate in tannin, high in the berrylike impressions of fruit promised by the bouquet. It is best when young. Rossese is made from the grape of the same name that grows near the pretty town of Dolceacqua, not far from the border where the Italian and French Rivieras meet. The best producer is Croesi.

❧ Sagrantino ☙
(D.O.C., UMBRIA)

A dark, strong red made near Perugia in the Montefalco appellation zone. The small, black grape variety was originally thought to have been brought to Umbria by one of St. Francis d'Assisi's followers, but it is now believed to have existed locally all along. The grapes are partly shriveled before crushing, as is done in Valpolicella to make Amarone, discussed on pages 55-7. Traditionally the wine is intended to be sweet, but since obtaining a D.O.C. designation, its producers are beginning to turn to a dry version. It is full, high in alcohol, and slightly bitter in taste.

❧ Salice Salentino ☙
(D.O.C., APULIA)

Full, warm, velvety wine, it is the best of the Salento reds. See also Copertino, discussed on pages 118-19. The producer is Apulia's largest privately owned winery, Leone de Castris.

❧ Savuto ☙
(D.O.C., CALABRIA)

Made in a valley of mountainous central Calabria, largely from gaglioppo, the region's prime red grape, plus a choice of four red and two white varietals. It is difficult to describe a wine that is the result of such a flexible formula and that is, moreover, easier to buy in twelve-gallon demijohns than by the bottle. From the sample I was able to obtain it appears to be an intensely fragrant, full, meaty red.

❧ *Squinzano* ☙
(D.O.C., APULIA)

Another Salento red. See Copertino, discussed on pages 118-19.

❧ *Torre Quarto Rosso* ☙
(VINO DA TAVOLA, APULIA)

A firm, round, unctuous red, delivering more fruit than finesse, but smooth and very easy to take. The grapes are principally malbec and a small amount of the local uva di troia. Torre Quarto is made on what was once a vast estate laid out in the 1840s by the French dukes de la Rochefoucauld.

❧ *Velletri Rosso* ☙
(D.O.C., LATIUM)

Everyday red of pronounced vinous odor, smooth and soft on the palate. Made near Rome of roughly equal parts sangiovese, montepulciano, and cesanese.

The Light Red Wines

Immediate appeal, vivacity, a rush of fresh fruit are what we should expect when the wines in the category of Light Reds show their best. They are not a thought-provoking lot, but their fruitiness cheers the palate and provides the carefree delight in drinking that is at the origin of our pleasure in wine. They are the kind of wines that Italy has always excelled in producing, and although they may be small-scale, they should not be belittled, unless one is ready to belittle charm.

FAMILIES OF LIGHT RED WINES

The Corvina, Rondinella, Molinara Family

One of the most interesting achievements of winemaking is the blending of several varieties of grapes to make a wine superior to any each of the single varietals alone could produce. The popular light reds of Verona —Bardolino and Valpolicella—are a notably successful example of this pratice.

The grapes used for both wines are corvina, rondinella, and molinara, all native to the Veneto. Corvina is the principal component of the blend. As the name suggests—it comes from *corvo*, Italian for crow—it is a very dark variety that contributes depth of color, alcoholic strength, and tannic firmness to the wine. Of the other two grapes, rondinella is the more important. Both help to soften corvina's harshness, lighten and brighten the wine's hue, and enrich its fragrance.

❧ *Bardolino* ❧
(D.O.C., VENETO)

Hills and vines always make pretty scenery. But there is no prettier landscape anywhere than the sweet hills of Bardolino facing Lake Garda and the sunset, a serene pattern of vineyards, olive trees, cypresses, castles, and Veronese villas in pale pink stone, arranged on gently inclined slopes, lit by the cheerful shimmer of the lake-reflected light. It deserves to be called charming as well as any place on earth, probably more so than most, and produces a wine to match.

Bardolino is a blend of Verona's basic red grapes—corvina, molinara, rondinella—plus a fourth, negrara. They make a pale red wine (pink in the Chiaretto version), with brilliant bursts of light that it is not far-fetched to associate with the reverberating radiance from the great lake at the vineyards' feet. The bouquet is delicate but drawn out, clearly anticipating the light, vivacious fruitiness that is caught immediately in the taste. A slight prickliness is sometimes present and not unwelcome. The aftertaste ends cleanly with a suggestion of bitterness.

The most representative examples of Bardolino come from the central, original production zone entirely fronting the lake and are labeled *classico*. Clamped behind the traditional zone, and bracketing it at the north and south ends, is a larger production zone entitled to the Bardolino appellation, but not to the qualification *classico*. The additional specification *superiore* is awarded when the wine reaches at least 11½ percent alcohol, 1 percent higher than the minimum standard for Bardolino, and is aged for one year before it is released.

My own preference is for the youngest possible Bardolino, when its qualities are closest to those of a freshly squeezed bunch of grapes. This is a wine that is best in its first year of life, before enforced inertia saps its vitality, slowing up the rush of fruit that is its most endearing feature.

Export Bardolino must be made to endure the wretched lot of transatlantic freight and to survive unaltered the two or three years' wait before it is consumed. Shippers cannot be faulted for sacrificing charm to stamina. This is not the same wine, however, that they themselves are likely to drink at home; those interested in the taste of authentic Bardolino cannot expect to find it very far from its source.

Good producers of Bardolino Classico, some of whom export, are Ca' Furia, Colle dei Cipressi, Fratelli Poggi, Girasole, Lamberti (with its single-vineyard bottling, Monte Ceriel), Le Tende, and Santi (with its special bottling, Cà Bordenis).

❧ *Valpolicella Classico* ☙
(D.O.C., VENETO)

A luminous ruby red color, a bouquet of scents that suggest ripe cherries and bananas, moderate sensations of alcohol, fresh, dry taste softened by fruit-sweet flavors, a clean finish with the faint bitterness of almonds are what we should expect of true Valpolicella. The lures of commerce—this is probably, along with Chianti, one of the Italian dry red wines that most frequently turns up abroad—have reshaped it somewhat. So what we have now is Valpolicella the world traveler, with much of its charm scuffed away, flatter, leaner, with less fruit to blunt the alcohol, offering consistency and shelf life in place of character.

The conditions for making Valpolicella that is truest to type exist in the original production area northwest of Verona. It was originally called Vallepolicella, and the wine took its name from the place. As the wine abbreviated its spelling and became better known, the place followed suit.

If one were to look down the Valpolicella zone toward Verona from a sufficient height, it would look like the back of an outspread left hand. From left to right, four knobby rows of hills, separated by narrow valleys, jab their way toward the Veronese plain. At the far right the broad curve of a shallow valley flattens out to the west, with Lake Garda flashing surprisingly near. The air over the Valpolicella vineyards trembles with the waves of light bouncing off that giant mirror of a lake, a quality of the landscape that the wine calls back with the shimmering luster of its color.

North of the vineyard line and sometimes inside it there are extensive plantings of cherry trees, which produce a particularly delectable variety of that fruit. What exchange takes place between orchard and vineyard is not clear, but it is indisputable that there is a sweetish, fruited cherry taste to Valpolicella.

Only wine made from grapes grown in this original production area is entitled to the qualification *classico*. Even within the *classico* area differences of character exist in Valpolicella, depending on the commune where it is produced. The easternmost valley of Negrar produces firmer, somewhat less fruity wines. Next to it, Marano, the most closed in of the four valleys, makes a lighter, more fragrant Valpolicella. The wines of Fumane are rounder and perhaps the most delicious. St. Ambrogio and S. Pietro Incariano make the biggest and most generous Valpolicellas. Unfortunately, these valuable distinctions are being lost through the indifference of the consumer and the requirements of the large shippers, into whose vats most of the grapes are now being conveyed to be blended and processed into the standard commercial product for which such a large market has been created.

The other areas where Valpolicella can be produced are to the east of the traditional zone. Immediately to the east is another valley, Valpantena, whose wine was once known by that name. Today it is identified as Valpolicella della Valpantena, a fresh and light but less fruity wine than Valpolicella Classico. The distinguished and long-established house of Bertani has consistently turned out some of the best wines from Valpantena, although even they have not been able to arrest the decline in quality for which excessive yields have lately been responsible. Further east is a large territory where Valpolicella without other geographic qualifications is produced. Its most notable communes are Illasi and Cazzano, and except for them most of the production is of indifferent quality.

In the blend of grapes for Valpolicella, corvina, rondinella, and molinara account for at least 85 percent of the total. The balance may include such grapes as barbera, sangiovese, Bardolino's negrara, or, if necessary, grapes and musts from other areas. The minimum alcoholic content must be 11 percent. If Valpolicella is aged for a year and achieves 12 percent alcohol, it can qualify as *superiore*. This last provision in the law has undoubtedly done as much harm as the permissiveness in yield per acre. Concentrated musts of various origin are often necessary to beef up the alcohol, to the detriment of the wine's character. And how a wine such as Valpolicella, whose most alluring quality is youth, can be qualified *superiore* after a year's aging is clear only to members of the appellation law panel.

Some of the producers whose wine best represents the original, nonindustrial character of Valpolicella are Allegrini, Bolla (with their single-vineyard bottling called Jago), Le Ragose, Giuseppe Quintarelli, Sanperetto, and Tedeschi.

VINTAGES: There is no reward in waiting for Valpolicella. It's a wine to be enjoyed young. The last great year was 1971, but that is of interest only to historians. Good wine was made in 1982 and 1983, acceptable wine in 1979 and 1980.

The Schiava Family

Schiava, or vernatsch, a pale red grape, is native to the province of Bolzano, also known as the Südtirol, the German-speaking northern half of the Trentino–Alto Adige region. It is by a substantial margin the most prevalent grape in Südtirol's production, making light-bodied, fragrant red wines that, if served slightly chilled to a blindfolded consumer, would be taken, for their freshness and thinness, as whites.

There are four types of schiava, some excelling in quality and others in productivity. Since the two characteristics are as mutually exclusive in schiava as they are in any other variety, wines from this grape vary broadly in distinction depending on the quantity of the less prolific, but finer schiava *gentile* variety present in the blend.

❧ *St. Magdalener* ☙
(D.O.C., TRENTINO–ALTO ADIGE)

When one steps off the train at Bolzano, one's eyes are drawn toward the north end of the station, where their gaze swings sharply upward as it follows the steep slope of the hills that rise just beyond the tracks. During harvest time one may see the tufted surface of the slopes break into motion. It is the grape pickers, moving from row to row of the vineyards that carpet the hills up to their crests, bobbing like shuttles on a great loom. This is where St. Magdalener is made, one of the two delicious wines produced inside Bolzano's suburban limits (see Lagrein Dunkel, page 114).

Producers of St. Magdalener are usually more generous with schiava *gentile* than their colleagues elsewhere in Südtirol and in Trentino, who swell their production with the more abundant, but duller schiava *grossa* variety. In addition to schiava, the blend is reinforced by small percentages of lagrein or pinot noir.

The color of St. Magdalener is a bright, deep ruby. The aroma is densely perfumed and flowery, suggesting candied violets. The taste is irresistibly smooth and soft, spreading lightly on the palate the gentlest, tenderest impressions of fruit, enlivened by an almondlike bitterness that rushes over other flavors in the aftertaste. No wine more neatly embodies the quality called charm.

Although it has next to no tannin to shed and little acidity to preserve it, some of the local enthusiasts propose St. Magdalener as a wine to lay down. There are no doubt examples of fuller, sturdier St. Magdaleners that can show endurance. But there are no transformations that age can bring that can equal the appeal of St. Magdalener in its fresh-tasting youth.

Good producers of St. Magdalener are Klosterkellerei Muri, Alois Lageder, and Schenck.

TRENTINO–ALTO ADIGE'S OTHER WINES FROM SCHIAVA GRAPES

✤ *Casteller* ✤
(D.O.C., TRENTINO–ALTO ADIGE)

It is produced in Trentino, within the provincial territory of its capital, Trento, from a blend of schiava, merlot, and lambrusco. There may be one or two small producers working with exceptional grapes grown in ideal circumstances who extract from this improbable blend an appealing, graceful, velvety wine that justifies the esteem it enjoys locally. One that I used to admire has since closed his winery. On the whole, Casteller is flimsy and uneven, with little body and less fragrance, sometimes turning up looking and tasting like a rosé.

Colli di Bolzano/Bozner Leiten

(D.O.C., TRENTINO–ALTO ADIGE)

This D.O.C. designation is restricted to schiava grown on the slopes of the hilly area between Bolzano and Terlano. Good examples of it can approach St. Magdalener in distinction, with customary, effusive flowery schiava bouquet and more body than ordinary Schiava dell'Alto Adige. Small percentages of pinot noir or lagrein are added.

Lago di Caldaro/Kalterersee

(D.O.C., TRENTINO–ALTO ADIGE)

Caldaro or Lago di Caldaro is the official appellation for a large quantity of wine produced both in Südtirol and in neighboring Trentino. Much of it is feeble stuff, particularly that produced in Trentino. A small proportion of it can reach high levels of quality, sometimes nearly equal to St. Magdalener. All of the better Lago di Caldaro is made in the original production zone in Südtirol overlooking the lake whose name the wine bears. Wine from this area carries the qualification *classico,* in addition to the wine name, which is usually given in German, Kalterersee. *Classico superiore* is a slightly better grade of the same, and finer yet is *auslese* or *scelto.* All of it should be consumed as early as possible after the vintage.

Some of the best producers of Kalterersee are Josef Brigl, Josef Hofstätter, Kellereigenossenschaft Girlan, Kellereigenossenschaft Terlan, Schloss Schwanburg, and W. Walch.

Schiava dell'Alto Adige/Südtiroler Vernatsch

(D.O.C., TRENTINO–ALTO ADIGE)

Meranese di Collina/Meraner

(D.O.C., TRENTINO–ALTO ADIGE)

Both the above appellations are for wines made from blends of at least 85 percent schiava, the first virtually anywhere in the whole territory of the province of Bolzano and the second only in the hilly districts near the city of Merano.

By and large it is likely to be a pale red wine, rather too fragrant

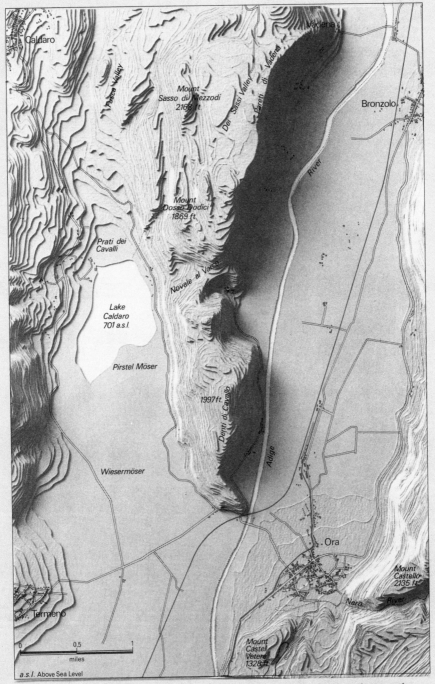

The site of Alto Adige's most popular red wine, the light red Lago di Caldaro / Kalterersee. Note also the town of Termeno, where the traminer grape is believed to have originated. See regional map of Trentino-Alto Adige, page 267.

for the thin flavor that follows. There are exceptions: In the Merano area a sturdy wine called Kuchelberger is made, blending lagrein with schiava; Kellereigenossenschaft St. Michael Eppan makes Kalvarienberger, a blend of pinot noir and schiava; Kellereigenossenschaft Girlan makes one of the best of all schiava wines, called Schreckbichler and qualified in great years with the barrel number, nine; and the producer Josef Hofstätter, often cited in these pages, makes a delicious version near the town of Termeno, a version that he calls Kolbenhofer and sells without D.O.C. designation, as *vino da tavola.*

⇜ *Sorni* ⇝
(D.O.C., TRENTINO–ALTO ADIGE)

A recently designated D.O.C. appellation, Sorni Rosso, from the northern tip of Trento province, is made of lagrein and schiava, with the addition of a little teroldego. It has more firmness than most schiava wines and a fine, flowery aroma. The producer is a cooperative, Cantina Sociale Lavis-Sorni-Salorno.

NOTE: By far the best wine from schiava in Trentino is made by Pojer & Sandri, who eschew a D.O.C. designation to sell it as Schiava di Faedo, an unclassified *vino da tavola.*

TWO OTHER MEMBERS
OF THE SCHIAVA FAMILY

⇜ *Cellatica* ⇝
(D.O.C., LOMBARDY)

Cellatica is produced just northwest of the city of Brescia. Schiava is its main component, plus barbera and marzemino. It is a darker ruby than most schiava wines, displaying that enticing mixture of floweriness and fresh vinosity in the bouquet typical of the grape. It is light but not frail, with considerable spryness to its taste impressions, which end somewhat abruptly with a touch of bitterness. A reliable source of Cellatica is Coop. Vitivinicola Cellatica-Gussago.

❧ *Valdadige Rosso* ❧
(D.O.C., TRENTINO–ALTO ADIGE AND VENETO)

A catchall appellation for wines produced in seventy-five townships within two regions. The territory consists of flats on the right and left banks of the Adige River, from Bolzano, past Trento, down to Verona. Besides the required schiava, producers may choose from six other grape varietals to blend into Valdadige Rosso. Tracts of the zone are, for part of the day, in the shadow cast by overhanging hills and mountains. How is one to describe this miscellany? As nondescript.

INDEPENDENT LIGHT RED WINES

CHIANTI DI PRONTA BEVA ("FOR EARLY CONSUMPTION")

❧ *Chianti* ❧
(D.O.C., AWAITING D.O.C.G., TUSCANY)

Vivacious and bright ruby red, this style of Chianti has the aroma of freshly squeezed grapes; prickly on the tongue, refreshingly acidulous, it is a delightfully fruity quaffing wine, to be used up within a year of its harvest. Maturer styles of Chianti are described on pages 31–43, and 102–3. In its straw-covered flask, it was primarily this kind of Chianti that originally won admirers beyond count. It was born as, and remains, a wine for local consumption, for its appeal is as short-lived and fragile as it is irresistible.

In the making of youthful Chianti, the practice of *governo*, which induces a second fermentation through the addition of partly shriveled grapes to the wine, is not only desirable, but indispensable. However debatable may be its merits in the production of slower-developing wines, without *governo* young Chianti would be too hard, too angular for ready drinking. A recent proposal would oblige this style of Chianti to carry on its label the qualifying term *governato*.

Even if produced within the Classico zone, Chianti *di pronta beva* is not permitted to bear a Classico designation because it does not meet the minimum aging requirements. The fresh youthful style of Chianti is associated instead with that vast area, surrounding Chianti Classico, that is generally referred to as Chianti Putto. *Putto* is Italian for cherub, which is the symbol of the consortium that has jurisdiction over the several districts outside the Classico zone that are permitted to make Chianti. (See regional map of Tuscany on page 275.)

The most engaging of these young wines comes from the district near Florence known as Colli Fiorentini. The town of Montespertoli in the Colli Fiorentini holds an annual celebration in late spring to welcome the new wine, an event of pure, guzzling joy. Another district known for the excellence of its young Chianti is Colli Aretini, in the province of Arezzo.

❧ *Freisa* ☙

(D.O.C. WHEN FOLLOWED BY ONE OF
TWO DISTRICT DESIGNATIONS, PIEDMONT)

To find oneself sitting before a plate of *salame* and a bottle of sweetish, frothy Freisa in a damp, smoky *osteria* ricocheting with the tight-lipped, impenetrable syllables of Piedmontese dialect is to have been dropped back a century or more into the old, and now largely forgotten, Piedmont.

Many of the wines that today make up Piedmont's family of majestic reds used to be sweet and bubbly. Occasionally today one may come across such a version of Nebbiolo or, more frequently, of Barbera. But the most common, the one still solidly entrenched in popular esteem, is Freisa.

The consumption of Freisa *amabile* ("sweet Freisa") is purely a local phenomenon, an arrangement as agreeable to its admirers as it must be to everyone else. For the rest of us, fortunately, Freisa is also made in a *secco* ("dry") version. It is a bright garnet wine whose berrylike aroma and flavor are usually thought to suggest raspberries. The freisa grape is rich in tannin and acid, which can make the wine hard and snappish. Two to three years' aging will soften it, but a longer period of maturation, while it might abate the tannin, will dry up the fruit.

New styles of vinification are producing a far less astringent and slightly prickly Freisa for immediate consumption. This is a welcome innovation that turns to greatest advantage the unique properties of a most interesting grape. The combination of firmness and vigor with emphatically fruity aroma and flavor puts Freisa in a category all its own.

The lack of complexity and the youthful, forward, one-dimensional taste make it a light wine that nevertheless possesses the solid, wirier structure of such bigger reds as Barbera.

Two production zones in Piedmont are entitled to D.O.C. appellations for Freisa: Asti and Chieri. Freisa d'Asti is by far more abundant. Freisa di Chieri, from the hills south of Turin, is the bigger wine of the two, but with fainter aromatic appeal. Most of the Freisa produced, however, bears no D.O.C. appellation at all.

Among the good producers are Bertolo, Aldo Conterno, Fratelli Biletta, Fratelli Oddero, Gaja, Bruno Giacosa, Prunotto, Scarpa, and Vietti.

VINTAGES: Freisa in the youthful, lightly effervescent style, of which Gaja's is the prime example, is drunk up quickly in Italy during the same year it is released. The more tannic Freisa will taste well after two to three years in the bottle but won't hold much interest thereafter. The most attractive recent years are 1980, 1982, and 1983.

❧ *Grignolino* ☙

(D.O.C. WHEN FOLLOWED BY ONE OF TWO
DISTRICT DESIGNATIONS, PIEDMONT)

In that ideal world where pure and simple joys flow like spring water, there must be a perpetual fount of Grignolino pouring in constant, uniform supply. In our world, sources of pure and simple joys, such as Grignolino, often run dry or turn brackish.

Grignolino can display the most refined, enchanting style of any of the world's light-bodied wines, and on those occasions it is indeed a joy. More frequently, alas, it is a disappointment. There are problems with the grape variety; too many inferior vines have proliferated and need wholesale replanting with selected stock. Even more than the other fine wines of Piedmont, Grignolino is extremely susceptible to the variables of vintage years. Moreover, the delicate fruit and fragrance that can make it so beguiling are fragile qualities that only scrupulous selection of grapes and patient vinification can conserve.

Buying Grignolino requires much more attention than drinking it. It is necessary to know what kind of year it was, where it was made, and by whom. To many drinkers, surrounding a wine of simple and casual appeal with so much connoisseurship may seem excessive. But it would not seem so to those who have once succumbed to the dainty blandishments of this gentle, fine-bred wine.

Grignolino is produced from the grape of the same name, most of it grown in the province of Asti in Piedmont.

The color is a brilliant, light ruby, with purplish reflections in young wines that turn to orange with age. The aroma is thin, but penetrating, combining a sweet, faintly flowery scent with herbal pungency. Flavors are grapy and lively, sharpened lightly by spicy sensations that are agreeably supported by moderate astringency and bitterness. It finishes with a flourish on the rising note of an extended aftertaste. The overall impression is that of freshness conveyed with racy elegance and firmness.

Like all light-bodied wines, Grignolino's appeal is strongest in its youth, within two years of the vintage. But unlike most other wines in its class, a well-made Grignolino from a robust year can continue to be drunk with delight well into its fifth year.

There are two D.O.C. appellations: the more important is Grignolino d'Asti; the other, Grignolino del Monferrato Casalese.

Some of the best townships in Grignolino d'Asti are Belveglio, Calliano, Castagnole Monferrato, Migliandolo, Mombercelli, Moncalvo, Penango, Portacomaro, and Rocchetta Tanaro. Among their most reliable producers we find Biggio, Carnevale, Bruno Giacosa, Aldo Margarini, Pio Cesare, Poncini, Rabezzana, and Tenuta dei Re.

In the Monferrato Casalese appellation, outstanding townships are Altavilla, Olivola, and Vignale. Good producers from this area are Cantina Sociale di Altavilla, Castello di Gabiano, Castello di Lignano, Giorgio Cosseta, Amilcare Gaudio, Bruno Giacosa, Livio Pavese, and Riccardi Candiani.

VINTAGES: 1978 was a great year, but it will not live forever, nor is any of what is left likely to turn up outside a producer's private cellar. The best vintage in Grignolino is always the most recent successful year.

❧ *Lambrusco* ☙

(D.O.C. WHEN FOLLOWED BY ONE OF FOUR DISTRICT
DESIGNATIONS, EMILIA–ROMAGNA)

For an unpretentious, if beguiling, little wine, Lambrusco has made a big stir. It is the object of condescending and derisive remarks from most critics, which have not prevented it from outselling, by an enormous margin, every imported wine in the American market. It has been called "bizarre," "nearly undrinkable," "not a wine for serious drinkers." I am not sure what is meant by a serious drinker. I know what a solemn drinker is, however. I have known enough of those, and Lambrusco is certainly not for them.

Before going any further, one must distinguish between the Lambrusco consumed in its native Emilia-Romagna and the export variety. The first is indeed a wine; the second, a beverage.

In Emilia-Romagna, Lambrusco is purplish and naturally frothy, with a sprightly, flowery, winy smell and the lightest body of any red wine I know. Dry, tart, faintly bitter, it possesses a brisk style that rouses and freshens the palate but quits it abruptly in a short, clean finish.

This is the wine that gastronomic pilgrims will find served at all restaurants from Parma through Modena to Bologna. It is not to be approached reverentially but is to be enjoyed for the delicious, light-hearted counterpoint it offers to the savory cuisine of the region. In Parma with *tortelli di zucca,* pumpkin- and cheese-stuffed pasta. In Modena with *bollito misto,* the steaming platter of boiled meats that always includes the local specialty, *zampone*—a thick, exquisitely creamy pork sausage. In Bologna with spinach lasagne, with tortellini, with breast of turkey *bolognese*—a sautéed turkey cutlet with Parmesan cheese, prosciutto, and white truffles.

No wine is so reviving to a toiling palate or to flagging spirits. Whenever I reach Bologna after a long, taxing drive on the high-speed Italian turnpikes, there is no other drink I want at the table.

Export Lambrusco is made from the same grapes, grown in the same region, but vinified in a substantially different style, boosting sweetness through the addition of concentrated musts. It was originally formulated by one of Italy's leading oenologists, Ezio Rivella, for Banfi, the importers of Riunite. Banfi believed that there was a place in the market for a wine low in alcohol, decidedly sweet and bubbly, a bottle that could be stored in the refrigerator alongside the sodas and six-packs and be consumed as casually, but with somewhat more stimulating results. How right they were! Their Lambrusco became the most successful wine ever brought to America, a bonanza for Riunite and for the other producers who duplicated the magic formula.

Of them all, Riunite is probably still the best, the fruitiest and least cloying. It would be difficult to imagine drinking it at the table, unless one is already accustomed to dining with cola or ginger ale. At the same time, it would be arrogant to ignore the pleasure it indubitably brings to so many people for whom Lambrusco is the first comfortable step away from the world of soft drinks and into that of wine.

Many different Lambruscos are produced in Emilia-Romagna for local consumption, of which four are entitled to a D.O.C. appellation. These are Lambrusco di Sorbara, Lambrusco Grasparossa di Castelvetro, Lambrusco Reggiano, and Lambrusco Salamino di Santa Croce. That is purely for the record, since the only one anyone ever asks for by name is Lambrusco di Sorbara, made in Modena province and by far the best of the lot. Of the non-D.O.C. Lambruscos, the best is the one made in the province of Parma, a dark, full wine that hints at a liaison between the lambrusco and the barbera grape that may have taken place some while ago in the more licentious days of Italian viticulture.

A word that may appear on a bottle of Lambrusco in Italy, and about which travelers should be warned, is *amabile*. It means sweet, and while it is improbable that any scrupulous restaurant would ever serve it before dessert, one never knows.

A selected list of the producers making the rarely exported dry version of Lambrusco should include Agostinelli, Casimiro Barbieri, Cancarini-Ghisetti, and Fini.

VINTAGES: When drinking Lambrusco in Italy, it is easy to choose the right year. It is the one of the most recent harvest.

❦ *Marzemino* ❧
(D.O.C., TRENTINO-ALTO ADIGE)

Marzemino started drawing the attention of wine writers as early as the sixteenth century; from the eighteenth century to the early part of the twentieth it was a frequently praised and much sought-after wine not only in its native Trentino, but throughout the Austro-Hungarian Empire. Of its many admirers the one most often quoted is Mozart's Don Giovanni, who finds it "excellent" when he drinks it at his last supper, before he is pulled into hell.

After a long period of success, Marzemino's career nearly came to an end as dire as the Don's. The battles of World War I devastated its vineyards, and the peace treaty, which amputated the territory of Trentino from Austria and awarded it to Italy, deprived it of the market through whose support it had flourished. Marzemino tottered on the edge of extinction for decades, and not until after World War II did it once again begin to thrive.

The wine is made from a blue black, thin-skinned grape of the same name cultivated on both sides of the Adige River, at the southern end of the Trentino region, in northeast Italy. The best vineyards are on the low, sunny volcanic slopes on the right bank of the river, specifically between the villages of Isera and Nogaredo.

The color of Marzemino is dark, more garnet than ruby. Its fragrance is the most entrancing of any wine produced in Trentino, a striking blend of perfumes suggesting ripe fruit, violets, and almonds. In the mouth the wine is silky, although less well-endowed versions may seem thin or even threadbare. The impression of fruit is firm and distinct, but refined rather than opulent. The bitter almond sensation in the nose is confirmed by the palate and restated in the elongated aftertaste.

The vibrant, abundant Merlot-like flavor described by the old writers is so hard to relate to contemporary renditions of Marzemino that one wonders if they had not been drinking wine made from some other grapes. My friend Giorgio Grai (see note, page 78) of Bolzano once provided a stunning reply to this query by producing a ten-year-old bottle of Marzemino whose texture was as voluptuous as a fine Pomerol and the seemingly unending sequence of flavors was simply dazzling.

Grai's bottle was a tribute to the skills this wizard of winemaking possesses and exercises, but it is not typical of what one may expect of Marzemino today. The best that generally awaits us is a light-bodied wine, quick and pleasing, in which the shadowy presence of potential greatness is sometimes sufficiently discernible to endow it with soft-stated elegance.

Two good producers of Marzemino are Bossi Fedrigotti and Letrari.

VINTAGES: Great vintages of the past are of little interest, first, since they are nowhere to be found, and second, save for a few prodigious bottles, there is little an aged Marzemino has to say to us that we want to hear. The most recent good vintage is the one to look for and to consume.

[4]

THE WHITE WINES
OF ITALY

When speaking of the difference between red wines and white, winemakers will say that reds are made in the vineyard, whites in the cellar. It's a pithy way of saying that good quality in red wines depends on the raw material that soil, weather, and vines produce, while in white wines it's the technique of vinification that counts. Like most dictums, this one emphasizes one truth at the expense of another. To make a fine wine, whether red or white, you need both good grapes and good hands. It's like pulling sound from an instrument. Put a Stradivarius into a musician's hands, and if he has the talent, he will make it sing. Give him a cracked bell, and he can do little to sweeten its clank.

It is true, however, that the white wines we drink today are the product of a special technology, pioneered in Germany and in California. It is Italy's recent mastery of these techniques, coupled with the matchless variety of its grapes, that has made its white wines so attractive and successful.

The juice of all grapes is colorless, or nearly so; all the color is in the skins. Red wines are red because they are fermented in contact with dark skins. In addition to color, skins contain other substances, among them tannin, whose hardness and bitterness are undesirable in white wine. Therefore, when making white wine, the juice, before it begins to ferment, is run off, separating it from the skins. Thus one can also make white wine from red grapes, as is often done in Champagne with pinot noir.

The absence of grape skins, however, drastically alters the structure of wine. Stripped of its tannin, wine must is left with a fragile constitution that may buckle as it undergoes the violent metamorphosis of fermentation. It must be fermented slowly, in temperature-controlled containers, preferably made of stainless steel, to extract, boost, and protect the delicate fragrances that remain. Even after a successful fermentation, white wine lacks the natural endurance of a red, and the winemaker may intervene with one or more stabilization techniques, including flash pasteurization, to keep the wine unaltered along its many stops as it travels from the bottling line to the dining table.

The freshness and vivacity that are indispensable to a white wine's appeal are manifestations of acids in the wine. If left to their own devices, young wines undergo a secondary fermentation, called malolactic, that transforms sharp malic acid into soft lactic acid. In red wines this is desirable. In most white wines it is not, and the winemaker must intervene again to block it. The smell of apples often detected in white wines signals the presence of malic acid (*malic* comes from *malum*, Latin for apple).

Constant intervention is the strategy in modern white wine technology, intervention with cold and with heat, with centrifuging machines to spin out solids, with filters, bleaches, acids, disinfectants. In some instances, in the south of Italy and in the islands particularly, where only oxidized, flat-tasting wines used to be made, this approach has produced a new class of wines, fresh, clean, and crisp. Examples are Sicily's Corvo and Sardinia's Sella & Mosca whites. Elsewhere, the new breed of cellar engineers has gone about stripping wines of all defects with such zeal that they also stripped them of most of their character. Examples are the bland, massproduced versions of Soave and Verdicchio that dominate the market.

We must not allow these bright, transparent, and oversanitized wines, however frequently they may turn up, to distort our view of Italian whites. No other country produces so large a variety of interesting white wines, with clearly expressed and widely differing characters. In terms of flavor, fragrance, delicacy, vivacity, or overall harmony there exist Italian wines that will often outperform all others in the equivalent price class.

What is absent from the spectrum of dry Italian whites are examples that match the power, fullness, and intensity of a few expensive Burgundies and their counterparts, the California Chardonnays. It's conceivable that they could be duplicated in northern Italy, if tradition and local taste prized such qualities in a white wine over freshness and immediacy.

With rare exceptions, Italian white wines are not aged in wood nor made to be laid down. The transformations that aging in new, small, oak barrels works upon bouquet and flavor are fascinating, and they have influenced our notions of style in great wines. But concepts of wine style, however slowly they may evolve, are manifestations of taste that are ultimately as mutable as concepts of style in clothes, in furniture design, in painting, or in language. We may be at the threshold of such a change, and the day might not be far off when we shall look on the practice of flavoring wine with wood as an anomaly no less strange than flavoring it with resin, as the ancients did, and the Greeks still do.

Sound, simple, attractive everyday whites are produced everywhere in Italy, in as broad an assortment as anyone could want, perhaps broader than anyone compelled to describe them would prefer. But white wines with more elevated qualities—wines that offer refinement, delicacy, gracious character—are almost without exception produced solely in the North, mostly in the Northeast, and largely of grape varietals not native to Italy.

In the competition with red wine in Italy, white has historically come off second-best. Nearly all the choicest plots with the best exposure and soil have been planted for red. And no native white varietal has ever developed that quite matches the noblest reds. Fortunately, such French and German varieties as pinot blanc, pinot gris, and riesling have put down solid roots in Italy.

The one area of the country where the white grape has always enjoyed the same respectful treatment as the red is the Northeast, in the regions of Veneto, Friuli, and Alto-Adige/Südtirol. A section of Friuli near the Yugoslav border bears the two geographic appellations that are most important to those looking for fine whites: Collio and Colli Orientali del Friuli. Here, a white wine tradition that parallels Piedmont's devotion to reds, supported by splendidly exposed hillside vineyards, gives us Italy's most distinguished white wines. These are all known by their varietal grape names, and those of foreign extraction—Pinot Bianco, Pinot Grigio, Riesling Renano—appear on some elegant bottles indeed.

Veneto's whites are not quite in the same league as Friuli's, but are nonetheless among the most engaging, certainly the most popular, produced in Italy. Native grapes, of which Soave is the best-known product, do particularly well here, as well as the usual French and German transplants.

Alto-Adige/Südtirol excels in perfectly balanced and exquisitely perfumed whites from pinot, sylvaner, and riesling as well as from the native traminer.

On the northwestern side of the peninsula, Val d'Aosta and Piedmont are not major sources of white wines, at least not from the point of view of quantity. Val d'Aosta's mountain vineyards are niggardly producers of a few rare but subtle, memorable wines made from local varieties seen nowhere else in Italy. In Piedmont the supremacy of red wines leaves little room for whites, but one native white grape, cortese, is responsible for a wine, Cortese di Gavi, of uncommon grace and delicacy, one that on occasion may even reach for greatness. And a recent entry, Arneis, may turn out in time to be one of Italy's finest whites.

With the exception of a small, high-altitude enclave near Naples that produces two remarkable wines, Fiano di Avellino and Greco di Tufo, the white wines of the other regions are less striking. This is not to say they are poor or do not deserve interest. No one is faring badly when he can choose for his table a wine from the roster that includes Vernaccia or Pomino from Tuscany, Orvieto or Torgiano from Umbria, Lugana from Lombardy, Albana from Emilia-Romagna, Frascati or Colli Lanuvini from Rome, Etna Bianco or Corvo from Sicily, Vermentino from Sardinia. With more or less pronounced individual character, all these possess those universal qualities that make white wine useful in the first place: vitality, freshness, and clear, zesty taste. It is pointless to reproach the wines of central and southern Italy for not delivering more, when it is precisely within their limits that our everyday expectations are most comfortably satisfied.

Estate-bottled white wines with subtle aromas, rich texture, nuances of flavor, lingering finesse are in as short supply in Italy as they are anywhere else. The joy of discovering an unctuous Pinot Bianco from one of the craftsman producers of the Collio, or an ethereal Riesling from Alto Adige, should be accompanied by the understanding that for these gems of winemaking the most appropriate settings are those thoughtfully ordered occasions when unhurried pleasures play to heedful senses.

A Note on Vintages

There are no vintage recommendations for all but two of the white wines listed here. While some Italian white wines are sturdy enough to with-stand aging, practically none, in my opinion, benefits by it. The changes that age brings, however interesting they may be in a few fortunate and largely unpredictable circumstances, invariably erase those qualities of animation and spontaneity that distinguish all well-made Italian whites, from the humblest to the noblest. This is not to say that vintages do not vary in quality. They do indeed, particularly in the North. And a three-year-old white from an exceptional vintage will have more to offer than a scrawny yearling from a weak harvest. There are sources more frequently updated than this work—newspapers, magazines, wine newsletters—that can inform the interested consumer on the merits of the available recent vintages.

Two Categories of Italian White Wines

The taste sensations we expect from white wines are different from those that red wines give us, and so are the categories we need to identify them. The conventional approach would be to group white wines according to their degree of dryness, beginning with bone dry and ending with intensely sweet, and to subdivide these into light, medium, and robust wines. To make matters simple for the reader, and for myself, I have devoted the discussions that follow just to such wines as we customarily drink with food, thus eliminating those of either subdued or openly declared sweetness, save for an occasional passing reference.

At the same time I have avoided creating categories coupled to varying states of dryness. I am aware that medium dry, dry, or bone dry are acceptable descriptive terms, but I am nonetheless uneasy about using them to pin down the character of a wine. Too often they serve as substitutes for keener and more useful perceptions. People will sip and say, "Ah, that is a good wine, so nice and dry!" But impressions of dryness are partly subjective, and the inexperienced easily confuse them with manifestations of fruit, of acid, or of mineral values. Furthermore, a white wine need not be bitingly dry to be fine, nor does response to such steely dryness automatically reveal a discriminating palate.

All wines examined here are technically dry, and I invite the reader to let that suffice while concentrating with me on other attributes that will lead us to a larger and more enjoyable appreciation of wine character.

The most noteworthy Italian white wines are divided here into two categories, each distinct enough to mark the boundaries of the two large basic groups within which we can expect to find nearly all dry white wines, and loose enough to accommodate without strain a multitude of individual styles.

One category is Light and Crisp, the other Full and Fruity. Light and Crisp wines are those in which impressions of alcohol and weight are played down in favor of such qualities as freshness and vivacity. Their impact is immediate, sharp, and stimulating. Full and Fruity wines are larger, more mouthfilling, conveying sensations of weight, sometimes palpable thickness, and ample, emphatic flavor.

In white wines, Italian whites in particular, bigness should not be expected to hold the promise of a superior order of sensations, as it does in reds. The qualities we ultimately hope for are elegance, delicacy, finesse, and as these are more related to style than to power, we shall as easily find them among white wines that are light as those that are full.

A note of caution: Much as I believe that basic categories are useful in organizing information, it is the information that matters, not the category. Wines are individual creations, and like all individuals, they have their share of ambivalence. Some of the wines placed in the Light and Crisp category could as easily have been grouped with the Full and Fruity. Or the reverse. Moreover, a region or a winemaker may extract different values from the same grape varieties. A Pinot Bianco from Terlano will be much lighter than one from the Collio. A Frascati from a small producer may be a plumper wine than one from an industrialized winery. I have tried to supply enough information for the reader to infer such distinctions.

On the whole, the groupings that follow are valid, I am convinced. But they are no substitute for the reader's careful evaluation of the descriptions given and, ultimately, of the wine itself.

Light and Crisp White Wines

FAMILIES OF
LIGHT AND CRISP WHITE WINES

The Cortese Whites of Piedmont

❧ *Cortese di Gavi* ❧
(D.O.C., PIEDMONT)

The overweening shadow of Piedmont's gigantic reds has made it difficult for the whites of the region to earn their place in the sun. Like scrawny children in a family of champion athletes, they can expect tolerance but not respect. In recent years, however, the Piedmontese have learned that in the outside world white wines are not only accepted but may even be sought after. At the same time they have learned to use the highly controlled white wine techniques that produce wines with character and stability from what used to be considered doubtful grapes. In Piedmont the chief beneficiary of these circumstances has been Cortese di Gavi.

The Gavi production zone is in the balmiest portion of Piedmont, at its southeastern tip, jutting almost into Liguria, the region of the Italian Riviera. It is a fetchingly pastoral area, with rings of fleecy, fertile hills and their best vineyards furring sunny slopes at six hundred to a thousand feet. The soil is loose and fine, with an abundance of marl and occasional sand. Here the golden cortese grape produces a wine low in alcohol, but charged with acidity.

It is a grape vulnerable to mold, particularly when it nears maturity, placing the grower in a dilemma: harvesting while the berries are still sound, but sour and underripe, or deciding to risk exposure to mold while waiting for more sugar to develop in their juice.

When all goes well, Cortese di Gavi is a wine of remarkable delicacy. The color is a brilliant straw yellow shot with green. The fragrance is light and fresh, with a small but fine, keen-edged bouquet. The flavor has the snappish vitality one expects from high acidity, fleshed out by firm, if lean, impressions of fruit enriched by candylike sensations.

The choicest sites in this appellation lie by the hamlet of Rovereto, in Gavi township, where more sugary grapes grow and rounder, fuller wines are made.

The outstanding producer is Soldati, who bottles three different Gavis. His finest, probably made from the free-run juice, is called Gavi dei Gavi and commands the highest price of any Italian white wine. Other admirable sources are Nicola Bergaglio, Castel di Serra, Luigi Gemme, La Giustiniana, and La Piacentina.

◆◢ Cortese dei Colli Tortonesi ◣◆
(D.O.C., PIEDMONT)

Immediately northeast of Gavi another zone is entitled to a D.O.C. appellation for Cortese. It is the Colli Tortonesi, the hills of Tortona, an area that takes its name from the largest town within its boundaries. Production of Cortese here is tiny compared with Gavi, and it is just as well, because the wine is sharper and thinner, stopping considerably short of the refinement and delicacy of its more fortunate neighbor.

❧ Cortese dell'Alto Monferrato ❧
(D.O.C., PIEDMONT)

The thinnest of the Corteses, whose production is scattered over a large district in central Piedmont. It is a very pale, green-tinged wine, acidulous and thereby fresh: a quick-flowing, lean, summer white.

The Müller-Thurgau Wines
of the Northeast

The amorous intrigues of grapes would not seem to be a subject of gripping interest. For some time, however, serious men in white coats have been scrutinizing the parentage of the Müller-Thurgau variety. It is known that the godfather was Dr. Müller-Thurgau, a Swiss botanist teaching at Geisenheim, Germany, at the end of the nineteenth century. Originally it was believed that the offspring issued from the coupling of riesling and sylvaner vines, inheriting some of the finesse of the first and the hardiness of the second. Subsequently, the prevailing opinion has been that sylvaner had had no part in the affair, whose most likely protagonists must have been two incestuous clones of riesling. While we wait for the whole truth to come out, we can turn our attention to the wine, about which there is no mystery whatever.

Its color is a pale straw yellow with flashes of green. The bouquet is full and seductively aromatic. The body favors softness at the expense of acidity, and fruity taste impressions spread silkily on the palate. Of all Teutonic wines, Müller-Thurgau is perhaps the most instantly appealing.

D.O.C. legislation has granted controlled appellations to Müller-Thurgau only in Trentino–Alto Adige, in whose northern half the most intense versions of the wine are made.

❧ Alto Adige Müller-Thurgau/
Südtiroler Müller-Thurgau ❧
(D.O.C., TRENTINO–ALTO ADIGE)

This is from the central portion of Bolzano province, elsewhere described in the sections on Pinot Bianco, pages 181–92, Gewürztraminer, pages

197–8, Riesling, page 150. Here Müller-Thurgau turns out somewhat duller and heavier than in the higher-altitude appellations. A good producer in this area is Kellereigenossenschaft Girlan.

❦ *Terlano Müller-Thurgau/*
Terlaner Müller-Thurgau ❧
(D.O.C., TRENTINO–ALTO ADIGE)

An exemplary wine, ethereal in aroma and vivacious in flavor, made from grapes grown on the steep vineyards of a mountainous zone west of Bolzano. The producer is Terlano's celebrated cooperative cellar, Kellereigenossenschaft Terlan.

❦ *Valle Isarco Müller-Thurgau/*
Eisacktaler-Müller Thurgau ❧
(D.O.C., TRENTINO–ALTO ADIGE)

As you cross from Austria into Italy through the Brenner Pass, you come to the valley of the Isarco River, the northeastern portion of Alto Adige, where the Alpine landscape gives way startlingly to the sight of improbably high vineyards rooted to the mountain sides. Here is where the Müller-Thurgau grape displays its uncommon endurance, producing aromatic wines with piercing bouquet, light body, and exceptionally delicate flavor. The best-known source is the abbey of Novacella, Stiftskellerei Neustift. A less famous but better producer is the local cooperative, Eisacktaler Kellereigenossenschaft.

❦ *Trentino Müller-Thurgau* ❧
(D.O.C., TRENTINO–ALTO ADIGE)

The official appellation in the province of Trento for this wine is Riesling, in which riesling renano, riesling italico, or müller-thurgau may be used singly or combined. When the principal grape is müller-thurgau, its name customarily appears on the label in addition to the Trentino Riesling denomination.

Trento's Müller-Thurgau is not as effusively scented as the Alto Adige versions, nor does it have the same palpably fruity flavor, but it can nonetheless be an appealing, smooth, light, well-balanced wine. I have been particularly charmed by the one produced by Giuliano Bolner at Villa Borino. Two equally admirable producers are Remo Calovi and Pojer & Sandri.

UNCLASSIFIED MÜLLER-THURGAU
(VINO DA TAVOLA)

Small productions of the wine are scattered in northern Italy outside the area prescribed by the controlled appellation statutes. They are of little interest except for the astonishing Müller-Thurgau made by Mario Schiopetto in the Collio zone of Friuli. It is one of the most sought-after wines among Italian connoisseurs and, regrettably, one of the rarest. In the measured elegance of its aromas, the plush texture of the body, the development of exquisite flavors that lingers in the sustained echo of the aftertaste, Schiopetto's Müller-Thurgau soars to peaks of refinement that elsewhere appear to be beyond the reach of this grape. It is a pity that there is no D.O.C. appellation for this variety in the Collio, particularly since another fine example, bottled nearby by Buzzinelli, indicates Schiopetto's achievement need not be a solitary one.

The Riesling Family

In Italy the name riesling is shared by two grape varieties whose only common feature is that they both make white wine. One is the same variety from which emerge the great wines of the Rhine and Moselle, called riesling renano in Italian. The other, known as riesling italico, Italian riesling, is of uncertain origin, although some specialists detect in it a similarity to the Neapolitan grape greco, described on page 210. Riesling italico makes a plain wine, vinous in fragrance, rather flat in body, coarsely fruity, a tolerable if charmless addition to the populous ranks of commonplace whites.

Rhine riesling, in its most complete manifestations, generates wines of heady perfume, deep, full flavor, and singular refinement.

The problem in choosing an unfamiliar Italian riesling by the label is that it sometimes does not state whether it is *italico* or *renano*, or a blend of both. Unless the wine merchant is able to tell you—an unlikely occurrence—the only way to identify it before stocking any quantity is to take a bottle home and taste it.

ALTO ADIGE'S RIESLING

It will not surprise those fortunate enough to have sampled some of the better Alto Adige wines, or patient enough to have read about them here, that Italy's finest Riesling is produced in this ex-Austrian province on Italy's northernmost border. The Teutonic style of winemaking, with its emphasis on fragrance, on clarity of flavor, on balance, finds its happiest application in Riesling.

These wines do not ask to be closely compared with Germany's Rieslings of spaetlese class or better. They are not so luscious nor intense, but they can be nearly as delicate, and most important, they are dry and consequently more useful for the table.

Here true Riesling is labeled Riesling Renano or Rheinriesling; and the lesser variety, Riesling Italico or Welschriesling.

Alto Adige Riesling Renano/
Südtiroler Rheinriesling
(D.O.C., TRENTINO–ALTO ADIGE)

The Alto Adige/Südtirol appellation covers the central and largest portion of the province of Bolzano. The Riesling that I have most consistently enjoyed here has been that bottled by Hofstätter. Other no less distinguished producers are von Elzenbaum, Giorgio Grai under the labels Herrnhofer or Bellendorf, Laimburg, and Kellereigenossenschaft Margreid/Entiklar.

Terlano Riesling Renano/
Terlaner Rheinriesling
(D.O.C., TRENTINO–ALTO ADIGE)

The mountain-raised wines from this small appellation west of Bolzano are lighter, more delicate than the ones bearing the Alto Adige denomination, with a bouquet less densely fruity and more flowery. The principal producer is Kellereigenossenschaft Terlan. Another is Alois Lageder.

TRENTINO'S RIESLING

In Trento's half of the Alto Adige/Trentino region, wine labeled Riesling may be made from riesling renano, riesling italico, or even müller-thurgau, alone or in any combination. In reality, nearly all of it is riesling italico, and none worth mentioning has come to my notice.

FRIULI'S RIESLING

Among the many gems in this region's treasury of white wines, Riesling shines faintly. It is produced in small quantity and not in every zone. In Friuli's most esteemed appellation—Collio—the D.O.C. statute admits only riesling italico, which is what you get when you pick up a bottle labeled Collio Riesling. Some Collio producers do make unclassified Riesling Renano, and among these Mario Schiopetto shows all the virtuosity of which his master hands are capable, but his Riesling is as scarce as it is good.

Colli Orientali del Friuli Riesling Renano
(D.O.C., FRIULI-VENEZIA GIULIA)

In Colli Orientali, the other notable zone in Friuli, true riesling is officially admitted, and it is here one should look for the region's most readily available fine editions of the wine. Although not so elegantly scented as Alto Adige's Riesling, it has a boldly fruity bouquet and the solid flavor and sumptuous texture we expect from a Friulian wine. The best producers are Livio Felluga, Ronchi di Manzano, Selva, Valle, and Volpe Pasini.

Aquileia Riesling Renano
(D.O.C., FRIULI-VENEZIA GIULIA)

Isonzo Riesling Renano
(D.O.C., FRIULI-VENEZIA GIULIA)

The plains of these two zones—the first coastal, the second riverine—bear the only other D.O.C. Rhine Rieslings in Friuli. Their wines are weightier than the Colli Orientali's, somewhat musky and earthy, but of generally good quality. The Isonzo wines are finer and more complete than Aquileia's. In Aquileia a good producer is Molin di Ponte; and in Isonzo, the cooperative cellar Cantina Produttori Vini del Collio e dell'Isonzo.

NOTE: In Friuli, Vittorio Puiatti, the colossus—both physically and intellectually—of Italian white wine makers, produces wines for his company, Enofriulia, unclassified, which are generically labeled Delle Venezie. This enables him to blend and buy grapes from anywhere within the large northeastern territory. Puiatti reasons that his civilized palate and technical wizardry make the Enofriulia name as reliable as any D.O.C. appellation. He may be right. There is no Riesling Renano in the country that gives such a penetrating yet so delicately balanced experience of the aromas and tastes of this varietal as Enofriulia's. Puiatti also produces a scintillating series of other white wines among which the Pinot Bianco, Chardonnay, Sauvignon, and Traminer Aromatico are conspicuously fine. Puiatti's finest production goes into his *linea verde,* with the wine name written in green.

OTHER RIESLINGS

The Veneto has no Riesling appellations, but a moderate quantity of wine from riesling italico alone, or in combination with riesling renano, is produced there, mostly near Treviso. In the Colli Berici zone two producers bottle unclassified but sought-after whites from riesling renano. They are Count da Schio at Costozza and Alfredo Lazzarini at Villa Dal Ferro. The latter's Riesling, bearing the coined name Busa Calcara, is decidedly the better balanced of the two.

❦ *Riesling dell'Oltrepò* ❧
(D.O.C., LOMBARDY)

In Lombardy the prolific Oltrepò Pavese zone has a Riesling appellation that envisages the possibility of a 100 percent riesling renano varietal wine. All the ones that have come my way, however, have been either Riesling Italico or a blend of the two varieties. Much of it is sound, fresh, full-flavored wine and would be easy to accept under any other label but Riesling, whose refined excitement in scent and taste it is unable to deliver. If one puts aside the expectations aroused by the name, Oltrepò Riesling is a wine worth trying, on its own simple terms. Some of the producers to look for are Cella di Montalto, Dal Pozzo, Denari, Il Frater, Nazzano, Oliva, and 4 Castagni.

The Sauvignon Family

An acquaintance with the whites of the Loire and of Graves, with California's various styles of Fumé or Sauvignon Blanc, discloses the many transformations of which the sauvignon grape is capable, expressed in wines that may range from light and tart to lush and overpowering. Italian Sauvignon manifests characteristics that can be clearly identified as those of the French varietal—a pungent, grassy, slightly aromatic nose and fresh, herbaceous flavor—in a style that is distinctly Italian—light, fruity, ripe, easy to drink.

Production of Sauvignon, like that of other wines from French grapes, is concentrated in the Northeast, specifically in the province of Bolzano (the Germanic half of Alto Adige/Trentino region), in Friuli, and in the Veneto's Colli Berici. Some is also produced closer to central Italy, in the Colli Bolognesi zone southwest of Bologna. In Tuscany, sauvignon is used occasionally to improve the blend of local whites.

ALTO ADIGE'S SAUVIGNON

There are not many growers cultivating sauvignon in Alto Adige and even fewer wineries bottling it. These are mostly in the northwest part of the province, between the towns of Bolzano and Merano, where they are entitled to the D.O.C. appellation Terlano. But they may also use the broader denomination Alto Adige/Südtirol.

The character of Bolzano's Sauvignon is more weakly enunciated than that of Alto Adige's other thickly scented whites. It is a pale straw yellow wine, tinged with green, with muted, herbal aromas and slight, fruity flavor served up on a bony frame. It is the lightest Sauvignon one is likely to find, but gracefully balanced and skillfully made, as the high standards of this province lead us to expect. Good examples of it are bottled by Kellereigenossenschaft Terlan, Alois Lageder, and Schloss Schwanburg.

FRIULI'S SAUVIGNON

In Friuli, Sauvignon gives its strongest performance. There are three D.O.C. appellations for Sauvignon in the region, the two hilly districts of Collio and Colli Orientali del Friuli and Isonzo, the riverine plains immediately south of Collio.

✤ *Sauvignon del Collio* ✦
(D.O.C., FRIULI–VENEZIA GIULIA)

✤ *Sauvignon dei Colli Orientali del Friuli* ✦
(D.O.C., FRIULI–VENEZIA GIULIA)

A brilliant, straw yellow wine with flashes of gold, a distinctive, aromatic bouquet, and firm, flinty flavor. In the Collio some of the best producers are Attems, Borgo Conventi, Buzzinelli, Drufovka, Formentini, Gradnik, Jermann Pighin, Princic, Schiopetto, Scolaris, Subida di Monte, and Villa Russiz. In the Colli Orientali: Cantarutti, D'Attimis, Livio Felluga, Selva, Cisiro Snidero, and Volpe Pasini.

✤ *Sauvignon dell'Isonzo* ✦
(D.O.C., FRIULI–VENEZIA GIULIA)

A pale gold Sauvignon, slightly less aromatic than its Collio counterpart, but fuller on the palate, approaching lushness on occasion. Recommended producers: Bader, Prandi d'Ulmhort, S. Elena, and Tenuta Villanova.

THE VENETO'S SAUVIGNON

✤ *Sauvignon dei Colli Berici* ✦
(D.O.C., VENETO)

The hills near Vicenza known as Colli Berici are the only district in the Veneto entitled to make a D.O.C. Sauvignon. It is an excellent, pale straw yellow wine, of which unfortunately not much is yet available. The aromas are markedly grassy and the taste light, fresh, agreeably tart. Castello di Belvedere and Nani Rizzieri are reliable producers.

EMILIA-ROMAGNA'S SAUVIGNON

✒ Sauvignon dei Colli Bolognesi di Monte San Pietro ✑
(D.O.C., EMILIA-ROMAGNA)

The steep hills southwest of Bologna are slowly establishing a reputation for the rich-flavored wines they produce, a reputation supported more by their dark intense reds than by their flatter whites. The Sauvignon here, because of its high alcohol and low acidity, resembles the soft, full wines of the South rather than the animated wines of northern Italy.

Colli Bolognesi Sauvignon is golden yellow, plainly vinous in aroma, strongly fruity in flavor and aftertaste. While it cannot be judged by the same standards as a Sauvignon from Friuli, it can be enjoyed as a modest, rustic example of the species. Good producers of it are Aldo Conti, Bruno Negroni, Palazzo S. Martino, and Terre Rosse.

✒ Bianco di Scandiano ✑
(D.O.C., EMILIA-ROMAGNA)

Produced near Reggio Emilia of a blend of sauvignon plus small percentages of malvasia and/or trebbiano. A very pale, often spritzy wine, usually vinified with a soft touch of sweetness.

The Soave Family and Its Near and Distant Relatives

✒ Soave ✑
(D.O.C., VENETO)

Soave is such an inoffensive, good-natured wine that to reproach it for not having a bolder personality seems peevish. Its role is to soothe, not to arouse.

I like to drink Soave from a carafe during one of the most deliciously inconsequential moments of an Italian summer afternoon: the late lunch by the pool at the Cipriani in Venice, keeping equally abreast of gossip and the procession of antipasti, painlessly bridging the gap between a midday swim and the predinner nap.

I like to drink it again in the evening at Harry's Bar, when one's attention is divided between watching the coming and going of beautiful women and choosing the most tempting of the day's *risottos*.

I like to drink it at the shore, where what I am really drinking in are the smells of fish grilling and of the spiced sea air.

I like to drink Soave best when I have to think about it least. But not because it is a poor wine. If it were, its defects would be distracting. Soave balances firm but unobtrusive fruit with a neat measure of acidity, wrapping it up with a tart yet not emphatic aftertaste. It is clean-tasting and refreshing in a pleasingly self-effacing way. These are the qualities that have made it popular and at the same time so adaptable to large-scale production.

Soave is produced on primarily flat land midway between Vicenza and Verona. The luxuriant vineyards, from which very large yields are permitted, are plainly visible from the superhighway that runs parallel to them. The more desirable portion of a now greatly enlarged zone is the traditional production area around the pretty town of Soave. Wine from this area bears the qualification *classico*.

Soave is a blend of two grapes, garganega and a local variety of trebbiano called trebbiano di Soave. The latter is a lighter and more delicate trebbiano than the varieties referred to elsewhere in these pages, in descriptions of Tuscan whites, Frascati, and Trebbiano di Romagna. The ratio of garganega to trebbiano is approximately 80 percent to 20 percent. The two grapes are widely cultivated in the Veneto and in neighboring Lombardy, where they are used in varying proportions, or sometimes just one or the other grape is used alone, for other white wines.

Soave Bolla, which some people think is one word, has earned its vast market through its soundness, reliability, and uniformity. Like all virtues, these too have their dark side. In the achieving of a never varying standard of taste, charm is blurred and those small peaks of character of which even Soave is capable are flattened.

For a more complete manifestation of Soave's winning ways one may look to Bolla's own fine estate-bottling, Soave di Castellaro (not yet available for export); to Pieropan (although this erratic producer can falter); and to Tedeschi's Capitel delle Lucchine.

Among the producers of commercial Soave, Bertani offers a product as consistent and acceptable as Bolla's.

WINES RELATED TO SOAVE

❧ Gambellara ☙
(D.O.C., VENETO)

It is the closest wine to Soave, both in geography—its territory is an extension of Soave's eastern district—and in grape composition—it is composed of similar proportions of garganega and trebbiano di Soave. Not astonishingly, it strongly resembles its neighbor, although it is a bit rounder and more aromatic, less fresh and delicate. Most of the wine comes out of Cantina Sociale di Gambellara, a cooperative.

❧ Colli Berici Garganego ☙
(D.O.C., VENETO)

Also known as Garganega, it is produced east of the Gambellara area, in the Berici hills south of Vicenza. It is usually made entirely of garganega, thus conveying a slightly more accentuated impression of the bitterness that is characteristic of the grape. Reliable producers are Castello di Belvedere, Fratelli Montagna, Franceschetto Rizzieri, and Nani Rizzieri.

❧ Colli Euganei Bianco ☙
(D.O.C., VENETO)

Here the standard Soave proportions are completely reshuffled, and some new grapes are introduced. Garganega accounts for 50 percent or less of the blend, which includes such varieties as prosecco (here called serprina), tocai, and sauvignon. Colli Euganei is adjacent to Colli Berici, with the city of Padua just beyond its eastern limits. Although I am assured that it has great potential, the zone is now more entitled to renown for the spas that its volcanic soil has spawned than for its wine, which is of uniformly flimsy quality.

❧ Bianco di Custoza ☙
(D.O.C., VENETO)

An increasingly popular wine, made west of Verona on territory partly its own and partly overlapping Bardolino country on the southeastern shore of Lake Garda. It is a slim but perky, slightly aromatic, frank-tasting wine, a thoroughly worthy member of this group. Bianco di Custoza is made up of a cosmopolitan assemblage of grapes, the ubiquitous garganega in it for up to one-third, in addition to Tuscan trebbiano, tocai from Friuli, and Piedmont's cortese. Some of its most quality-conscious producers are Gorgo, Le Tende, Menegotti, Piona, and Tebaldi.

◄ Colli Morenici Mantovani del Garda Bianco ►
(D.O.C., LOMBARDY)

Here is an example of the work that committees do when they go about devising a memorable name for a wine. Its translation is White from the Moraine Hills of Mantua on Lake Garda. Try it sometime on your friendly wine merchant.

The zone is a semicircle of hills facing the southern end of the lake, whose soil is composed of gravel, sand, and clay left behind in prehistory by the glaciers' wrenching slide into oblivion.

Colli Morenici Bianco is a blend of garganega and a heterogeneous assortment of trebbianos—the Tuscan, the Roman, and the Veneto's own trebbiano di Soave. This is a firm, sharp, fruity wine, little known outside its territory.

◄ Lugana ►
(D.O.C., LOMBARDY AND VENETO)

This is one wine in which trebbiano di Soave (locally known as trebbiano di Lugana) has an opportunity to show all its charm and delicacy, since no other grape is used. Lugana is a bright, very pale straw yellow wine. The bouquet is shy and low-key, but appealingly fruity. The tasting qualities are represented by a cool, gentle combination of smoothness and tartness, without any snappishness in the aftertaste.

Although some Lugana is produced in the Veneto and sold by shippers of Bardolino, most of its zone of production, the lowlands on Lake Garda's southern tip, is in Lombardy.

Among the best of its many producers are Ambrosi, Bordignon, Ca'Furia, Co de Fer, Fratelli Fraccaroli, Pelizzari di S. Girolamo, and Zenato. My favorite Lugana is the one that Pierantonio Ambrosi serves in unlabeled bottles as the house wine at that gem among country restaurants, La Vecchia Lugana, near Sirmione.

The Trebbiano Family

The wines in this group are made principally from trebbiano, known as ugni blanc in France, where it is used to make cognac. The variety used in the following wines is mainly the Tuscan one, but the somewhat different varietals grown in Romagna and in Latium are also employed. Trebbiano is more amply discussed on page 162 in the section on Tuscan and Umbrian whites and also on page 199 under Roman whites.

❧ Bianco dei Colli Maceratesi ❧
(D.O.C., MARCHES)

Made from Tuscan trebbiano together with a nearly equal quantity of a local variety of the greco grape known as maceratino. One of the most amiable wines in the trebbiano family, with a thin, breezy bouquet, fresh, if neutral, flavor, a light, easy flowing body. The best producers are Compagnucci Compagnoni and Attilio Fabrini.

❧ Galestro ❧
(VINO DA TAVOLA, TUSCANY)

A wine formulated in 1980 by a group of independent producers in Chianti and Chianti Classico looking to establish an outlet for the white grapes they are no longer incorporating in the traditional Chianti blend. Galestro's name is taken from that of a crumbly rocky formation typical of Chianti soil and present to some extent in its best vineyards.

Although it is still an unclassified *vino da tavola,* Galestro has a clearly defined production code and zone of origin, which its promoters hope will eventually win it the official status of a D.O.C. designation. The principal grape is trebbiano, to which up to 40 percent other white grapes may be added. The producers' committee is experimenting with blends that include chardonnay, pinot bianco, and vernaccia and will by 1984 or 1985 recommend the most suitable varieties to be employed.

An innovation in the Galestro code is that a maximum, rather than a minimum, level of alcohol is established: 10½ percent. The emphasis is not on weight, but on freshness, and to this end grapes are to be picked early.

Galestro is not intended to satisfy those looking for richness of flavor. It is the archetypal technological white, a quaffing wine, pale, clear, bright, with clean but faint grape aromas and, in the mouth, impalpable impressions that are directed exclusively to the surface, bringing sensations of freshness, liveliness, crispness. Among the prime movers of Galestro are Antinori, Frescobaldi, and Ruffino.

⋙ *Montecarlo Bianco* ⋘
(D.O.C., TUSCANY)

From this appellation, placed east of Lucca and close to Montecatini, issues the one D.O.C. Tuscan white with claims to refinement. Tuscan trebbiano accounts for two-thirds of the blend of white grapes in Montecarlo. Among the others we find such French varietals as pinot bianco, pinot grigio, sauvignon, and semillon. The result is that the angular tasting qualities of trebbiano have been rounded off, producing a wine in which straightforward flavors are polished by smooth, flowing texture and graceful development of fruit on the palate. The small quantity made is distributed among several good producers. Among them are Fattoria del Buonamico, Fratelli Guarino, Fattoria Montecarlo, and Passaglia.

⋙ *Trebbiano d'Abruzzo* ⋘
(D.O.C., ABRUZZI)

Although Trebbiano d'Abruzzo may be made either partly or entirely from Tuscan trebbiano, the traditionally dominant grape in this white from the southeastern region of Abruzzi is not trebbiano at all, but bombino bianco. Bombino is a greenish yellow grape stippled faintly with brown and cultivated in southern and central Italy, mainly in Abruzzi. Small amounts of it are used in such Roman whites as Frascati. Used alone, it makes a flowery, velvety, but somewhat nerveless wine.

Since producers of Trebbiano d'Abruzzo are allowed complete latitude in the matter, the proportions of trebbiano and bombino bianco vary, and so does the wine. Those with more bombino will taste milder and softer, while the ones with more trebbiano feature a sharper attack on the palate.

The most widely distributed maker is Casal Thaulero. More beguiling versions are bottled by Baron Cornacchia, Dino Illuminati, and Emidio Pepe.

❧ *Trebbiano di Aprilia* ❧
(D.O.C., LATIUM)

Produced on reclaimed marshland south of Rome from a blend of Tuscan trebbiano and the native trebbiano giallo. It is markedly vinous to the nose, soft and insipid on the palate. Recently it has been introduced to America by Bolla, the Soave firm.

❧ *Trebbiano di Romagna* ❧
(D.O.C., EMILIA-ROMAGNA)

When we lament the immoderate application of technology that rubs so hard at a wine's defects that it ends by erasing its character, it is soothing to recall those occasions when out of ordinary materials it has given us something drinkable, and even likable.

My acquaintance with Trebbiano, one of the two white wines of my native Romagna, goes back to when it was a scrawny beverage fit only for the distilleries. But in recent years I have come to know it as a wine of well-balanced if modest proportions, cleanly vinous to the nose, taut and tingling on the palate, a neutral but refreshing summer accompaniment to simple seafood dishes.

The grape of which it is made is trebbiano romagnolo, one of many varieties of trebbiano spread throughout the Italian peninsula. For descriptions of other wines based on trebbiano, refer to page 162, Roman whites, page 199, Lugana, page 158. It is most closely related to the Veneto's trebbiano di Soave, although not anywhere so delicate.

Out of hundreds of bottles of Trebbiano di Romagna I have had, the ones from the following producers have left the kindest memories: Cesari, Francesco Ferrucci, Guarini Matteucci, Giuseppe Marabini, Monsignore, Pasolini dall'Onda, Picchi, Fratelli Ravaioli, Fratelli Vallunga, and Zanetti.

❧ *Trebbiano di Sicilia* ❧
(VINO DA TAVOLA, SICILY)

A spritzy wine made from Tuscan trebbiano in western Sicily by a company called Enorcarboj. I find it coarse and wholly unappealing, but it must have an appreciative public somewhere, judging from the substantial quantity produced.

NOTE: A recently created appellation, Capriano del Colle Bianco, located near Brescia, in Lombardy, is a pure varietal Trebbiano, either of the Tuscan or Soave variety. It is listed for the record since there has been no opportunity to taste it.

The Trebbiano and Malvasia Family in Tuscany and Umbria

There is a large family of white wines from Tuscany and Umbria in central Italy that share a common parentage. Their similarities are more significant than their differences, however slighting that may seem to their respective partisans; we may, therefore, find it more practical, and certainly less repetitive, to examine broadly the traits common to the whole group before narrowing our acquaintance to individual members.

A genealogical chart would show that the entire family is descended from the union of trebbiano and malvasia, two grapes that for centuries have had featured roles in Italian winemaking.

The existence of trebbiano in central Italy goes back past the time of the Romans to at least that of the Etruscans. One variety or another of this ubiquitous vine is planted throughout Italy, where it is used to make wines as different as Soave and Frascati and serves as a component of a dozen or more central Italian reds, of which Chianti is the most conspicuous example. The same grape is known in France as ugni blanc, used in Charente to make a thin sour wine that is transformed into Cognac.

Tuscan trebbiano is a yellow grape tinged with green or with rust that produces a sharply acidic wine with neutral aroma and firm, moderately fruity flavor.

Malvasia has an even longer and more tangled history. It originated in ancient Greece, then became successfully established in Crete. When the Venetians were masters of Crete, they brought the wine home, where it became so popular that in the Venetian republic wineshops themselves came to be called *malvasie*. In England, Malvasia was known as Malmsey, a name familiar to those who recall Shakespeare's account of the execution by immersion of Richard III's nephews in the Tower.

There are so many vines now called malvasia, bearing not only white fruit but red, that even the authors of Italy's encyclopedic official ampelography, *I Principali Vitigni da Vino Coltivati in Italia,* found themselves unequal to the task of identifying more than eleven basic varieties.

Malvasia *bianca del Chianti,* the variety with which we are concerned here, is a pale, dusty, greenish gold grape that yields a delicately fragrant, pleasing, silky wine.

Most Tuscan and Umbrian whites, whether they are D.O.C. or unclassified, whether one finds them in bottle or served as house wines in carafe, owe their basic character to the coupled attributes of these two grapes. From trebbiano they derive their appetizing tartness, their vivacity, their emphatic flavor and aftertaste; from malvasia they inherit delicacy and whatever fragrance and tenderness of flavor they may possess.

The added influence of other grapes, the natural advantages of a choice vineyard's soil or exposure, the skills or advanced equipment available to a few winemakers will make some of the wines in this group emerge with finer features than their fellows. But to expect them to be distinguished or memorable can lead to disappointment. What makes these wines appealing and easy to live with is their freshness, their plainspoken flavor. They are straightforward sometimes to the point of coarseness, but at least one can say for most of them what cannot often be said for so many of the white wines we drink every day: They are rarely boring.

The following are all the D.O.C. and some of the better unclassified wines in this category.

THE TUSCAN BRANCH OF THE FAMILY

Bianco della Valdinievole
(D.O.C., TUSCANY)

Made in the province of Pistoia, in north-central Tuscany. Fresh, grapy aromas and crisp, firm flavor.

Bianco di Pitigliano
(D.O.C., TUSCANY)

The most abundant wine of the lot, produced in the province of Grosseto, in Tuscany's southern tip. In addition to trebbiano and malvasia, grechetto and verdello grapes may be used. The color is pale straw tinged with green; the taste lean, slightly bitter, quickening to the palate, and deliciously mouth-cleansing. Bottled by the cooperative cellar of Pitigliano.

❧ *Bianco Pisano S. Torpe'* ☙
(D.O.C., TUSCANY)

Produced east of Pisa on both sloping land and riverine plains. S. Torpe' is one of the city's two patron saints. Paler and flintier than most of the others listed here. The best producers are Fattoria di Gello and Fattoria di Piedivilla.

❧ *Bianco Val d'Arbia* ☙
(VINO DA TAVOLA, TUSCANY)

The production zone marches alongside the river Arbia from the town limits of Montalcino, south of Siena, moving north, deep into Chianti Classico territory. A large area indeed. The wine, on the other hand, is small, the most modest probably of the whole group.

❧ *Bianco Vergine della Valdichiana* ☙
(D.O.C., TUSCANY)

The immense, ghostly white steers of the Chiana Valley, famous in Italy for beefsteak, are gradually surrendering their pasture to vines for the increasingly popular Bianco Vergine. This wine's fast-rising reputation is based not so much on any single outstanding characteristic, but on the delicate, pleasing balance of its simple virtues. The color is a pretty straw yellow, sometimes brilliant in fine examples. It has the fresh, fruity aroma of freshly squeezed berries and a flavor that, while light, is firmly expressed. As one swallows, a pleasing, bitter, slight suggestion of almonds rises in the back taste. Among its worthier producers are Mario Baldetti, Fattoria Manzano, Spalletti (the same who makes Chianti at Rufina), and Aldo Casagni. The last is a small grower-winemaker, of whose delightful wine the only complaint one can make is that too little of it is available.

❧ *Montescudaio* ☙
(D.O.C., TUSCANY)

Produced in a hilly area near the Tuscan coast and east of Leghorn. Montescudaio has a high percentage of trebbiano and some vermentino, in addition to malvasia. It is a bright, pale straw yellow, with barely perceptible fragrance, but firm flavor. A good Montescudaio is made by Fattoria Santa Maria.

❧ *Parrina* ❧
(D.O.C., TUSCANY)

As one travels south in Tuscany, this is the last classified wine one finds before crossing the border into the Lazio region. Its center of production is Orbetello, near the resort towns of Porto Ercole and Porto S. Stefano, where much of the wine is consumed. It is also close to Tarquinia, whose vividly frescoed Etruscan tombs have been a source of inspiration for the graphic design of some Parrina labels.

Parrina contains, in addition to the customary blend of trebbiano and malvasia, a small amount of ansonica. This large, amber gold, smooth-tasting grape originates in Sicily, where it is used in the blend of many white wines, among them Corvo. The color of Parrina is straw yellow with flashes of gold; the bouquet is shy, delicately flowery; perhaps because of the presence of ansonica, this is one of the most velvety, easy-drinking Tuscan whites. Its best-known producer is Fattoria La Parrina. A possibly even better one is Fattoria Chiusone.

UNCLASSIFIED TUSCAN WINES IN THE FAMILY

❧ *Ardenghesca* ❧
(VINO DA TAVOLA, TUSCANY)

One of the best out of a legion of single-owner, proprietary wines. Unusually firm, sumptuous flavor. Made in southern Tuscany by Giorgio Cabella's Fattorie di Monte Antico e dell'Abbadia Ardenghesca.

❧ *Bianco della Lega* ❧
(VINO DA TAVOLA, TUSCANY)

It is the name adopted in 1980 by the members of the "black rooster" Chianti Classico consortium for the whites that they have been turning out with their surplus trebbiano and malvasia grapes. These wines are representative of their category, crisp, short on fragrance, long on emphatic taste and aftertaste. Like Chianti itself, many are ordinary, some are decently made, and a few are fine. One can expect the most reliable examples to come from the producers of the choicest Chianti. (A selection of recommended producers appears on pages 36-41.)

❧ *Bianco di Maremma* ☙
(VINO DA TAVOLA, TUSCANY)

To Italians this partly savage zone back of the southern Tuscan coast calls to mind malaria and wild boars. The malaria is gone, the boars remain (both the four- and the two-legged variety), and many new vineyards tame the landscape. For Bianco di Maremma, ansonica grapes are added to trebbiano and malvasia. Like Parrina, described on page 165, these wines are light, flowery, and smooth. The name Bianco di Maremma, while it is commonly employed in speech and geographically correct, does not appear on labels. The whites of Maremma are bottled under individual proprietary names, the best of which are: Capalbio, Montecucco, Montepescali, La Pievanella–Bianco di Monte Antico (do not confuse with Ardenghesca Monte Antico, page 165), and Poggetti.

❧ *Bianco Montosoli* ☙
(VINO DA TAVOLA, TUSCANY)

A flowery, vivacious wine produced in Montalcino by Altesino, a good maker of Brunello.

❧ *Bianco di Nugola* ☙
(VINO DA TAVOLA, TUSCANY)

A delicate and spry pale gold wine made from the standard trebbiano and malvasia combination found in nearly all Tuscan whites, to which verdicchio and vernaccia are added. It has grace and more than average endurance. Produced by Fattoria di Nugola Nuova.

THE UMBRIAN BRANCH OF THE FAMILY

❧ *Colli Altotiberini* ☙
(D.O.C., UMBRIA)

The production zone is in the upper valley of the Tiber, the river that on its way to Rome slices through Umbria from north to south, severing the region into two nearly neat halves. The appellation has achieved D.O.C. status only recently and has yet to acquire the kind of recognition that encourages quality production, but it promises well. Like most Umbrian whites, the Altotiberini are light, delicate, agreeably tart, and the best of them also possess the elusive quality Italians call *genuino*—the taste of authenticity. Of many good and enthusiastic producers, one that stands out is Colle del Sole.

❧ *Colli Perugini* ☙
(D.O.C., UMBRIA)

Another new D.O.C. appellation whose large territory rambles up and down the slopes of hills south of Perugia. Whites tasted from this area, while they are consistent with the general character of this class of Umbrian wines, have yet to exhibit any features that would make their specific zone of production distinctive.

❧ *Colli del Trasimeno* ☙
(D.O.C., UMBRIA)

The notoriety of this appellation must be attributed largely to the tireless promotions of an adopted son, Ferruccio Lamborghini, who would like his wine to become as celebrated as his tractors and sports cars. They are certainly vigorously flavored, sound, sturdy examples of the breed, but considerably short of elegance. Lamborghini's Villa Fiorita is no doubt the most desirable of the Trasimeno whites. The bulk of the production issues, at a distinctly less ambitious quality level, from the Cantina Sociale, the cooperative cellar at Castiglione del Lago.

❧ *Orvieto* ❧

(D.O.C., UMBRIA AND LATIUM)

Orvieto, a blend of trebbiano, malvasia, and grechetto, is a wine in transition whose past, and possibly its future, are more fascinating than its present. At the moment, Orvieto is a serviceable white, made in a fresh, clean, even style, interchangeable with many technically sound central Italian wines from Tuscany, Umbria, or Latium. Whether one chooses a bottle of Orvieto *secco,* or Torgiano bianco, or Bianco della Valdichiana, or Frascati is more a question of convenience than of discernment. They can all be depended upon to deliver similar relief to a tolerant thirst.

It was not always so. Midway into this century, when Orvieto was still a "handmade" wine, most of it cellared in the grottoes scooped out of the volcanic rock below the town whose name it shares, it had a personality that could not be taken for any other. It was nearly invariably sweet *(abboccato)* with a reticent sweetness that rarely intruded upon the enjoyment of food. It was delicate, but not feeble. It felt fat and smooth in the mouth, with a lengthy development of close-textured, silky, fruit flavor. When Orvieto was consumed close to its source, still cool from the cellar, with the simple, earthy, aromatic cooking of its region, nothing ever was more delicious.

As Orvieto stumbled into the modern age, submitting to intense exploitation of its vineyards and industrialized production, it joined the scores of new, superclean, nearly neutral, dry white wines, leaving most of its character to survive in the memory of its former admirers.

After a period of neglect, the fortunes of Orvieto are beginning to be revived, mostly by the Tuscan houses that dominate its production and, building upon the past glory of its widely recognized name, are committed to making a wine of broad yet distinct appeal. Unless it was coincidence that this area has made captivating wine for centuries, it may not be wishful speculation to trust in the Orvieto to come.

To date, the most successful has been Antinori, with their Castello della Sala Orvieto Classico. In parenthesis, Antinori's sweet version of Orvieto—Orvieto *abboccato*—is a masterpiece, although too dense and luscious to drink with anything but a ripe peach or mango and most suitable perhaps for after-dinner sipping.

In addition to Castello della Sala, good Orvieto Classico is produced today by Barberani and Le Velette.

The D.O.C. appellation embraces a large zone, some of it spilling over from Umbria into Latium. The wine with the most explicitly defined character comes from the territory closest to the town of Orvieto and is designated as *classico*.

❧ *Torgiano* ☙
(D.O.C., UMBRIA)

Although a D.O.C. appellation, Torgiano is all but the trademark of Giorgio Lungarotti, the man who virtually controls the production of both Torgiano white and red (for the red, refer to Rubesco *riserva,* discussed on pages 48–50). Lungarotti's Torgiano shares the lightness of typical Umbrian whites, the briskness of the common trebbiano parentage, but tastes with a delicacy that is its own.

A major influence in its personality is the large presence of grechetto, a gentle, refined grape, but credit must also go to the control that this estate exercises over quality, from the vineyard to the cellar. Selected lots of Torgiano from exceptional vintages are bottled as *riserva.* These are deep, full whites in sloping-shouldered burgundy bottles. They seem to be stepping out of character, however, to strain for profundity and refinement, which elude their grasp. One misses in them the easy charm of the younger, simpler wine.

The Torgiano area is large for a single family's fief, but diminutive when compared with other D.O.C. zones in Umbria. It is a wedge-shaped section of low slopes and plains immediately south of Perugia, tapering to an end near the point where two rivers meet, the Chiascio and the Tiber.

COUNTRY WINES

Anyone traveling in Tuscany and Umbria will find a dozen or more members of this wine family that have no D.O.C. appellation. They are humble local wines whose names are no better known than they need to be. Their reputations and capacity to please are wholly confined to their place of origin.

INDEPENDENT LIGHT
AND CRISP WHITE WINES

❧ *Alcamo* ☙
(D.O.C., SICILY)

At a dinner party in Rome, the talk had been mostly about wine and food, and somehow it had come out that I was working on this book. As we left the table, the somber Sicilian member of parliament who had sat across from me touched my arm and said, "Please, when you write about Alcamo, say something kind." I promised him I would be fair, a promise that did not seem entirely to reassure him.

I have tried Alcamo many times, before that evening and since. The fairest comment I now can make about this wine from the western end of Sicily is that what is remarkable is not how dull it often is but, in the face of conditions that would seem so unpromising for winemaking, how good it sometimes can be.

In order to turn its vast vineyards into a source of desirable light table wines, Sicily has had to shed traditions and equipment that were obsolete, while finding ways to circumvent the hazards of a fiery climate. With liberal infusions of public funds and northern skills, Sicilian winemaking has leaped with startling swiftness out of its feudal past into the modern age. Alcamo is one of the principal products of this transformation, and upon it and similar wines rest the island's hopes of winning a place in the market for better wines.

The Alcamo zone of production is in the heart of the province of Trapani, whose provincial capital is considerably closer to North Africa than it is to continental Italy. The searing African winds and scanty rainfall notwithstanding, more vines grow here than in nearly every other Italian province. The predominant grape is catarratto, of ancient native lineage. In the blend of four white grapes that go into Alcamo, 80 percent is catarratto, in a subvariety known as bianco lucido.

The muted aroma and flavor catarratto produces suited the vermouth industries of the North, which acquired it by the tankload as a neutral base for the aromatic components of their aperitifs. Its high alcohol and tendency to oxidize made it attractive to producers of Marsala. When catarratto was made into table wine, however, before new methods of cultivation and winemaking were adopted, the result was a wine the color of amber with the flat, oxidized, hot alcohol taste we used to identify as the Sicilian style.

Today, Alcamo is turned out at a little over 11 percent alcohol, its color is a pale straw yellow quickened by glints of green, and it offers a subdued grapy aroma with straightforward, crisp, spirited flavor.

Unfortunately, most of Alcamo's production is entrusted to cooperative wineries whose indifference to quality justifies the low esteem in which cooperatives are held in Italy.

Discouragingly lackluster as may be the bottles that come off the cooperatives' assembly lines, enough decent Alcamo exists to earn our continued faith in this wine. The outstanding example is Rapitala', produced by Count de la Gatinais on a hilly estate in the center of Alcamo territory. It is deeper and more brilliant in color than standard Alcamo, with a penetrating herbal fragrance and pronounced flavor. Another Alcamo, not quite so fine as Rapitala', but more appealing than most, is produced by one of the rare diligent cooperatives, Cantina Sociale S. Antonio.

❧ *Bianchello del Metauro* ☙
(D.O.C., MARCHES)

Bianchello may be translated as "little white," and of the thousands of Italian wine names none is so aptly descriptive. Little should not be confused with insignificant. This is the very model of a fresh, charming young white, small but comely. On those occasions when we want to take our pleasures simply, Bianchello delivers them, with style.

The color of Bianchello ranges from a pale, transparent parchment to light straw yellow. The fragrance is cool and clean, with the most restrained accent of fresh, slightly underripe fruit. The taste is delicate, yet firm and steely, with a taut, mouth-quickening finish.

Bianchello is produced on the slopes of the valley of the Metauro River, near the Adriatic city of Fano, in the Marches region. It is overshadowed by that region's celebrated, but not more distinguished, white wine, Verdicchio. Although substantial quantities are available and consumed locally, the only Bianchello to have crossed the regional and national borders, so far, comes from just one producer, Anzilotti-Solazzi.

❧ *Blanc de La Salle* ☙
(VINO DA TAVOLA, VAL D'AOSTA)

❧ *Blanc de Morgex* ☙
(VINO DA TAVOLA, VAL D'AOSTA)

No one knows how it came to be there, but when the northern barbarians retreated from Italy and the people of the Val d'Aosta again began to cultivate their high-perched plots just below Mont Blanc's perennially white peak, they found a vine producing good grapes at the improbable altitude of three thousand and more feet. The vine, which came eventually to be known as blanc de morgex, buds very late, past the season of nipping cold, and matures completely before the autumn frosts, making small bunches of perfectly ripened, golden yellow fruit. Another name for this varietal is blanc de valdigne, Valdigne being the northern part of the Val d'Aosta region.

The wine from blanc de morgex is a true creature of the north: pale, lean, somewhat aloof. The color is cool, transparent, greenish yellow. The bouquet is fresh, clean, direct, and daintily herbal. The body can perhaps be best described as wiry, closely knit, and animated by substantial yet well-balanced acidity. The total impression is one of delicacy moving with vivacity.

Two towns, La Salle and Morgex, each give their name to substantially similar wines. (The Morgex name is also used for the varietal.) The lilliputian size of the vineyards and the unrelenting hardship of growing and harvesting grapes on a mountainside make it impossible ever to make much Blanc de La Salle or Blanc de Morgex. Moreover, three times as much wine is consumed in Val d'Aosta as can be produced from its skimpy vineyards, so very little of the output ever finds its way outside. Nevertheless, if there is strong enough interest, and the rewards of selling exceed those of drinking, it is not unreasonable to expect a small but steady quantity of these wines to trickle down from the mountain and flow into a connoisseurs' market.

In both towns the growers have banded into a producers' cooperative, an Association des Viticulteurs. In La Salle a single producer bottles outstanding wine under his own label, Constantino David.

❧ *Verdicchio* ☙
(D.O.C., WHEN FOLLOWED BY ONE OF TWO
DISTRICT DESIGNATIONS, MARCHES)

During the first months of my marriage I lived in my wife's home town of Cesenatico, a fishing village on the Adriatic, where once a week we used to eat at Titon's, a dockside *trattoria* that one of the town's fishermen had recently opened. Each day the fish came straight from the boats, usually still palpitating, into Titon's kitchen, where it was either fried or grilled over natural charcoal. It may have been then the best-tasting seafood to be had in Italy. I have seldom had its equal anywhere, and never better. When no more fish was left at the end of the evening, Titon used to sit in the dining room, share a grappa with the remaining customers, and accompany himself on the guitar.

We routinely drank local wine, Albana or Sangiovese, until Titon suggested we try a wine, which he had just received, called Verdicchio. The name—pronounced *Verdíkkio*—was instantly appealing, beginning with the word for green and ending in the sharp rap of the hard, double *c,* an irresistible suggestion of freshness and verve. The wine lived up to its promise: the color a lively straw green; the smell delicately and pervasively vinous; the taste unlike that of any other white, full, robust, but brisk, with an exhilarating suggestion of citrus fruit. A mounting and pleasantly clean sensation of bitterness followed the first impressions on the palate deep into the aftertaste.

Our Verdicchio was one of the early examples in the amphora-shaped bottle devised by Fazi-Battaglia. Before Fazi-Battaglia, Verdicchio was made in a spritzy to fully sparkling style. This was the company responsible for transforming it into a still wine and marketing it in the bottle that has since become so familiar. Fazi-Battaglia deserves credit not only for that, but for continuing to maintain the appealing qualities that first made Verdicchio so popular. Of all the wineries that must necessarily conduct business on an industrial scale, it perhaps does its job best.

Fazi-Battaglia's Verdicchio may leave us with an unsatisfied yearning for greater character, but it consoles us with reliable delivery of the basic satisfactions one demands of this wine. If the highly permissive yields were reduced and small estate-bottlings encouraged, more richly expressed versions of Verdicchio would become available. But at probably twice the price, would importers and merchants take a chance on them?

Verdicchio takes its name from the greenish yellow grape from which it is made, although up to 20 percent trebbiano and malvasia of the Tuscan varieties are admitted into the blend. It is produced in the Marches, the coastal region on the Adriatic on whose territory northern Italy ends and the South begins.

There are two appellations for Verdicchio, Castelli di Jesi and Matelica. The first, located in the northeastern section of the region and closest to the coast, is by a large margin the more productive of the two and the variety you are most likely to find in shops or on restaurant wine lists. Matelica is farther inland and to the west. It makes a fuller, more alcoholic, heavier wine that is much admired by those who manage to find it.

Good producers of Verdicchio dei Castelli di Jesi, besides Fazi-Battaglia, are M. Brunori, outstanding among the small growers, and the Cantina Sociale di Cupramontana, which, unlike most cooperative cellars, turns out a fine wine, often better than that of private wineries. Other good bottlers are Castellucci, Garofoli, Fratelli Torelli, and Umani Ronchi.

The best-known producer of Verdicchio di Matelica is La Monacesca. Equally good, and fully representative of the ample-bodied character of this appellation, is Mattei's Verdicchio.

The choicest Verdicchios of all are probably two unclassified bottlings, one known as Verdicchio di Montanello, produced by Compagnucci Compagnoni, the other, Verdicchio Pian delle Mura, made by Attilio Fabrini.

Other Light and Crisp White Wines

❧ *Cartizze* ❧
(D.O.C., VENETO)

Please see Prosecco, discussed on pages 176-7.

❧ *Castel del Monte Bianco* ❧
(D.O.C., APULIA)

The principal grape in this mountain-grown Apulian white is a local varietal called pampanuto, blended with Tuscan trebbiano and bombino bianco. Castel del Monte is very pale, indistinct in aroma and neutral in flavor, but fresh, sound, and pleasant. The only important producer is Rivera, better known for their immensely popular Castel del Monte rosé.

❧ Corvo ☙
(VINO DA TAVOLA, SICILY)

A combination of public funds, modern technology, and Piedmontese skills have transformed this once aristocratic holding into a vast, modern plant processing Sicily's best-known wines. The whites exemplify those qualities that characterize up-to-date, industrialized winemaking of a high order: consistency, freshness, balance, and adequate flavor without the distracting presence of pronounced character.

There are two Corvo whites, Marca Verde (once known as Prima Goccia) and Colomba Platino. The first, under its green label, is the one familiar abroad, a smooth, firm, zesty wine. The second, more delicate but tarter, is one that fancy restaurants in Palermo often recommend.

Both are made from the fine, native inzolia grape, blended with other Sicilian varietals, acquired in different climatic zones of the island to compensate for vagaries of vintages and to assure the wines the constant tasting qualities one expects of Corvo.

❧ Erbaluce ☙
(D.O.C., PIEDMONT)

Spry, lightly acidulous wine, with gently refreshing, slightly bitter flavor. Made on the low slopes of hills near Turin from the grape of the same, poetic name, which can be translated as sunlight grass. Its best producers are Corrado Gnavi, Filiberto Gnavi, and Istituto Professionale di Stato "Carlo Ubertini."

❧ Etna Bianco Superiore ☙
(D.O.C., SICILY)

Sicily's most charming white, made almost entirely from Mount Etna's native carricante grape. A softly stated floweriness in the nose leads to nimbly delivered, gracious flavor in the mouth. The best producer is Villagrande.

Faustus Bianco
(VINO DA TAVOLA, SICILY)

It is made from inzolia grapes grown near the town of Bagheria, just outside Palermo, where this prized native variety develops best. A fine, stylish white, it offers the nose delightful suggestions of jasmine, followed by supple yet vivacious flavor.

Locorotondo
(D.O.C., APULIA)

Offering a cool, clean, neutral taste, this is a modest wine for casual consumption, no worse, and possibly better, than many mass-produced whites from the Veneto. Made from a blend of verdeca and bianco d'alessano, grapes long established in central Apulia.

Monterosso Val d'Arda
(D.O.C., EMILIA–ROMAGNA)

Soft, lightly aromatic, and spritzy, it is a small but appealing wine, never so enjoyable as when consumed with a platter of the marvelous local salami and prosciutto. Made near Piacenza from malvasia and other local grapes.

Nuragus
(D.O.C., SARDINIA)

Sardinia's most abundant wine, having once a rather heavy, but to-day a much lighter and brisk, neutral taste. The nuragus grape is said to be the island's most ancient, established there for perhaps thousands of years.

Prosecco di Conegliano and/or Valdobbiadene
(D.O.C., VENETO)

An appley, light, tangy sparkling wine, the most popular of its type in Italy. It is made with the grape of the same name in the northernmost controlled appellation zone of the Veneto. Prosecco may bear either the

Conegliano or Valdobbiadene district designation or both, but when it is only Valdobbiadene it is better.

When produced in a tiny area near the town of S. Pietro in Barbozza in Valdobbiadene, it is further qualified as Superiore di Cartizze, an irresistibly fresh and delicate sparkler. Its best producer is Nino Franco.

A still Prosecco also exists, a full, tart white, but, given the demand for the sparkling version, rather scarce.

⊷ *Regaleali Bianco* ⊷
(VINO DA TAVOLA, SICILY)

This white is the best of the highly touted but unremarkable Regaleali line. Modestly fragrant, light in flavor, it is a standard, serviceable white. It is made from the native catarratto and inzolia grapes plus a little sauvignon.

⊷ *Ribolla* ⊷
(D.O.C. IN COLLI ORIENTALI DEL FRIULI, VINO DA TAVOLA
ELSEWHERE IN THE REGION, FRIULI-VENEZIA GIULIA)

A light-bodied, very crisp, rustic white, fruity in the nose and spirited in flavor. See also Bianco del Collio, described on page 212.

⊷ *San Severo Bianco* ⊷
(D.O.C., APULIA)

It is produced on flat land in northern Apulia from a blend of Tuscan trebbiano and bombino bianco. A fresh and neutral white, it is not disagreeable but not very interesting, either.

⊷ *Torbato di Alghero* ⊷
(VINO DA TAVOLA, SARDINIA)

Freshly vinous in aroma, lively in flavor, with soft suggestions of fruit. A Spanish grape established in northwestern Sardinia, torbato used to make a high-alcohol, sweet wine. It was skillfully transformed by Sella & Mosca, the winery that has been so successful in giving formerly stout island wines a slim, contemporary profile. Also see Vermentino di Alghero, described on pages 204–5.

❧ *Torre Quarto Bianco* ☙
(VINO DA TAVOLA, APULIA)

An unclassified white made in Apulia by the Cirillo-Farrusi brothers from a blend of Tuscan trebbiano, bombino bianco, and greco. It is almost parchment white, vigorously fragrant, with stronger flavor and firmer character than other traditional Apulian whites.

❧ *Trebbianino Val Trebbia* ☙
(D.O.C., EMILIA-ROMAGNA)

It is made in Piacenza, in the Emilia half of the Emilia-Romagna region, in the valley of a river whose name, Trebbia, gives some support to the claim that here is where trebbiano originated. Despite the name of the place and of the wine, trebbiano's contribution to the formula, which is a blend of several white grapes, is minimal. Probably because of the presence of muscat grapes, the otherwise vinous smell of Trebbianino is lightly underscored by an aromatic scent. This is a thin, soft, vaguely sweet wine, neither nasty nor particularly appealing.

In the same zone, from a similar formulation, Valentino Migliorini makes an engaging, unclassified lightly sparkling wine he calls Trabense.

❧ *Tudia Bianco* ☙
(VINO DA TAVOLA, SICILY)

At a tasting in 1980 of Sicilian whites sponsored by the region, this—the least known in the field of twenty-nine—was the best. A pale, straw yellow wine, it tastes clean and fresh, with an appealing almondy nose taken up in the crisply bitter aftertaste. Made from inzolia grapes blended with trebbiano by Baron Pucci di Benisichi.

❧ *Verduzzo del Piave* ☙
(D.O.C., VENETO)

Pale golden wine smelling of almonds, with firm, lively flavor. Made from the green verduzzo grape on the flats of the Piave River district in the provinces of Treviso and Venice. A wine with a similar name, Verduzzo Friulano, made from a different variety of the verduzzo grape, is described on page 213.

Full and Fruity White Wines

FAMILIES OF
FULL AND FRUITY WHITE WINES

The Malvasia Family

In Italy a greater variety of grapes and wines go by the name Malvasia than by any other. Malvasia may be dry or may range from implicitly to intensely sweet. It may be an aperitif, table, or after-dinner wine. It may be light or strong, white or red, still or sparkling. Malvasia grapes are blended into Chianti and into dozens of whites.

FRIULI'S MALVASIA

The Malvasia we are concerned with here is the dry, still, white version, chiefly represented by the one produced in Friuli–Venezia Giulia, the most northeasterly of Italy's regions, bracketed by the Veneto on the west and Yugoslavia on the east.

The grape is a native species, called malvasia istriana, whose loosely bunched, greenish yellow berries have none of the lush, aromatic taste associated with many other malvasias.

The wine is a pale golden yellow, with simple vinous and grapy smells. Faintly astringent in the mouth, it has full body and an appealingly citric flavor whose lurking bitterness surfaces cleanly in the finish and aftertaste.

Malvasia del Collio
(D.O.C., FRIULI-VENEZIA GIULIA)

Malvasia dell'Isonzo
(D.O.C., FRIULI-VENEZIA GIULIA)

These are the only two D.O.C. appellations for Malvasia in Friuli. The first, a zone of sloping vineyards, yields finer wines than the second, which is composed mainly of riverine plains.

In the Collio some of the good producers are Attems, Borgo Conventi, Manferrari (bottled by Buscemi), Schiopetto, and Villa Russiz. In Isonzo we have Bader, Prandi d'Ulmhort, and Tenuta Villanova. Excellent unclassified Malvasia is available from estates producing outside the officially recognized D.O.C. zones, and these are D'Attimis, Budini, Germano Filiputti, Geremia, and Conti di Maniago.

EMILIA-ROMAGNA'S MALVASIA

❧ *Malvasia di Ziano* ❧
(VINO DA TAVOLA, EMILIA-ROMAGNA)

Made near Piacenza from an aromatic variety of the grape. It is soft-bodied, and much of it is spritzy and slightly sweet, with a delicious taste of ripe peaches. Good dry versions do exist and may become better known when granted pending D.O.C. recognition. Reliable makers are Giancarlo Molinelli and Italo Testa.

❧ *Malvasia Terre Rosse* ❧
(VINO DA TAVOLA, EMILIA-ROMAGNA)

An unclassified Malvasia made in the Colli Bolognesi area by Dr. Enrico Vallania. It is the closest to Friuli's version, but coarser and earthier.

SARDINIA'S MALVASIA

❧ *Malvasia di Cagliari* ❧
(D.O.C., SARDINIA)

A strong, nutty wine made in the style indigenous to Sardinia, high in alcohol—as high as 16 percent—and low in acidity. Although it may be most suitable as an aperitif, I have found it an excellent accompaniment to very ripe or sharp cheese. The best-balanced example I have tasted is produced by Vini Classici di Sardegna.

OTHER MALVASIAS

❧ *Fiorano Bianco* ❧
(VINO DA TAVOLA, LATIUM)

A bright, straw yellow wine made exclusively from Latium's malvasia di candia on Prince Boncompagni Ludovisi's vineyards just outside Rome on the Appian Way. Its bouquet is light yet pungent. The austere taste is characterized by flinty, mineral impressions supported by a touch of bitterness that persists in the lingering aftertaste. In its combination of steely flavor and velvet texture it displays an aristocratic elegance that is shared by no other Roman white.

❦ *Donna Marzia* ❦
(VINO DA TAVOLA, APULIA)

Another varietal Malvasia, produced near Lecce in Apulia by Count Zecca. It presents the aromatic side of malvasia's character, with firm, lengthy flavor layered on a plump, satiny body.

The Pinot Bianco Family

Of the white varietals of foreign origin that are cultivated in Italy, the one that generates the most distinguished wines is pinot bianco. It is a French vine, whose grapes in France are sometimes blended with chardonnay for Champagne and used in Burgundy to make Mâcon-Villages and other lesser whites.

Pinot bianco, like any finely bred varietal, is miserly with quantity, but bountiful with quality. Its undersized bunches of yellow gold berries yield a wine with a throng of distinctive smells in which the appley and flowery odors common to other whites are often joined by sensations of nuts, amber, and bread crust.

All the D.O.C. appellations and, with few exceptions, the choicest examples of Pinot Bianco are found in northeastern Italy, in the regions of Alto Adige–Trentino, Friuli, and Veneto.

TRENTINO–ALTO ADIGE'S PINOT BIANCO

❦ *Alto Adige Pinot Bianco/ Südtiroler Weissburgunder* ❦
(D.O.C., TRENTINO–ALTO ADIGE)

The appellation Alto Adige/Südtirol encompasses most of the towns in the province of Bolzano, and it identifies the finest Pinot Bianco produced in this German-speaking territory, where the grape as well as the wine are usually called weissburgunder.

In Alto Adige Pinot Bianco the color goes from deep straw yellow to light gold, the aroma clearly enunciates the nutty, crusty characteristics of the varietal, and on the palate one savors that ideal balance between freshness and fullness that makes a successful Pinot Bianco so fine.

Some of the best producers of it are Antonio von Elzenbaum, Giorgio Grai under the labels Herrnhofer or Bellendorf, Hofstätter, Kellereigenossenschaft Girlan, Kellereigenossenschaft Margreid/Entiklar, Kellereigen St. Michael, Kellereigenossenschaft Tramin.

❧ Terlano Pinot Bianco/ Terlaner Weissburgunder ☙
(D.O.C., TRENTINO–ALTO ADIGE)

Within this small appellation are high, sloping vineyards north and west of Bolzano, whose loose, well-drained soil is formed largely of glacial debris, sand, and feldspar. The Pinot Bianco made here is fine, but somewhat paler and lighter than the one made under the Alto Adige/Südtirol appellation, less emphatic in aroma and body.

Preeminent producers of Terlaner Weissburgunder are Kellereigenossenschaft Terlan, Klosterkellerei Muri, a Benedictine convent, and Schloss Schwanburg.

NOTE: When the name Terlano/Terlaner appears alone without the qualification Pinot Bianco/Weissburgunder, it denotes a blend of several white grapes in which pinot bianco has the largest share. The other varieties are riesling, sylvaner, and sauvignon. In Terlaner, a pale yellow wine with faint bouquet, it is difficult to recognize the more substantial properties of pinot bianco. Its producer is Kellereigenossenschaft Terlan.

❧ Pinot del Trentino ☙
(D.O.C., TRENTINO–ALTO ADIGE)

The D.O.C. statute does not require that Trentino's white Pinot be qualified as Bianco. This was done to sanction the widespread practice in the zone of blending pinot bianco with the lesser pinot grigio grape. Pinot bianco nevertheless dominates the blend. It is in fact the most prevalent white grape cultivated in Trentino, where much of it goes into the best champagne-method sparkling wine produced in Italy.

A considerable number of vineyards officially producing pinot bianco are actually planted in chardonnay, a grape whose existence the Italian wine laws, through a mysterious lapse, failed to acknowledge.

The Trentino appellation includes the whole province of Trento; but save for rare, scattered sites, the most suitable land for pinot bianco is in the northern section of the province, particularly in the townships of Lavis and S. Michele.

The wine is without question Trentino's finest white, but in comparison with the neighboring Alto Adige version it shows less character, more coarseness, once again testifying, as do Trentino's Cabernet and Merlot, to the less selective standards of cultivation and vinification prevalent in Trento's half of this part-Austrian, part-Italian region. This is not intended to depreciate all Pinot del Trentino, whose better producers are capable of bottling some worthwhile wine, indeed.

The outstanding maker is Roberto Zeni. Other good names to know are De Cles, Foradori, Istituto Agrario Provinciale S. Michele all'Adige, Cantina Sociale Lavis-Sorni-Salorno, and Villa Borino.

FRIULI'S PINOT BIANCO

In the Pinot Bianco of this half-Slavic, half-Venetian region we find the most complete expression of those traits that cause Pinot Bianco to emerge from the ranks of Italian whites. The two Friuli appellations that excel in Pinot Bianco, as they do in nearly every white wine they produce, are the Collio and Colli Orientali del Friuli.

Collio Pinot Bianco
(D.O.C., FRIULI–VENEZIA GIULIA)

Colli Orientali del Friuli Pinot Bianco
(D.O.C., FRIULI–VENEZIA GIULIA)

These adjoining zones, consisting of low, unspectacular hills, seem to have been arranged by nature to favor the making of some of the world's finest wines. They turn their backs to the north, against a mountain chain that shelters them from the ice-fed winds of the Alps. They spread open their fertile valleys to the south and to the sun, a few hundred feet above the coastal plains that bring in the temperate, benign sea breezes of the

Adriatic. Their soil is loose, primarily marly, sometimes rocky, sometimes mixing sand and limestone, always well drained, encouraging vines to put down strong roots.

Intensity is the hallmark of the wines of the Collio and Colli Orientali. Their Pinot Bianco is an instance of power gracefully deployed. The color is a lustrous golden yellow. The bouquet is a sustained, but not indelicate, declaration of the flowery and fruity fragrances natural to the grape, with the accent on almondlike nuttiness and bread crust. In the flavor there is a finely tuned understanding between ripeness and acidity, between mouthfilling roundness and vivacity.

Some of the Collio's better producers are Borgo Conventi, Buzzinelli, Formentini, Gradnik, Gravner, Humar, Princic, Scolaris, and Villa Russiz. Gaspare Buscemi is a one-man cooperative turning out impeccable bottlings from the grapes of small growers, such as Furlani, Komjanc, and Zampar, to whom he gives principal billing in the labels. One of his masterpieces is an unclassified wine called Runk, a dazzlingly elegant blend of pinot bianco and tocai. The ultimate standard of quality in Collio Pinot Bianco is set by the monarch of all Collio producers, Mario Schiopetto.

In the Colli Orientali the wines of Livio Felluga stand out. Other good producers are Mario Budini, Valentino Butussi, Cantarutti Alfieri, Ronchi di Manzano, and Volpe Pasini.

Grave del Friuli Pinot Bianco
(D.O.C., FRIULI–VENEZIA GIULIA)

Isonzo Pinot Bianco
(D.O.C., FRIULI–VENEZIA GIULIA)

Aquileia Pinot Bianco
(D.O.C., FRIULI–VENEZIA GIULIA)

Latisana Pinot Bianco
(D.O.C., FRIULI–VENEZIA GIULIA)

If the Pinot Bianco of these remaining four appellations in Friuli, particularly that from Grave, were produced in any other region, we would have heard much more about it. But attractive though it is, it is eclipsed by the far more fascinating specimens from the hills of the Collio and the Colli Orientali.

The hills of the Collio, facing the sun and the fresh Adriatic breeze, producing some of Italy's finest white wines. See regional map of Friuli-Venezia Giulia, page 271.

The wines of Grave, Isonzo, Aquileia, Latisana come almost entirely from lowlands, some of them riverine plains, others coastal. Their fragrance is more muffled, their flavor less sumptuous, their body less buoyant and leaner than the slope-grown Pinot Bianco. These are, nonetheless, authentic wines of Friuli, benefiting from the region's benevolent climatic location and most of all, perhaps, from the meticulous, dedicated workmanship of the Friulani growers and winemakers. Their claims are modest but not invalid and repay our attention with some of the best values to be had anywhere in white wine.

In this relatively large area the producers are legion. Some of the good ones are Duca Badoglio, Cantoni, Paolo De Lorenzi, Fratelli Pighin, Pittau, Pradio, Prandi d'Ulmhort, Russolo, Villa Ronche, Volderie, and Aldo Zaglia.

THE VENETO'S PINOT BIANCO

To the sea of wine produced each year by Venice's home region, Pinot Bianco contributes only little puddles. The bulk of the Veneto's white wine consists of Soave, Tocai, Garganega, and Prosecco. A good portion of the Pinot Bianco that is made goes into blends to improve other whites. The remainder is divided into two appellations, Colli Berici and Breganze.

❧ *Colli Berici Pinot Bianco* ❧
(D.O.C., VENETO)

This appellation encloses the intensely cultivated hills immediately south and partly to the west of Vicenza. The best Pinot Bianco in the Veneto is produced here. It is not so full a wine as that of the Collio nor so intensely fragrant. The permitted addition of up to 15 percent pinot grigio dilutes some of its varietal character, but for its small scale, and on its own terms, it can be most appealing. The delicate bouquet, the light but firm body, and the tender fruitiness are representative of the graceful style of this region's wines.

An exceptionally fine Pinot Bianco is made by Alfredo Lazzarini, who calls it Bianco del Rocolo. Of lesser, but good quality is the wine of Cantina Sociale dei Colli Vicentini, Severino Muraro, and Nani Rizzieri.

❧ *Breganze Pinot Bianco* ❧
(D.O.C., VENETO)

The low hills, shallow valleys, and foggy plains of Breganze form one of the smallest D.O.C. areas in the Veneto, in the center of the region, north of Vicenza and west of Asolo. Breganze's Pinot Bianco is blended from nearly equal parts of pinot bianco and pinot grigio. Which of the two caps the other is left to the discretion of the producer.

The wine is a very pale straw yellow color with flashes of green. The fragrance is fresh and predominantly flowery, followed in the mouth by crisp, tart, persistent impressions of fruit.

A dynamic, enthusiastic young producer, Fausto Maculan, makes a delicious Breganze Pinot Bianco. An excellent wine is also made by Gino Novello.

UNCLASSIFIED PINOT BIANCO IN THE VENETO

Most of the non-D.O.C. Pinot Bianco is of dubious authenticity and variable quality. But a few bottlings are equal to any bearing recognized appellations. These are Ca' Furia's Pinot, from Sirmione on Lake Garda; Angelo Serafin's del Col de i Gai, made near Treviso; and Venegazzu Bianco, made north of Treviso in the Montello-Asolo area.

LOMBARDY'S PINOT BIANCO

In Lombardy there are two D.O.C. appellations for Pinot Bianco: Franciacorta and Valcalepio. Franciacorta is by a wide margin the more important and better wine, benefiting from the loose, well-drained soil of sloping vineyards and from the reflected light issuing from Lake Iseo, just north of the growing area.

❧ *Franciacorta Pinot Bianco* ❧
(D.O.C., LOMBARDY)

It is spare in style, with a pale, greenish yellow color, a light, sharp fragrance, and smooth but narrowly cast flavor to which accentuated acidity contributes a sustained impression of freshness.

In Franciacorta, which has successfully publicized all its wines, red, white, and sparkling, many good producers are active. Some of them are Barboglio de' Gaioncelli, Bersi Serlini, Ca' Del Bosco, Convento SS. Annunciata, Faccoli, Fratelli Berlucchi, Monti della Corte, Mosnel, and Villa.

Valcalepio Pinot Bianco
(D.O.C., LOMBARDY)

A recent appellation covering a partly hilly area southeast of Bergamo. The zone has never been known as a source for particularly fine wines, and its edition of Pino Bianco is a very plain one indeed. The producer is Cantina Sociale Bergamasca.

OTHER PINOT BIANCO WINES

Pinot Bianco di Fontanafredda
(VINO DA TAVOLA, PIEDMONT)

In Piedmont there is no D.O.C. appellation for Pinot Bianco, but the largest estate in the region, Fontanafredda, makes one all the same and with good reason, for it is an admirable specimen. Nutty and herbal odors mingle in the vigorously expressed bouquet, and there is fullness and strength in the ample-bodied flavor. The sensation of almonds becomes deliciously explicit on the palate and ends in the back taste without coarseness.

Colli Bolognesi di Monte San Pietro Pinot Bianco
(D.O.C., EMILIA–ROMAGNA)

The growers in the hills west of Bologna nurse considerable enthusiasm for their Pinot Bianco. It is probably the best white wine of the zone, but that is qualified praise since this appellation excels not in whites but in reds. It is a firm, strong wine that is stingy on fragrance, assertive in flavor, rugged, not to say rough, in style. The most genteel Pinot Bianco of the Colli Bolognesi is produced by Bruno Negroni.

❧ *Pomino Bianco* ❧
(VINO DA TAVOLA, AWAITING D.O.C., TUSCANY)

It has always been assumed—both by those who enjoy Tuscany's white wines for what they are and by those who, for the same reasons, disparage them—that the whites of this region could never achieve anything more than rustic, simple appeal based on frank flavor and appetizing acidity. In recent times, however, attempts have been made to achieve greater distinction by the planting of imported grape varieties sanctioned by neither tradition nor the D.O.C. statute and through the sensitive application of advanced winemaking technology. The most successful of these efforts is responsible for Pomino.

Pomino is made from pinot bianco blended with pinot grigio, sauvignon, and chardonnay grapes grown in high-altitude vineyards on the Frescobaldi estate in Chianti country, north of Florence.

It is a very pale, parchment-colored wine with glints of yellow gold. The bouquet is fine and delicate. Tasting qualities are crisp, even, and gracefully fruity, unblemished either in their development or in their aftertaste by the coarse texture one associates with central Italian white wines.

❧ *Favonio Bianco* ❧
(VINO DA TAVOLA, APULIA)

Favonio, a 100 percent Pinot Bianco, is made by Attilio Simonini in Apulia, the southernmost region in eastern Italy, the heel of the boot when you look at the country's map. For Apulia, pinot bianco is as exotic as cabernet franc and chardonnay, the other French grapes that Simonini, who is from the Veneto, planted here. The instinct that led Simonini to cultivate in the South varietals that are supposed to thrive only in his native Northeast did not mislead him. No other wines of the region match his for delicacy.

Favonio Bianco is a bright, straw yellow wine, with a small but appealing bouquet and bold, lasting flavor. There is a suggestion of greenness to it, as though the grapes had been picked just short of ripeness, and it is not as complete a wine as the best of the Friuli, but then no other Pinot Bianco is. When we take into account what are the climatic conditions in which Favonio is made and how ordinary are other white wines in Apulia, Simonini's achievement compels not only admiration but amazement.

The Pinot Grigio Family

The small, grayish purple berries of the French varietal pinot gris produce Italy's most fashionable white wine. Why it should have been Pinot Grigio to achieve such popularity rather than Pinot Bianco, which can deliver finer and more complex taste sensations, is a puzzle. Or it may be that the explanation lies precisely within those circumstances, since the demand for whites comes mostly from those who are more comfortable with a wine of uncomplicated personality. The name, too, must have a part in its success: There is something alluring and elegant about a white wine called *grigio*.

Pinot Grigio is made in disparate styles that change not merely from region to region but from producer to producer. The differences are immediately apparent in the color, which may go from light straw to yellow gold to a lovely, transparent, pale copper tint. Such variations usually reflect the differing intentions of the winemakers.

The theory is that the palest Pinot Grigios, made from must that has had no contact with the grapes' dark skins, are fresher and more delicately fragrant, while the deeper-hued ones achieve their prettier color at the risk of those oxidized, off odors to which white wines are subject when they undergo even slight maceration—fermentation on the skins.

In practice, some of the superscrubbed, pale wines are indistinct in aroma and flavor, while there are copper-tinged Pinot Grigios that are beautifully perfumed and taste perfectly clean and fresh.

The principal areas of Pinot Grigio production are in the Northeast —in Alto Adige/Südtirol (where it is also called Ruländer) and in Friuli —and in the north-central region of Lombardy.

ALTO ADIGE'S PINOT GRIGIO

❧ *Alto Adige Pinot Grigio/Südtiroler Ruländer* ❧
(D.O.C., TRENTINO–ALTO ADIGE)

Within this appellation are wines produced in the central portion of the province of Bolzano, which constitutes the German-speaking half of the

Alto Adige/Trentino region. Pinot Grigio here has the intense fragrance that can be attributed both to the grape and to the Teutonic style of winemaking. Tasting qualities present an attractive balance between body and vivacity. Some of the top producers are Kellereigenossenschaft Girlan, Hofstätter, Magrè-Niclara, and Schloss Schwanburg.

❧ Terlano Pinot Grigio/Terlaner Ruländer ☙
(D.O.C., TRENTINO–ALTO ADIGE)

The wines of Terlano, from steep slopes between Bolzano and Merano, are the elite of this already elite zone. Regrettably, they are often bottled under the better-known Alto Adige/Südtirol appellation, to which they are equally entitled. Their fragrance is appealing but not showy; flavor is firm but not earthy. Terlano Pinot Grigio accurately represents this appellation's qualities. The principal producer is Kellereigenossenschaft Terlan. A good, smaller one is Alois Lageder.

❧ Valle Isarco Pinot Grigio/Eisacktaler Ruländer ☙
(D.O.C., TRENTINO–ALTO ADIGE)

The spicy aromas of Pinot Grigio from the Alpine vineyards of the Isarco River valley are typical of this appellation in the far northeast corner of Bolzano province. So is the thinner, sharper body. The choicest producer here is Eisacktaler Kellereigenossenschaft.

In the province of Trento—the southern, more Italianate half of the Alto Adige/Trentino region—the presence of Pinot Grigio is negligible. Most of the grapes grown are blended with pinot bianco to make the wine designated as Trentino Pinot. From those few that have been vinified separately, I have tasted no wine worth recalling.

FRIULI'S PINOT GRIGIO

❧ Collio Pinot Grigio ☙
(D.O.C., FRIULI-VENEZIA GIULIA)

❧ Colli Orientali del Friuli Pinot Grigio ☙
(D.O.C., FRIULI-VENEZIA GIULIA)

On the slopes of these two high-ranking appellations of the region where some of Italy's most distinctive whites are made, Pinot Grigio puts on the most flesh and weight. Fruit aromas dominate the bouquet. Taste impressions are round and smooth, featuring a generous body occasionally overcharged with alcohol. In the Collio some of its better producers are Borgo Conventi, Buzzinelli, Formentini, Gradnik, Jermann, Schiopetto, Scolaris, and Villa Russiz. In the Colli Orientali: D'Attimis, Dorigo, Livio Felluga, Francesco Lui, Ronchi di Manzano, Isidoro Tilatti, and Volpe Pasini.

Pinot Grigio delle Grave
(D.O.C., FRIULI–VENEZIA GIULIA)

Isonzo Pinot Grigio
(D.O.C., FRIULI–VENEZIA GIULIA)

Aquileia Pinot Grigio
(D.O.C., FRIULI–VENEZIA GIULIA)

Latisana Pinot Grigio
(D.O.C., FRIULI–VENEZIA GIULIA)

Pinot Grigio from the plains of the other four Friuli appellations is generally shorter on aroma and blunter in flavor than its Collio and Colli Orientali counterpart, but it is, by and large, an agreeable wine, vigorous, fruity, straightforward. Some of the bottles from Grave can, in fact, be rather fine.

Recommended producers from Grave are Molino delle Streghe, Pighin, Pittau, Pradio, and Villa Ronche. From Isonzo: Bader, Prandi d'Ulmhort, S. Elena, and Tenuta Villanova. In Aquileia the large Cantina Sociale Cooperativa del Friuli Orientale bottles Pinot Grigio under the Molin di Ponte label and also produces it for Valdo. In Latisana the most reliable name to look for is Isola Augusta.

LOMBARDY'S PINOT GRIGIO

Pinot dell'Oltrepò Pavese
(D.O.C., LOMBARDY)

One of the most attractive of Pinot Grigios is made south of Milan, in the zone called Oltrepò Pavese. There is not as much of it as in Friuli, nor is it nearly as well known; its identity is often lost under the D.O.C. name Pinot, which can be applied to Pinot Bianco or Pinot Grigio or any blend of the two.

The bouquet of Oltrepò Pinot Grigio is frankly vinous, supported by delicate suggestions of fruit. On the palate, fresh and simple flavor travels smoothly on a sturdy body. Excellent bottlings are produced by Duca Denari's Il Casale, Membretti-Balestreri, and Tenuta di Oliva.

₰ *Clastidium* ₰

(VINO DA TAVOLA, LOMBARDY)

It is made from a combination of both pinot grigio and pinot noir, vinified white. When I worked in Milan as a copywriter in the 1960s, it was my favorite white, steely fresh, compact, rich in flavor, helping to extend even further that essential feature of the Italian advertising process, the creative lunch. Clastidium is made by the firm of Ballabio, which was then, several years before the founder's death, one of the finest producers in the Oltrepò zone. Recent samplings suggest that the transition to new management is having its ups and downs, mostly downs.

The Tocai Family

If you are drinking Tocai on its home ground in Friuli, it may not be possible to be wholly objective about it. You might be at table with a hospitable grower, the plate before you covered by rose-pink slices of San Daniele, the sweetest ham you have ever tasted, soon to be followed by a thick soup of beans, corn, potatoes, and smoked pork. In the hearth nearby, over a slow wood fire, birds are turning on a spit. From the rough, thick hands of your host, a bottle spills a scintillating, pale gold liquid into your glass. He waits for your first swallow, looks at you with bright, exultant eyes, and asks, "Isn't that an extraordinary wine?" Gladly surrendering to the occasion's enveloping sense of well-being, you lower your eyelids and nod assent.

Even in more detached moments one must concede that Friuli's Tocai is a wine of unmistakable character, not easily confused with other whites. It is certainly not like its namesake, Hungarian Tokay, a wine from a totally different grape. Nor does it resemble Tokay d'Alsace, which is made from the grayish purple grape known in Italy as pinot grigio.

Tocai's whispery bouquet is a combination of fruity, floral, and herbal aromas, in which one might distinguish the scent of almonds and, more faintly, of fennel. Flavor reaches the palate with a solid impact, cushioned by impressions of roundness and warmth. Acidity is moderate, but sufficient to impart vigor. The aftertaste is emphatic, with clearly emerging sensations of fennel and of an agreeable, peachpit-like bitterness.

FRIULI'S TOCAI

Tocai del Collio
(D.O.C., FRIULI–VENEZIA GIULIA)

Tocai dei Colli Orientali del Friuli
(D.O.C., FRIULI–VENEZIA GIULIA)

Friuli, the northeastern region adjacent to Yugoslavia, is the prime source of Tocai; and within Friuli, the two choicest appellations for this, and for all other white wines of the region, are the hilly zones of the Collio and the Colli Orientali. Nowhere else does Tocai achieve the same perfect balance or comparable depth of flavor.

In the Collio some of the best producers of Tocai are Al Cret, Attems, Berin, Buzzinelli, Ca' Ronesca, Formentini, Gradnik, Humar, Pighin, Princic, Schiopetto, Scolaris, and Villa Russiz. In addition, a talented young oenologist, Gaspare Buscemi, issues separate bottlings of first-rank wines from grapes grown by Furlani, Komjanc, Manferrari, and Zampar.

In the Colli Orientali, most worthy of mention are D'Attimis, Dorigo, Livio Felluga, Francesco Lui, and Ronchi di Manzano. These are lengthy lists, but not long enough to accommodate all of these districts' good makers of the most popular wine in the region.

❧ *Tocai delle Grave del Friuli* ☙
(D.O.C., FRIULI-VENEZIA GIULIA)

❧ *Tocai dell'Isonzo* ☙
(D.O.C., FRIULI-VENEZIA GIULIA)

❧ *Tocai Friulano di Aquileia* ☙
(D.O.C., FRIULI-VENEZIA GIULIA)

❧ *Tocai Friulano di Latisana* ☙
(D.O.C., FRIULI-VENEZIA GIULIA)

The remaining four appellations in Friuli consist of gravelly plains (Grave), riverine plains (Isonzo), and coastal flatlands (Aquileia and Latisana). Wine of respectable quality is produced, but on the whole it is duller, less graceful than that of the Collio and the Colli Orientali. Some of Grave's Tocai can be quite good and generally has an edge in length of flavor over the other three appellations.

Of the many producers in Grave, by far the largest zone in Friuli, a few of the good ones are Duca Badoglio, Cantoni, La Delizia, Pittau, Pradio, and Villa Ronche. In the other appellations reliable names are Bader, Cantina Produttori Vini del Collio e dell'Isonzo, Isola Augusta, and S. Elena.

THE VENETO'S TOCAI

Tocai will never displace Soave and its siblings in the hearts or, more exactly, in the throats of the people of the Veneto, but it has its share of popularity, and at least one of the appellations has established its reputation beyond the region's borders.

❧ *Tocai di Lison* ☙
(D.O.C., VENETO)

A full, satiny wine, with a sharp scent of spiced fruit. Produced in easternmost Veneto, adjacent to the Friuli appellation of Latisana. The older, finer portion of the zone is entitled to the qualification *classico*.

Tenuta S. Anna of Loncon has been responsible for the success Tocai di Lison has had, a success that must be attributed at least in part to the beautiful S. Anna labels reproducing details from paintings of the old masters. Other producers deserving more recognition are Club Produttori Associati, Antonio Dal Moro's La Fattoria, Paolo De Lorenzi, and Conti di Porcia.

❧ *Tocai del Piave* ☙
(D.O.C., VENETO)

An attenuated version of Tocai di Lison, with fruity but muted aromas and leaner flavor and body. The largely flat Piave zone begins at Lison's western limits and ends just east of Treviso. Some of its good producers are Marcello del Majno, Liasora, Mercante, and Stepski-Doliwa.

❧ *Breganze Bianco* ☙
(D.O.C., VENETO)

This small, hilly zone in the Veneto's center makes a pale, light, vivacious, frankly fruity Tocai in which there may be up to 15 percent of other white grapes. Its best bottler is Maculan.

❧ *Tocai dei Colli Berici* ☙
(D.O.C., VENETO)

A soft, nutty, round wine from the hills south of Vicenza. The best example of it is Alfredo Lazzarini's Costiera Granda.

LOMBARDY'S TOCAI

❧ *Tocai di S. Martino della Battaglia* ☙
(D.O.C., LOMBARDY AND, IN SMALL PART, VENETO)

Here, on the plains of Lake Garda's southern shore, the tocai vine makes its final stop in its western migration from Friuli. It evidently likes to travel light, for it has shed along the way most of the qualities that make a Tocai Friulano so memorable.

S. Martino's wine is mild in fragrance and flavor to the point of indistinctness, save for an accentuated bitterness that is not as agreeable as when it is part of a more complete range of flavors.

The same area is successful in producing another white, the charming Lugana, a precedent that encourages hope of a brighter future for Tocai di S. Martino. Even now, small, unsung producers, such as Ercole Romano and Torretta Spia d'Italia, are giving convincing proof with their well-made wines that the generally mediocre performance of this appellation is not inevitable.

Traminer Aromatico/Gewürztraminer

The feature of the wines made from the traminer grape that fascinates those who prize them, while it discourages those who don't, is their piquant aroma. The explicitness of its primary grape fragrance makes Gewürztraminer unlike other wines and superficially similar to those made from muscat grapes. The parallel ends there, for, whereas that aroma dominates all other impressions in the taste and aftertaste in muscat wines such as Asti Spumante, it is only the precursor of more developed and elegant sensations in fine Gewürztraminers.

In Italy the most desirable Gewürztraminer or Traminer Aromatico is produced in the German-speaking Alto Adige/Südtirol. There is reason to believe, although the evidence is not conclusive, that the grape itself originated near the Alto Adige town of Termeno (in German, Tramin). (See the map on page 131.) The obvious question is, How does Alto Adige's Traminer Aromatico compare with the better-known, and justly admired, Gewürztraminer of Alsace? The equally obvious answer is that it is different.

One should not expect from the Alto Adige wine the highly charged attack on the senses, the unfettered opulence, of the Alsatian variety. In fact, to producers in Alto Adige the assertiveness of Alsatian wines approaches vulgarity. That is not my opinion, but to be aware of that attitude is to be prepared for the restrained, ethereal style of Traminer Aromatico.

The color of the wine is pale, burnished gold. The bouquet is full and penetrating, swollen with the characteristically spiced aroma of the grape. Flavors carry forward on the palate some of the aromatic sensations of the bouquet that develop into more complete, smooth, delicate impressions of fruit. It closes gracefully, with lingering, but subtle evocations of the initial aroma and a clean, softly stated suggestion of bitterness.

❧ *Alto Adige Gewürztraminer/*
Südtiroler Gewürztraminer ❧
(D.O.C., TRENTINO–ALTO ADIGE)

❧ *Valle Isarco Gewürztraminer/*
Eisacktaler Gewürztraminer ❧
(D.O.C., TRENTINO–ALTO ADIGE)

The finest Gewürztraminer is produced near the town of Termeno on the right bank of the Adige River, in the southwest portion of Alto Adige. It is the one entitled to the Alto Adige/Südtirol appellation. There is a separate appellation for Valle Isarco/Eisacktaler Gewürztraminer, made in the Isarco River valley in northernmost Alto Adige. It is a paler, thinner, less heady wine, than the one made in Termeno.

The standout producer of Termeno's Gewürztraminer is Antonio von Elzenbaum. Other distinguished producers are Hofstätter, Alois Lageder, and Schloss Schwanburg. In Valle Isarco it is Eisacktaler Kellereigenossenschaft and Stiftskellerei Neustift.

❧ *Traminer Aromatico del Trentino* ❧
(D.O.C., TRENTINO–ALTO ADIGE)

It is produced in the northern townships of Trento province, where it meets the southern end of Alto Adige. Most of it is feebler than the Termeno version, but two excellent Traminers are bottled by Bossi Fedrigotti and Villa Borino.

FRIULI'S TRAMINER

❧ *Traminer del Collio* ❧
(D.O.C., FRIULI–VENEZIA GIULIA)

❧ *Traminer dell'Isonzo* ❧
(D.O.C., FRIULI–VENEZIA GIULIA)

The Collio and Isonzo appellations press against the Yugoslav border in Friuli, the supreme white wine region of Italy. Collio vineyards are on sloping ground, Isonzo on the plains; and the former almost invariably excel. But in neither case, as far as Traminer goes, can they match the Gewürztraminers of Alto Adige.

Collio's Traminer is fragrant enough, but it is heavy and sluggish, lacking in charm. The Isonzo is more muted in aroma, to the extent of smelling simply vinous, and plainer in flavor.

The Trebbiano and Malvasia
Family of Roman Whites

When we looked at the white wines of Tuscany and Umbria, we found most of them belonged to a single family begot by trebbiano and malvasia grapes. Nearly all the whites produced in the Roman region of Latium are similarly related members of a large clan, whose sires are once again trebbiano and malvasia.

The trebbiano is sometimes the Tuscan variety, but more traditional is the native trebbiano *giallo*—yellow trebbiano—which makes a less acidic, plushier, deeper-colored wine than Tuscany's varietal. Two native malvasias are used: malvasia bianca di Candia, also known as malvasia rossa after the pink color of the plant's flowers, and malvasia del Lazio, also called puntinata because of its speckled berries. The first is by a large margin more prevalent. Unlike the Tuscan malvasia del Chianti, it yields a faintly aromatic, perceptibly nutty wine. The second variety, the speckled malvasia, is the finer of the two, but less productive and consequently less popular with farmers, who, unfortunately, are steadily growing less of it.

In Roman whites, malvasia dominates the blend, reversing the Tuscan proportion, which favors trebbiano. In comparing the better wines of Latium with those of Tuscany, one finds them more aromatic, with a deeper, more golden color, more velvet in their texture and roundness in the body. They lack, however, much of the vitality, the crispness of the Tuscans and may even taste flat and flaccid.

In homage to the fashion for totally dry wines, Latium's producers have stripped their whites of their once characteristic, usually understated sweetness, which seemed such a delightful and harmonious extension of their softness.

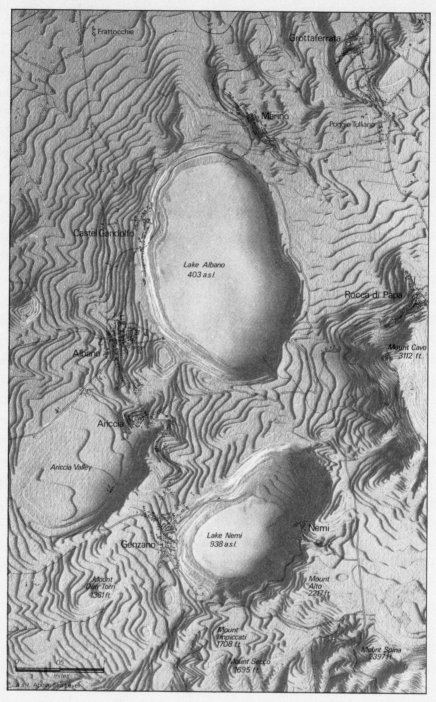

A section of the Castelli Romani zone where Roman whites are produced. The lakes fill the craters of extinguished volcanoes. See regional map of Latium, page 281.

CASTELLI ROMANI WHITES

Most representative of Roman whites are the wines of the Castelli Romani. The Castelli ("castles") refer to the hills formed by the volcanic puckering of the land southeast of Rome and to the collection of towns, princely villas, and vineyards on their slopes. Included in Castelli Romani are the following appellations.

Colli Albani
(D.O.C., LATIUM)

A large area, enclosing several towns, whose wine is hard to distinguish from the many others, except perhaps for being at the same time coarser and thinner. Production is dominated by the cooperative cellar Cantina Sociale Cooperativa Colli Albani.

Colli Lanuvini
(D.O.C., LATIUM)

This zone is adjacent to, but smaller than, Colli Albani. Some of the best wine of the entire Castelli Romani area is made here, endowed with delicacy and length of taste. Good producers are Colle Rubro and Colle San Gennaro.

Frascati
(D.O.C., LATIUM)

Of all the Castelli wines, its vineyards are closest to Rome. It is also the most plentiful of the lot, although production cannot be so abundant to account for all the house wine passed off as Frascati in the *trattorias* of the capital. The Frascati of old, particularly the very sweet *cannellino* type made partly with grapes shriveled by the noble mold, was a deep gold wine, plump, unctuous, and simply delicious. Modern Frascati, certainly the dry version, is a pale copy both literally and figuratively. Much of it is made to an unvarying standard in the vast, automated cellars of Fontana Candida. Other, less widely known but worthy producers are De Sanctis, Cantina Produttori di Frascati, Cantina in S. Matteo, Sant'Anna, and Zandotti.

❧ *Marino* ❧
(D.O.C., LATIUM)

To the west of Frascati are the vineyards of Marino, on generally flatter land. It is here that the lean, pared-down, new look in Castelli wines was launched—precisely at the giant cooperative Cantina Sociale Cooperativa di Marino, which bottles, under its label, wine made from the grapes supplied by more than four hundred growers.

❧ *Montecompatri-Colonna* ❧
(D.O.C., LATIUM)

This curious appellation straddling the superhighway southeast of Rome has the choice of using both names on its labels or just Montecompatri or Colonna alone. It remains a choice unexercised, since there is not much wine and most of it is sold in bulk. The only bottler I am aware of is Cantina Sociale Cooperativa di Montecompatri.

❧ *Velletri* ❧
(D.O.C., LATIUM)

This southernmost of the Castelli whites emphasizes the aromatic fragrance and the bitterness that characterize the malvasia del Lazio varietal. A representative example is bottled by the Cantina Viticoltori di Velletri.

OTHER ROMAN WHITES

Outside the Castelli Romani zone there are several whites produced north and south of Rome that deliver to a more or less marked degree the aromas and taste impressions common to Roman whites. There is nothing about them that deserves special comment beyond acknowledgment that the following D.O.C. appellations exist: Capena, Cerveteri, Zagarolo. Better than any of the three is an unclassified white produced by the Maccarese winery north of Rome's Fiumicino airport. It is a clean-tasting, full-bodied blend of the classic Roman trebbiano and malvasia, called Maccarese Bianco.

There is also Est! Est!! Est!!! di Montefiascone. If, so far, you've been spared having to hear the legend of the origin of the wine's name, it is now about to catch up with you. A twelfth-century bishop traveling to Rome sent his servant Martin ahead to mark with the word *est* the places where good wine was served. After presumably many happy *est* stops, the tippling prelate found to his joyous amazement, on arriving at Montefiascone, that his diligent scout had scrawled on the wall of the inn "Est! Est!! Est!!!" He thereupon unloaded all his considerable baggage and never moved on, for shortly thereafter he died. As a comment on the wine's virtues or on Martin's discernment, the story may be interpreted two ways, the more prevalent and more favorable one not being the more accurate. Est! Est!! Est!!! is in fact the most dismal member of this group of wines, whose frailties this too-often-told tale has exposed to more public scrutiny than they can decently withstand.

The Vermentino Family

❧ *Vermentino di Gallura* ☙
(D.O.C., SARDINIA)

Before my first visit to Sardinia, I had been drinking on the mainland a pale, crisp, perfectly balanced, light Sardinian white called Vermentino di Alghero. The morning I landed in Cagliari, the island's major city, my first order of business, after a brisk, exploratory walk, was lunch. With it I asked for a bottle of Vermentino, but not from Alghero, hoping to expand my experience of the wine. That experience was stretched farther and faster than I could have imagined with the first taste of the deep gold, powerful, soft, strong-flavored wine I had been brought. It was a prompt and often-to-be-repeated demonstration of the heavy, alcoholic wine-making style traditional to the island.

The wine I had with lunch was a Vermentino di Gallura, from the northeastern tip of the island. Gallura's green hills, partly sloping vineyards, and forests of cork-bearing oaks set it apart from the unconfined plateaus that distinguish Sardinia's stark, often fierce landscape. This is also the district that has opened the island to international tourism through the gilded resort on the Costa Smeralda.

The D.O.C. statute requires from Vermentino di Gallura a minimum alcohol content of 12 percent and grants the qualification *superiore* to wines with 14 percent alcohol or better. In practice, the standard version is closer to 13 percent, and the *superiore* easily reaches 15 percent or more.

Despite the high alcohol, the smoothness of the wine, combined with rich, ingratiating flavor, makes it surprisingly—a more appropriate word might be treacherously—easy to drink at table. When it reaches *superiore* levels, however, it can only serve, for all but Sardinian palates, as a before- or after-dinner drink.

The finest producer is Cantina Sociale del Vermentino, who, up to the present, has preferred to market its wines as *vino da tavola,* under coined names. For the lower-alcohol version it uses S'Éleme and for the stronger *superiore,* Aghiloia. It is one of many cases in Italy, even more frequent in Sardinia than on the mainland, where a producer chooses to sell his wine under an unclassified proprietary name rather than with a D.O.C. designation.

❧ *Vermentino di Alghero* ☙
(VINO DA TAVOLA, SARDINIA)

The Vermentino di Alghero I mentioned earlier is produced on the northwestern side of Sardinia, inland of the handsome coastal town of Alghero. Just as the heavier Vermentino is a fine example of a wine respecting native tradition and satisfying local taste, the other is a perfect model of a wine skillfully tailored to suit the modern fashion for light whites.

If we were to adhere inflexibly to the organization of this book, Vermentino di Alghero should be placed in the category of light wines. It favors our understanding of the wine, however, to examine it here, against the background of the fuller Vermentino from whose traditional style its makers have turned away.

Vermentino di Alghero is one of several white and red wines produced by Sella & Mosca, the largest private estate in Sardinia and one of the largest in Europe. They make wines in Sardinia to sell on mainland Italy and abroad, where lightness and balance are marketable virtues. To achieve these virtues, alcohol levels must go down and acid go up; more emphasis is put on fragrance, less on body.

On the vast plains of its property Sella & Mosca trains vines in the *tendone,* or canopy, method that increases the yield per acre to two or three times that of conventional cordon-trained vines and to several times that of head-trained vines once prevalent on the island. The more grapes per square foot of soil, the less sugar in each berry and, consequently, the less alcohol in the wine. The grapes grow under the cool canopy of their own leaves, sheltered from the acid-destroying heat of the Sardinian sun and high above the reflected heat of the soil. When crushed, the must is instantly separated from the skins and subjected to slow, cool fermentation in steel tanks. As soon as the wine is finished and clarified, it is bottled.

This is contemporary white wine technique done by the book and done well. No one else in Sardinia and few on the mainland can match Sella & Mosca's total control and results.

Vermentino di Alghero satisfies neither the alcohol nor the geographic requirements of the D.O.C. appellation, and it is sold as unclassified *vino da tavola,* which diminishes its appeal not one bit, as can be deduced by its popularity in the mainland's restaurants.

Another unclassified Vermentino is made in Alghero by the Cantina Sociale Riforma Agraria. Its high alcohol and traditional tasting qualities relate it to Vermentino di Gallura. It is marketed under the name Aragosta ("lobster") and it is a suitably substantial accompaniment to the succulent Sardinian crustacean.

LIGURIA'S VERMENTINO

Sardinia's vermentino grape is native to Spain; but before it reached Sardinia, it stopped and settled in Liguria, Italy's half of the Riviera coast. It is used as a minor component of a blend of white grapes that produce the region's most celebrated wine, Cinqueterre. Authentic Cinqueterre exists in such small quantity and has been the object of such fanciful adulation in Italian letters that it may be more at home in a book of fairy tales than in a book of wine.

There is also a wine called Vermentino that is produced at the western end of the coast from the single varietal alone. It has attracted less notice than Cinqueterre and cannot even claim D.O.C. status, but it is nonetheless a far more attractive white, with an abundance of fresh, vivacious flavor and satiny texture. Good producers of it are Calleri, Crespi, and Vairo.

The most fascinating and elegant example of a Vermentino in Liguria is a wine called Linero Bianco, in which vermentino is blended with trebbiano and malvasia. Linero is made by Tognoni. A similar wine, marked by delightful freshness and vigor, goes by the coined name Sarticola Bianco. It is produced by Musetti, on Liguria's southern end close to the Tuscan border.

INDEPENDENT FULL AND FRUITY
WHITE WINES

◆ *Albana Secco* ◆

(D.O.C., AWAITING D.O.C.G., EMILIA–ROMAGNA)

If you should visit Ravenna to make the rounds of the mosaics that illuminate its churches, you would likely be most dazzled by the brilliant, jewellike surfaces in the mausoleum of Galla Placidia, a fifth-century Roman empress. And upon coming out, perchance, into the light and heat of a summer afternoon, you might sit down at a cafe for refreshment and ask for a cool glass of the best local wine. It is not improbable even now, as once it was almost inevitable, that you would be served a wine looking like molten gold and tasting of honey. This is Albana, one of Galla Placidia's favorites, fifteen centuries ago, and still the paramount white wine of the region, although the dry (*secco*) version has begun to replace the traditional sweet (*amabile*) variety.

The color of Albana *secco* is paler than that of the sweet, closer to straw than to gold. The fragrance is light but keen, gently aromatic. The sugary grapes yield as much as 13 percent alcohol, so it follows that the impression on the palate is warm and round, balanced in well-made examples by vivacious acidity and deep fruit flavors. It finishes cleanly with a nutty, reticently bitter, almondlike back taste. A choice Albana is an intriguing, delicate wine whose first simple smells and flavors develop in the nose and mouth into rapidly expanding sensations of herbs and ripe fruit.

The controlled appellation restricts the production of Albana to Romagna, the southeastern triangle of the Emilia–Romagna region, wedged between the Apennine hills and the Adriatic Sea. Several sub-varieties of the grape are cultivated. Tradition associates the finest with those grown on the slopes surrounding Bertinoro, a town from whose perch atop a sharp-rising hill one can see, beyond the vineyards, orchards, and wheat fields below, the nearby Adriatic, a streak of pale blue wash rimming the horizon. The reputation of Bertinoro's grapes is based on the unctuous *amabile* style of Albana, semisweet to intensely sweet. But the most suitable varieties of albana for dry wines are produced a short distance to the north, in the hills near the towns of Faenza and Imola.

Some of the most consistent producers in this area are Pasolini dall'Onda, Tenuta Panzacchia, Tenuta Zerbina, Valeriano Trere', and Vallunga.

❧ *Arneis* ❧
(VINO DA TAVOLA, PIEDMONT)

The grapes of arneis, like the gifts of a ghostwriter, have long been used to advance other reputations than its own. In its native Piedmont this lovely green gold grape is used to improve white wines such as Favorita and Cortese or to refine the coarse address of some Barberas or other harsh reds.

Although it is a vigorous and generous vine, not much arneis has been cultivated. Problems with vinification are cited (it is supposedly easily disposed to oxidation), but the truth is that the Piedmontese have never had much patience with white grapes, save for the muscat that goes into Asti Spumante. Now that the public's thirst for white wine seems to have become unquenchable, a few producers have begun to make a 100 percent varietal Arneis, thus rescuing from anonymity a wine of the greatest promise.

Its rich straw yellow color with flashes of brilliant gold signals from the first Arneis's notable character. The aroma is subtly fruited, possibly recalling that of pears, and the bouquet is fine and forthright. The succulent taste flows with velvety smoothness toward a buoyant aftertaste wherein for long moments a rich succession of flavors continues to develop and expand. Alcohol is substantial, between 12 percent and 13 percent, but in elegant balance with acidity and fruit.

It is still too soon for Arneis to be granted a D.O.C. appellation, and whether it gets one or not is not as important as the need to protect it from hasty commercialization and dilution of quality, since this wine clearly has the potential to reach the pinnacle among Italian whites.

The choice production zone has been identified. It is on the left bank of the Tanaro River in that range of hills known as Roero, exposed to the cool morning sun and already responsible for the fruitier, more graceful examples of Barbera, Nebbiolo, and Dolcetto. In particular, the most favored vineyards for Arneis are in the central portion, in the townships of S. Stefano Roero and Monteu Roero.

Three producers so far are making a pure varietal Arneis. Bruno Giacosa, whose name appears on the labels of some of the most skillfully made wines in Piedmont, and the first-rate house of Vietti make a wine that fits the description above. A third, Cornarea, makes a crisper, less "ripe" version. Cornarea is at present the only one vinifying Arneis from grapes grown on its own estate and is assisted by the Ceretto brothers of Barolo and Barbaresco fame.

Tenuta Carretta makes a wine called Bianco dei Roeri, in which arneis is blended with nebbiolo vinified white, that is, without its skins. It is paler and steelier than pure Arneis, without the 100 percent varietal's unctuousness, but with more freshness and sprightliness.

◄ *Fiano di Avellino* ►
(D.O.C., CAMPANIA)

Fiano, produced less than an hour's drive from Naples, is sometimes cited as proof that despite the hot climate fine wines can be made in southern Italy. Perhaps it's perversity on my part, but it seems to me that its very distinction is a demonstration of the contrary, for Fiano is like no other white wine of the South. It owes its quality not to its generic geographic origin, but to a cool mountain climate, to a rare and noble grape, and to the singular talents of its winemaker, Antonio Mastroberardino.

The color of Fiano is a brilliant, pale straw yellow. In the bouquet there are delicate suggestions of spice and flowers. The taste is distinguished by aristocratic, even austere firmness. As one rolls the wine around in the mouth, there is a marvelous evolution of flavors that culminates in the sensation of toasted hazelnuts persisting into the aftertaste. The compelling personality of Fiano makes it a wine one can enjoy on its own before a meal, sniffing and sipping thoughtfully.

Fiano is made in the mountainous province of Avellino, where vineyards climb to a thousand feet or more above sea level. The vine was known to the ancient Romans, who called it *vitis apiana;* the root of the word *apiana* is the Latin for bees, whose gluttony was presumably strongly stimulated by the fruit's honeyed pulp. The berries are a beautiful tawny gold, but the skin is thick and the bunches small, producing little wine; these qualities led many peasant growers to uproot the vine and substitute it with humbler, but more prolific varieties such as trebbiano and sangiovese.

There are no large vineyards, but scattered patches are planted in fiano, usually close to bushes of the hazelnut for which Avellino is celebrated. In fact, one of the two words in Italian for hazelnut is *avellana*.

The man responsible for the revival of Fiano and for its present

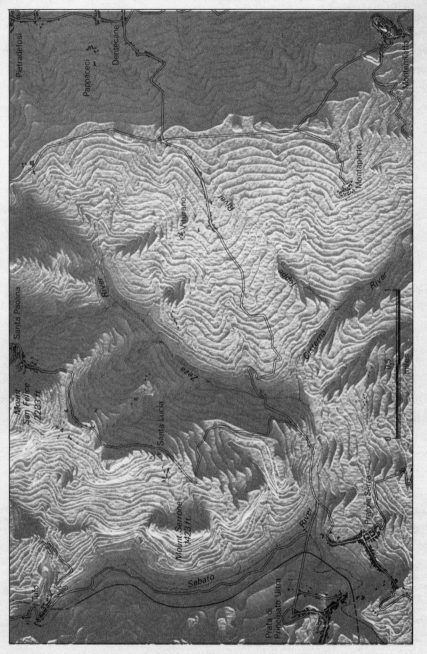

A portion of the mountainous Avellino township where Greco di Tufo, Fiano di Avellino, and Taurasi are produced. See regional map of Campania, page 287.

exalted state is Antonio Mastroberardino, whose family has been making wine in the same area since the eighteenth century. From Mastroberardino's training in chemistry and oenology and from his scholarly immersion in local tradition has emerged his own sensitive approach to winemaking, which connects the most valid methods of contemporary technology to the valuable experiences of the past. His wines are not only technically sound, as are many commercial wines today, but fully express their native character, as no commercial wines do.

Mastroberardino knows about soft presses and cold fermentation, but he has not discarded the older practice of giving even white wines some barrel age. In most instances, barrel aging is fatal to a white wine's freshness, and few are doing it in Italy today; on the other hand, there are few Italian whites that can match the elegance of Fiano.

VINTAGES: Fiano is that rare Italian white that improves with a little bottle age.
Good Years: 1978, 1979, 1980, 1982
Great Years: 1977, 1983

❧ *Greco di Tufo* ☙
(D.O.C., CAMPANIA)

One or two of antiquity's most highly praised wines—Falernian and Aminean—were probably made from greco grapes. Not since the liquidation of the Roman Empire, however, had anything been done with them to attract serious notice until Antonio Mastroberardino began producing his Greco di Tufo.

Mastroberardino has already been mentioned elsewhere in descriptions of the kingly red, Taurasi, on pages 60–1, and of the equally aristocratic white, Fiano, just above. Greco di Tufo comes from the same province of Avellino, in the rugged mountains east of Naples; it takes the second part of its name both from the town Tufo and from tufa, the volcanic rock where it grows best.

Greco is an unusual-looking fruit, the grayish berries flushed with gold or amber, forming small bunches that separate into twin clusters. To greco is added another varietal, called coda di volpe ("fox tail") because of its curved tip, in proportions of one to four or five.

The wine is a cheery, bright straw yellow color. In the assertive bouquet there is a penetrating suggestion of almonds and a thin, sharp whiff of aromatic fruit. The flavors are vigorous, sustained, and bracing, very lightly underscored by bitter impressions that recall the almond sensations in the nose. The character of the wine is full but not opulent, tonic rather than seductive, at the same time sturdy and spry.

ₑ Lacryma Christi del Vesuvio Bianco ₛ
(D.O.C., CAMPANIA)

This is a wine related by geography and grape variety to Greco di Tufo. It is produced closer to Naples, on the very slopes of Vesuvius. The predominant grape is coda di volpe rather than greco, whose presence in the blend is minimal. It is paler, more flowery and light-bodied than Greco di Tufo, but a firm and spirited wine nevertheless. The nonpareil producer is once again Mastroberardino.

ₑ Vernaccia di San Gimignano ₛ
(D.O.C., TUSCANY)

Michelangelo described Vernaccia as a wine that "kisses, licks, bites, tingles, and stings." He loved it. For that matter, many Tuscans still do and consider it their region's—which, for Tuscans, is the same as saying their country's—greatest white. There is no disputing that this pale gold wine from the many-towered town of San Gimignano has strength of character. If, in character, we are expected to appreciate force before other, more elusive attributes—such as refinement—we must then join the chorus of Vernaccia's admirers.

There is certainly nothing elusive about Vernaccia's attack on the palate or its aftertaste. The first is vigorously, one might even say raspingly, fruity and propelled by noticeable alcohol. The second comes with jolting impact, thrusting a tight knot of flavor down the throat.

Up to recently, it was believed that the way to tame this tough wine was with age, first in wood, then in the bottle. Some of the better traditional Vernaccias did in fact mellow with time, although too often they also picked up some of the stale odors and tastes of oxidation. Lately, conversion to more modern techniques of vinification and abandonment of barrel aging have taken much of the sting out of Vernaccia to produce a lighter, more flowery, better-balanced wine.

Vernaccia di San Gimignano is made from a yellowish green grape of the same name, not to be confused with the variety used in Sardinia to make the delectable, sherrylike Vernaccia di Oristano. The name is believed to have the same origin as our word *vernacular,* from the Latin *vernaculus,* meaning native or of this place. Consequently, many Italian grapes, for lack of other identity, are called vernaccia.

The most celebrated, and high-priced, producer of Vernaccia di San Gimignano is Pietrafitta. There are a host of others, some of whom do just as well. Among them: Riccardo Falchini, Frigeni-Sonzogni, Fattoria di Fugnano, Guicciardini-Strozzi, Fattoria La Torre, Fattoria di Monte Oliveto, Fattoria di Pancole.

VINTAGES: Vernaccia has endurance, and mature vintages from one of the better makers can be worthwhile. All the years from 1980 through 1983 have been good.

Other Full and Fruity White Wines

❧ *Bianco del Collio or Collio* ☙
(D.O.C., FRIULI-VENEZIA GIULIA)

Made from ribolla grapes blended with malvasia and tocai. A lighter wine, called Ribolla, is described on page 177. A more robust wine than straight Ribolla, but coarser and lumpish.

❧ *Chardonnay* ☙
(VINO DA TAVOLA FROM VARIOUS REGIONS)

Chardonnay is a late arrival on the Italian wine scene. Although the grape has long been grown in the northeastern region of Trentino-Alto Adige, it was always considered a variety of pinot bianco and blended into wines bearing the Pinot name. A few producers have recently begun to bottle unblended Chardonnay and label it as such. The best are in the Trentino, and among them are Pojer & Sandri and Bollini. In Fruili, Vittorio Puiatti of Enofriulia bottles a vigorous and fruity Chardonnay. Near Bologna, Enrico Vallania makes a 100 percent Chardonnay under his Terre Rosse label and, in Apulia, a small but respectable production comes from Attilio Simonini. Friuli and Tuscany are just beginning to take interest in the grape. With the 1981 vintage a highy perfumed, charming Chardonnay made its debut in Umbria, produced by Lungarotti. No one should expect to find traces of the complex styles typical of Burgundian or California Chardonnay in the Italian versions. These are wines that know nothing of barrel aging, made to be fresh, fragrant, and fleet of body, to be consumed as young as possible.

✒ Ciro' Bianco ✑
(D.O.C., CALABRIA)

Earthy, heavy white made from the greco grape in the district better known for its red, described on page 118.

✒ Favorita ✑
(VINO DA TAVOLA, PIEDMONT)

Coarsely fruity, teasingly bitter. Most of the small production of favorita grapes goes into blends, often with barbera.

✒ Melissa Bianco ✑
(D.O.C., CALABRIA)

Like Ciro' Bianco (see above).

✒ Ostuni ✑
(D.O.C., APULIA)

A blunt, full-bodied wine made near Brindisi from the local impigno grape blended with up to three other native varietals.

✒ Verduzzo Friulano ✑
(D.O.C., FRIULI–VENEZIA GIULIA)

Full, fruity, assertive, slightly astringent wine, made from the yellow verduzzo grape in several districts of Friuli. A solid white, very popular in its home region.

✒ Vespaiolo ✑
(D.O.C., VENETO)

Golden yellow wine with vigorous, slightly acerbic flavor. Made from the vespaiolo or bresparolo grape grown solely on the sloping vineyards of the Breganze district, north of Verona.

[5]

ITALY'S SWEET WINES

and Other Wines of Special Interest

The preference for dry wines is a modern one, formed upon the well-balanced, fully fermented, still wines the French learned how to make two centuries ago. But it was endearing sweetness that made wine popular for nearly all its long history, and it is in a perfectly made naturally sweet wine that we can experience in its purest form the full, luscious pleasure of drinking.

That sweet wines should be categorized solely as wines for dessert is regrettable. If anything, they *are* the dessert. A great sweet wine stands alone, demanding nothing to go with it but our attention. The joy it brings to the palate needs no mediation from cakes or creams or biscuits or any other food. It discloses to us, as no dry wine is capable of doing, the sensuous power of this miraculous drink, a transubstantiation of fruit and sun into honeyed liquid.

Italy has been preeminent in the making of sweet wines for centuries, and its fine hand has not lost its touch. The range of Italian sweet wines is dazzling, from palest gold to dark glowing red to deepest amber; from blithe, youthful wines to ones of seemingly deathless intensity; from those wines made by the timeless process of withering grapes on straw mats to concentrate their sugar to others made by the most advanced modern methods to preserve freshness and lightness. Unfortunately, some of the greatest sweet wines in Italy, among them many of the Muscats made from partly shriveled grapes, have become dishearteningly rare, because the cost and effort to produce them have failed to obtain the corresponding rewards in the marketplace.

As is indicated in the glossary at the back of the book, different terms are used to denote varying degrees of sweetness: *amabile, dolce* or *dolce naturale, liquoroso* or *dolce liquoroso*. *Amabile* is just past the threshold of sweetness. *Dolce* and *dolce naturale* mean explicitly sweet. *Liquoroso* in any context means alcohol has been added to fortify the wine. When a wine is known to be neither *amabile* nor *liquoroso*, but simply and naturally sweet, none of these terms may appear on the label. Although many of the wines listed below are available in both naturally sweet and fortified versions, descriptions have been based on the more desirable unfortified types. Some of them are also made into *spumante*, sparkling wine, but except where indicated, only the still version is described. Another term you may find on a label is *passito*. It means withered and is sometimes joined to the name of a wine made from partly shriveled grapes, as in Passito di Caluso. Some sweet wines are made by both the conventional and the *passito* methods. The *passito* will always be more intense and is usually more worthwhile.

THE MOSCATO FAMILY
OF SWEET WINES

All the varieties of the muscat grape that during the millennia of their stay in Italy have multiplied beyond count have, for simplicity, been officially reduced to two wine-producing groups: moscato bianco ("white muscat") and moscato giallo ("yellow muscat").

The first, moscato bianco, is by a great margin the most diffuse, responsible for wines as spread out geographically as Asti Spumante from Piedmont and Moscato di Siracusa from Sicily.

The second, moscato giallo, is cultivated almost exclusively in Trentino–Alto Adige.

The wines that issue from these grapes vary widely, some light and thin, some corpulent, some whispery, some intense, some fading quickly, some nearly imperishable. One trait they have in common, which indelibly marks all muscat wines, is the unforgettable aroma and flavor of the grape, a heady, musky, ripe peach scent that is equally explicit in its address to the nose and the mouth and that only the muscat delivers.

FROM THE MOSCATO BIANCO GRAPE

❧ *Asti Spumante* ❧
(D.O.C., PIEDMONT)

Pale gold and sparkling, it is the most charming of all sweet wines, manifesting delicious muscat aroma and flavor with the utmost delicacy and verve. Low alcohol, no more than 9 percent, and moderate sweetness give Asti a nimbleness no other sweet wine approaches. Stringent controls and sophisticated techniques distinguish Asti's production. Virtually all Asti houses use the charmat, or sealed vat, method of creating sparkling wines. The CO_2 gas that is a product of fermentation cannot escape from the pressure-controlled vats and is bonded to the wine in the form of tiny bubbles. The champagne method achieves a similar result far more laboriously by fermenting the wine in individual bottles. The charmat process, while producing a less elaborate wine, is ideally suited to the fresh, spontaneous style of Asti Spumante. Among the giants of Asti, Martini & Rossi and Cinzano deserve special notice. Of the slightly smaller producers, Fontanafredda makes a particularly distinguished wine, just a shade drier.

❧ *Moscato d'Asti* ❧
(D.O.C., PIEDMONT)

Like Asti, but less fine, more coarsely fruity.

❧ *Moscato Naturale d'Asti* ❧
(D.O.C., PIEDMONT)

Not a *spumante,* but a still wine, ingenuously sweet and irresistible, closer in flavor to wonderful grape juice than to wine.

❧ *Moscato dell'Oltrepò* ❧
(D.O.C., LOMBARDY)

Bright gold wine, intensely aromatic, with explicit sweetness, light body, and short life.

❧ Moscato dei Colli Euganei ❧
(D.O.C., VENETO)

Golden yellow color and thin, delicate structure. Moderately sweet, usually still, but also available sparkling. Best very young.

❧ Moscato di Trani ❧
(D.O.C., APULIA)

Golden yellow wine with intense aromas and generous sweetness. Luscious texture compensates for lack of vigor. Best in three to four years.

❧ Moscato di Noto ❧
(D.O.C., SICILY)

Pale gold wine. Delicately sweet in its natural version, becomes hot and overbearing when fortified. Best at under five years of age.

❧ Moscato di Siracusa ❧
(D.O.C., SICILY)

Rich, amber gold wine, with finely expressed aroma, deep, deep flavor on a sumptuously velvety body. Very rare. Moderately long-lived.

❧ Moscato di Cagliari ❧
(D.O.C., SARDINIA)

Full, golden wine, with openly declared aromas and flavor. Best within its first four years.

❧ Moscato di Sorso-Sennori ❧
(D.O.C., SARDINIA)

Sardinia's, and perhaps Italy's, finest muscat. A glossy, pale amber wine, carrying its honeyed load with extraordinary delicacy and lightness. Best when young.

❧ *Moscato di Tempio* ☙
(VINO DA TAVOLA, SARDINIA)

From the northern tip of the island; deep gold, densely sweet, and velvety. Moderately long-lived.

FROM THE MOSCATO GIALLO GRAPE

❧ *Moscato del Trentino* ☙
(D.O.C., TRENTINO–ALTO ADIGE)

Deep, straw yellow color, lightly aromatic, warm, intensely sweet flavor. Best when young.

❧ *Moscato Giallo dell'Alto Adige/*
Südtirol Goldenmuskateller ☙
(D.O.C., TRENTINO–ALTO ADIGE)

Light straw yellow color, intensely perfumed, slight in body. To be consumed as young as possible.

A SICILIAN WINE FROM
A DIFFERENT MUSCAT GRAPE

❧ *Passito di Pantelleria* ☙
(D.O.C., SICILY)

Made from shriveled zibibbo grapes, a table variety of the muscat family. Produced on the island of Pantelleria, close to the Tunisian coast. Amber-colored, intensely sweet, delectably warm and velvety, with sensations of concentrated, raisiny fruit. Does not improve past its fourth or fifth year.

INDEPENDENT SWEET WINES

Albana di Romagna Amabile
(D.O.C., AWAITING D.O.C.G., EMILIA–ROMAGNA)

A brilliant golden yellow wine made from albana grapes. (The dry version, Albana *secco,* is described on page 206.) In the bouquet there are softly stated suggestions of peaches and nuts; the flavor is fruity and mildly sweet. In Romagna many used to drink it with food, and some of the farmers still do. The choicest sites for Albana Amabile are on the slopes of the hill of Bertinoro, near Cesena.

Aleatico

Because of its penetrating aroma, the red aleatico grape was long believed to be an offshoot of the muscat, although aleatico's scents are a little finer, less vehement, more flowery than fruity. It makes a wine of very deep red color, ranging from blackish ruby to purplish garnet, depending on its provenance. The flavor is generously sweet, but not to excess. It is exceptionally long-lived.

Aleatico is produced in various parts of central and southern Italy. Two of its numerous incarnations have been granted D.O.C. designations, Apulia's Aleatico di Puglia and Latium's Aleatico di Gradoli. The most highly regarded, however, is the one produced in Portoferraio, on the island of Elba, an unclassified *vino da tavola.*

Anghelu Ruju
(VINO DA TAVOLA, SARDINIA)

A garnet red, spicily fragrant, densely sweet, portlike wine, made by Sella & Mosca from cannonau grapes that have been partly withered in the sun.

Brachetto
(D.O.C. WHEN FOLLOWED BY THE DISTRICT DESIGNATION
D'ACQUI, OTHERWISE VINO DA TAVOLA, PIEDMONT)

Pale, lively red, from the grape by the same name. An appealingly flowery, spritzy, faintly sweet wine.

❧ Caluso Passito or Passito di Caluso ☙
(D.O.C., PIEDMONT)

Made from partly shriveled, white erbaluce grapes. The dry version, called Erbaluce, is described on page 175. One of Italy's best. Delicately nutty bouquet leads to taste sensations that, remarkably, are both densely sweet and vigorous. Exceptionally long-lived wine: I've had forty- and even sixty-year-old Caluso that had lost nothing of its freshness and strength. The best producer is Corrado Gnavi. Great years that may still be available are 1946, 1958, 1961, 1964, and 1971.

❧ Girò di Cagliari ☙
(D.O.C., SARDINIA)

Produced from the increasingly scarce red girò grape grown on the plains north of Cagliari. A bright, pastel ruby wine, aromatic, flowingly sweet. Best when youngest.

❧ Greco di Bianco ☙
(D.O.C., CALABRIA)

Made from shriveled white greco grapes. A discouragingly rare but wonderful wine, exuberantly fragrant, with a sumptuous texture against which the exquisitely controlled sweetness is almost austere. The producer is Umberto Ceratti. His wine is best under five years from the vintage.

❧ Malvasia delle Lipari ☙
(D.O.C., SICILY)

Made from partly shriveled white malvasia grapes grown on the Aeolian Islands off Sicily's northeast coast. Bright, deep gold wine, intensely aromatic, with full, velvety sweetness. Moderate longevity.

❧ Malvasia di Casorzo d'Asti ❧
(D.O.C., PIEDMONT)

❧ Malvasia di Castelnuovo Don Bosco ❧
(D.O.C., PIEDMONT)

From the red malvasia grape. Faintly aromatic, light-bodied, mildly sweet, short-lived wines.

❧ Malvoisie de Nus ❧
(VINO DA TAVOLA, VAL D'AOSTA)

Made from a variety of white malvasia native to Val d'Aosta, sometimes, and probably incorrectly, believed to be related to pinot grigio. Amber-colored when mature, it has a pervasively perfumed, outspread bouquet and charged, vivid flavor on a close-knit, almost wiry body. The life span appears to be nearly indefinite. Produced in infinitesimal quantity by Don Auguste Pramotton, parish priest in Nus.

❧ Monica di Cagliari ❧
(D.O.C., SARDINIA)

A pale, ruby red wine, made from monica grapes usually allowed to wither briefly before crushing. Lightly aromatic, supple, and warm. Best within three years.

❧ Nasco ❧
(D.O.C., SARDINIA)

One of Sicily's most extraordinary wines, it is made from the nasco grape, found only on the island. The color is a lustrous, golden yellow; the bouquet exquisitely flowery, with suggestions of freshly opened, dewy field blossoms. In the flavor, a bitter nuttiness plays elegant counterpoint to the evenly strung out sweetness.

❧ Orvieto Classico Abboccato ❧
(D.O.C., UMBRIA)

The traditional version of Orvieto is sweet, *abboccato*. Its freshness, its quick-flowing texture, its clean flavor and dry finish display all the charm which originally made Orvieto one of Italy's most irresistible whites. Compare with Orvieto *secco,* described on pages 168-9.

❧ Picolit ❧
(D.O.C. IN COLLI ORIENTALI DEL FRIULI ZONE, VINO DA
TAVOLA ELSEWHERE, FRIULI-VENEZIA GIULIA)

Usually compared with France's Château d'Yquem, with which it shares only the distinction of being the highest-priced sweet wine of its country. A bright, golden yellow wine, it is characterized by a peculiarly "dry," aloof kind of sweetness that I have always found disappointing. Picolit is so extravagantly admired by people of unquestionable discernment that I can only conclude that all my experiences of the wine must have been based on unrepresentative examples. Judged to be extraordinarily long-lived.

❧ Recioto di Gambellara ❧
(D.O.C., VENETO)

Similar to Recioto di Soave (see below), but heavier, fruitier, not as fresh.

❧ Recioto di Soave ❧
(D.O.C., VENETO)

Made from selected, partly dried grapes of the same varieties used for Soave (see page 156). Gently, not cloyingly sweet, displaying the freshness and vivacity typical of Soave. Pieropan is a good producer. Even better is Masi, who bottles his version as unclassified *vino da tavola* under the name Recioto di Campociesa. Good for six to seven years or more.

Recioto della Valpolicella Classico
(D.O.C., VENETO)

Made from the ripest, and then shriveled, grapes of the same varieties blended into Valpolicella. The dry version of Recioto is discussed under Amarone, pages 55–7. With a beautiful, warm, ruby red color and a bouquet of fruit and spice that is exceptionally fresh for a wine made from nearly raisined grapes, Recioto brings to the fullest expression the dulcet, cherry-like flavor of Valpolicella. The triumph of its style is in delivering explicitly sweet taste sensations that, when they quit the palate, leave it dry and clean. It is a sublime accompaniment to strawberry ice cream, at once demolishing two popular beliefs: that sweet red wines are uninteresting and no wine goes with ice cream. Best producers are Masi and Tedeschi. Their Reciotos are easily good for eight years or more.

Verduzzo di Ramandolo or Ramandolo
(D.O.C., FRIULI–VENEZIA GIULIA)

Made of the full-bodied verduzzo friulano grape in the Colli Orientali zone, in a small locality called Ramandolo, north of the city of Udine. The color is a straw yellow flashing with gold; the bouquet, honeyed and fruity; the taste sensations, a finely bred combination of roundness and verve, the impressions of sweetness both sensual and vibrant. The best producer is Giovanni Dri. Ramandolo has moderate endurance, so it is best at about three to four years.

Vernaccia di Serrapetrona
(D.O.C., MARCHES)

A foamy wine made mostly from vernaccia nera and a little sangiovese. A portion of the vernaccia grapes is partly dried and added later to the fermentation vat, a procedure analogous to that of *governo* in Chianti. Deep purplish ruby color, aromatic bouquet, vivaciously sweet flavor thinly sheathed by tannic firmness, tonic bitter finish. Also made in a less entrancing *secco* ("dry") version. The producer is Attilio Fabrini. To be consumed young.

◄ *Vin du Conseil* ►
(VINO DA TAVOLA, VAL D'AOSTA)

Another of those frustratingly rare, superb wines from the Alpine vineyards of Val d'Aosta. Made from a grape called petite arvine. The color
is a limpid straw yellow; the bouquet pervasively flowery; the flavor
fugitively sweet, fresh, of great length and suavity. Produced by Ecole
d'Agriculture. Best when young.

◄ *Vin Santo di Gambellara* ►
(D.O.C., VENETO)

Produced from the white grapes used to make Gambellara (the same that
go into Soave) and allowed to dry briefly before crushing. Its first
fermentation is in small barrels; the second, in larger vats. It is bottled
younger than Vin Santo Toscano (see below), which it resembles but does
not equal. Moderately long-lived.

◄ *Vin Santo Toscano* ►
(VINO DA TAVOLA, AWAITING D.O.C., TUSCANY)

Much as Chianti has been synonymous abroad with Italian wine, Vin
Santo is in Italy the most immediate symbol of sweet wine. It is produced
in Tuscany, both in the Chianti zones and outside them, of trebbiano and
malvasia, preferably more of the latter. The grapes are hung from rafters
or spread on straw mats and left to dry for several weeks before they are
pressed. Their juice is poured into small oak barrels, without filling them
to the brim; the opening is shut and cemented airtight. Three to four years
later the barrel is opened and until then no one can predict with certainty
how it will turn out. As a friend in Chianti who makes a little of this
wine for his own use likes to say, if you are lucky, you have Vin Santo,
if not, very expensive vinegar.

During the wine's long confinement in wood, fermentation proceeds
slowly, at stops and starts, until the yeasts feeding on the sugar-rich must
have had all they can take and expire from, so to speak, overnourishment.
Usually there is still sugar left over, and then the wine is sweet. Sometimes, either because the grapes were too low in sugar, or the strain of
yeasts was uncommonly voracious, all the sugar is fermented out and one

has dry Vin Santo, a less common version than the sweet, but not necessarily less good. Good Vin Santo, whether sweet or dry, is worth the wait and the uncertainty. The color is a glossy, light amber; the bouquet intensely animated and with madeira-like odors; the flavor temperately sweet (when not dry); the texture piled deep with velvet.

Showing exceptional endurance, it often strides unflagging into its second or even third decade.

Vin Santo is also produced by similar methods in Umbria and in the Marches, but rarely with comparable results.

❧ *Vino Santo Trentino* ☙
(D.O.C., TRENTINO–ALTO ADIGE)

Made from the nosiola grape, a fine white variety native to Trentino. Like Vin Santo Toscano and other wines described here, its grapes are allowed to dry after the harvest; but unlike most of them, they are held back not for weeks, but for five to six months before crushing. The grapes, selected for perfect ripeness, are picked at the beginning of October and pressed at Easter. During this interval, botrytis, the noble mold of Sauternes and the Rhine, attacks the berries, favoring them with an even greater concentration of flavor.

The must is placed in small wood barrels to ferment, then to age for at least three to four years. An additional period of two or more years in the bottle is desirable before releasing the wine for sale.

Vino Santo Trentino is a far more opulent wine than the Tuscan variety, or of any other *vino* called *santo*. It is, indisputably, one of the pearls of Italian winemaking. The color is a light, luminous amber; the bouquet ample and stately with yeasty suggestions of warm bread; the flavor rich and dense, lusciously, but never oppressively, sweet.

The producer is Cantina di Toblino. Like Tuscan Vin Santo, its longevity is exceptional.

DRY VERSIONS OF SWEET WINES

There are a few Italian wines that can be sweet, but whose finest manifestations are dry. They have one advantage over their sweet kin: They may be taken at any time between meals, instead of shortly after them. They provide, indeed, the most stimulating prelude to dinner, as well as drinking pleasure wholly independent of the table.

❦ *Malvasia di Bosa* ❧
(D.O.C., SARDINIA)

It is produced on a small, hilly zone located on the western coast of Sardinia and crossed by the Temo, the only navigable river on the island, serenely flowing into the Mediterranean. The landscape is unusually tranquil for Sardinia, which, except for its fairy-tale tourist enclaves, elsewhere arouses feelings of awe and disquiet.

The vines of Bosa are meticulously pruned, low, head-trained *alberelli* —stunted trees—in the old island tradition, producing intensely ripe fruit. The wine, fermented off the skins, is aged several years in partly filled, small oak barrels. Its color is a light straw yellow; the bouquet is acute and fine, with prickly aromas of scented flowers and aromatic fruit; the closely knit flavor is warm and nutty, moving with finesse and unfaltering persistence into a loftily pervasive aftertaste. The best producer of Malvasia di Bosa is Salvatore Deriu Mocci.

❦ *Marsala Vergine* ❧
(D.O.C., SICILY)

There exist Marsalas of all descriptions, from very dry to intensely sweet, from pure wine to flavored beverages. The only one worth knowing about is Marsala Vergine, also known as Marsala Soleras.

It is one of the world's superb sipping wines, pale amber in color, with a musky bouquet in which aromas of jam, wild flowers, and nuts delicately mingle and with a flavor that is as succulent as it is dry.

Marsala Vergine is made almost entirely of the native grillo grape and aged for years in wood, using procedures either identical or equivalent to those employed in making sherry. The best producer is Diego Rallo.

❦ *Vernaccia di Oristano* ❧
(D.O.C., SARDINIA)

Another Sardinian gem, of a light, brilliant, topaz color; a penetrating, vigorous bouquet in which sensations of alcohol trail with them suggestions of fruit blossoms. Finespun flavor, faintly bitter, at once silky and fresh, is harmoniously completed by a sustained, caressing aftertaste.

Vernaccia is made in central Sardinia, just inland of the Gulf of

Oristano, from an island variety of the vernaccia grape grown on the lower valley of the Tirso River. The wine is aged in small, thin-walled chestnut barrels filled only to nine-tenths of capacity. They are kept above ground where the temperature stays near 75°, to favor the development of the special strain of yeasts (saccharomyces rouxii) responsible for the flavor of the mature wine.

Unblended Vernaccia earns the designation *superiore* when aged three years and *riserva* when aged four. Wines from superior harvests are aged even longer. I have tasted fourteen-year-old private stock still in the barrel that showed no sign of decrepitude.

The best producer of Vernaccia di Oristano is Fratelli Contini.

VINTAGES:
Good Years: 1960, 1961, 1962, 1963, 1966, 1968, 1970, 1971, 1972, 1974, 1975, 1977
Great Years: 1958, 1959

A SELECTION OF ITALIAN ROSÉS

I hope no one who likes rosés will take offense, but I am unable to conceal the fact that I find them nearly always boring. Beyond the charm of their color, with which I am quickly satiated, they have little to say to me. A few are undoubtedly more interesting than others, and those I have listed here.

Castel del Monte Rosato
(D.O.C., APULIA)

A vivacious, fruity, pale ruby wine with flashes of gold, made from bombino nero grapes grown on high-altitude vineyards. Produced by Rivera.

Cerasuolo di Vittoria
(D.O.C., SICILY)

Very pretty, pale cherry red wine, made from a blend of local grapes. Straightforwardly vinous to the nose, with a surprisingly full, warm flavor. But not too surprising when one discovers it is over 13 percent in alcohol.

❧ *Faustus* ☙
(VINO DA TAVOLA, SICILY)

Pale ruby tinged with garnet in color; fresh, crisp flavor.

❧ *Lacrimarosa* ☙
(VINO DA TAVOLA, CAMPANIA)

A beautiful, copper-colored rosé from mountain-grown aglianico grapes, created by a master winemaker, Antonio Mastroberardino. The combination of delicate flavor and firm body is exceptional for a rosé.

❧ *Riviera del Garda Chiaretto* ☙
(D.O.C., LOMBARDY)

There is also a Riviera del Garda Rosso—red—but for once, the pink is the more appealing wine. Both are made on the western shore of Lake Garda from the groppello grape blended with sangiovese, barbera, and marzemino.

In color it is pale cherry tinged with ruby. An airily floral bouquet and sprightly flavor charged by a thin current of nutty bitterness. It is delicious with *anguilla alla gardesana,* eel marinated in wine, stuffed with rosemary and sage, and charcoal broiled.

❧ *Rosa del Golfo* ☙
(VINO DA TAVOLA, APULIA)

A coral pink to pale cherry red wine with intensely perfumed nose, evenly sustained brisk flavor. Made by Giuseppe Calo' near the Gulf of Taranto from Apulia's best red grapes: negroamaro, mainly, and malvasia nera.

❧ *Sant'Anna Isola di Capo Rizzuto Rosato* ☙
(D.O.C., CALABRIA)

Usually referred to simply as Sant'Anna. A lustrous rose pink color, vinous nose, full and warm flavor. The red version of the same wine is duller.

APPENDIXES,
BIBLIOGRAPHY,
AND INDEX

When and How
to Serve Italian Wine

WINE AND FOOD AFFINITIES

The pairing of wine with food is one of those exquisite games that is best played with as much freedom as possible to devise one's own moves. While the combinations can be infinitely varied, their delights are basically of two kinds: one is the confirmation of pleasure anticipated; the other, blissful surprise. The first is the fruit of experience; the second, of experiment. In each there is a part of the other, for no recurring pattern is entirely gratifying unless it stirs perceptions freshly, and no discovery is pleasant unless our senses are predisposed to welcome it.

Yet the inevitable query continues to come up—What do I serve this wine with?—and it is hard to answer without giving too much or too little guidance. I would rather err by offering less guidance than more. To reflect on how the taste of wine suits the food it accompanies is often fascinating and sometimes instructive, but to transform such reflections into intransigent rules does not always enlarge our opportunities to appreciate wine. It is more likely to curtail them.

We do not need a great variety of wines to explore the diversity of their relationship to food. In fact, until we have acquired considerable experience, it is best to start with as few as possible, perhaps two, or even just one if it is a red. When we confine ourselves at first to drinking the same wine with different dishes—which happens to be what small wine producers do most of their lives—we discover the large repertory of responses of which even simple wines are capable. At the same time we are gradually tuning our discrimination, preparing ourselves for the

endlessly expanding range of sensations to which we gain access as we
begin to experiment with other wines and other combinations.

The relationship between wine and food should favor the lively
expression of the attributes of both. But the match needn't be evenly
weighted. It can be arranged so that the wine captures most of our
attention, if, for example, we serve a Rubesco Riserva or a Carema with
a roast chicken. Or it would work the other way around if with the same
dish we drink a Valpolicella. On the other hand, we can strive for a
harmonious combination of equally assertive wine and food, such as a
young Chianti served with a pasta sauced with garlic and olive oil or with
a rosemary-scented fricassee of rabbit.

The accumulation of experience suggesting that white wines drink
well with fish is a reliable guide, but we shouldn't feel uncomfortable
about making other choices. Some reds, served cool, are easily as suitable,
particularly the light reds from Lake Garda—Bardolino, Riviera del
Garda Rosso, or Chiaretto—or a St. Magdalener from the Tyrol, or a
Grignolino from Piedmont. With a fish soup or fish in a sauce flavored
with herbs or tomato, these would certainly be more interesting than a
light, crisp white. With dark-fleshed fish such as bluefish or tuna, Sangiovese di Romagna or Rossese di Dolceacqua can be as satisfying as any
full-bodied white.

If we are limiting ourselves to a single wine for an Italian meal
composed of the traditional two principal courses—a pasta, *risotto,* or
soup followed by any meat—a medium-range red would probably be the
most comfortable to stay with throughout the meal. A Merlot from any
of the northeastern regions is exceptionally adaptable; so is a Dolcetto
from Piedmont or a Chianti Classico from Castelnuovo township. If the
theme of the meal is fish, a good single white that can sustain interest from
the first course through the second would be one of the full, fruity ones,
such as Albana *secco,* or Malvasia del Collio, or a Friuli Pinot Bianco,
or a Greco di Tufo.

The selection of the menu usually precedes that of the wine, but that
order should be inverted when planning to serve a prime example of one
of the great Italian reds such as Amarone, Barolo, Brunello, Taurasi.
These are powerful wines that demand building up to.

The course they accompany—and here I shall risk being dogmatic by
saying it should be a game casserole or roasted or grilled meat or fowl
—should be prefaced by a restrained first course, an elegant Parmesan
risotto or homemade pasta with asparagus and cream, served perhaps with

a fragrant white such as a Friuli Sauvignon. Then, when the great red is poured, I would nurse it along, taking care that I leave a generous portion for the end of the meal, when I could finish it either alone or with the best of all cheeses for the purpose: an authentic Parmigiano-Reggiano, mature, but not dried out.

The most elaborate red wines have so much to tell that they should not be obliged to compete too closely with food for our attention. Food is necessary to set the scene for their entrance, but then the stage should be cleared of all but the most essential props and turned over to them exclusively.

Other wines do not speak as eloquently as the great reds, but all honestly made wines have something worthy to say, even if sometimes they only whisper it. If there exists a single principle at work in choosing wine well for the table, it is to gauge the intensity with which it delivers its message and to join it to the chorus of flavors in the meal so that it will either rise above them or blend harmoniously, but neither jar nor be submerged.

For those to whom the taste of much Italian wine is still unfamiliar, the classifications and descriptions in this book should help in forming preliminary judgments about what combinations may be most agreeable. Here are some specific examples of liaisons of wine and food I have experienced and enjoyed.

Prosciutto

With a salty prosciutto, such as you are likely to find in Tuscany and Umbria or closer to home, southern-style country ham, cured, but not smoked: Chianti from the Colline Senesi. With a sweeter prosciutto, like the Parma or San Daniele variety, or their American equivalents, combined with ripe melon or figs: Müller-Thurgau from the Tyrol's Valle d'Isarco, or an Alto Adige Gewürztraminer.

Salami

A tart, lively, but not overbearing red: Freisa, Barbera del Monferrato, or Sangiovese di Romagna.

Pasta

It's the sauce in the pasta that influences my choice of wine. With a delicately flavored fish sauce in which there is no tomato, hot pepper, or garlic: Bianchello, Cortese di Gavi, or Lugana. With a more ebullient seafood sauce: Parrina Bianco, Verduzzo Friulano, or Vernaccia di San Gimignano. With a Bolognese meat sauce: Valpolicella, Marzemino, or young Barbera from the Colli Bolognesi. In dealing with the unlimited variety of vegetable sauces, I consider whether they have an olive oil base and include tomato, garlic, or hot pepper, or whether they are cooked with butter and cream and exclude sharp flavorings. In the first case, I prefer a red: Buttafuoco, Dolcetto, or Montepulciano d'Abruzzo. In the second, a fragrant white: Sauvignon, for example, or Etna Bianco Superiore. With pesto on the pasta I love the floweriness of a Tyrolean Riesling or Sylvaner, providing the garlic presence is not too bold.

Game is sometimes used to sauce pasta, employing the dark juices from roast wild birds, or the minced remains of a stew of venison or hare, and a rich sauce can also be made from kidneys, sweetbreads, or wild mushrooms, either dried or fresh. On those occasions when such a dish is the principal feature of the meal and does not lead to a meat course, I pull out all the stops and bring on a large-scale red: Gattinara, Barbaresco, Chambave Rouge, or Castello di Monte Antico Riserva. Should the pasta precede a major meat course, I'd save the nobler red for the meat and begin with Bonarda dell'Oltrepò, Franciacorta Rosso, Etna Rosso, or Per'e Palummo.

With any pasta sauce in which the principal or sole element is tomato: a southern white, such as Ischia Bianco Superiore, or, if a red is desired, any of the medium-range Tuscan reds in the sangiovese family (pages 103–6).

Risotto

It should be evaluated according to the ingredients with which it is flavored, thus the same suggestions made for pasta are applicable. With *risotto alla milanese,* saffron *risotto,* traditionally served alongside ossobuco, an impeccable accompaniment is Lino Maga's Barbacarlo. Another is Donnaz from Val d'Aosta. An unorthodox choice, but one that I find equally enjoyable, is Lagrein Dunkel.

Sausages, with or without polenta

For an evenly balanced match: Ribolla from any Friuli zone or Cerasuolo di Vittoria from Sicily or Lacrimarosa, the copper-colored rosé from Avellino. For more vigorous emphasis on the wine: Valgella from Valtellina.

Beef

With steak or roast beef: Barolo, Spanna, Vino Nobile, Taurasi, or a strong southern red such as Salice Salentino. With casseroles: Chianti Classico, Chianti Rufina, Carmignano, all of *riserva* class. With boiled beef, particularly when it is a part of *bollito misto,* that prodigious Italian assemblage of boiled meats that includes *cotechino,* tongue, chicken, and calf's head: if you are in Italy, anywhere between Parma and Bologna, the happiest choice is a dry Lambrusco; if you are not, or are unable to overcome an aversion to spritzy red wine, Barbera d'Asti or Barbera dell'Oltrepò.

Birds

When roasted or grilled, whether they are chicken or game birds: any fine red wine from the nebbiolo grape (see Big Reds, pages 19–30 and Medium-Range Reds, pages 90–8), favoring the lighter examples for chicken or turkey and the more robust for the wild fowl. With casseroles: the same recommendation for beef casseroles is valid, which may be alternated with a full white such as Arneis, S'Éleme, or Verduzzo Friulano. With chicken breasts: for richly sauced ones, Fiano di Avellino; for light, freshly flavored ones, Riesling from Friuli or from Colli Berici.

Lamb

With a rack of lamb, a gigot, or a truly Italian lamb such as the pan-roasted one with juniper berries in Marcella Hazan's *Classic Italian Cook Book,* a deep and subtle red: Tignanello, Sassicaia, Brunello di Montalcino from Biondi-Santi or Emilio Costanti, or Masi's Campo Fiorin. With baby lamb braised in white wine, Roman style, I used to do as the Romans do, drink Frascati; but the unctuous Frascati that once went so well with that milky-sweet meat is nearly extinct, so a more congenial Roman wine today would be a red: Cesanese del Piglio or Fiorano Rosso.

Pork

The simplicity of Italian pork dishes makes this an ideal meat against which to set off a good red wine. Any will do, but some I have liked particularly well are Pinot Nero, Teroldego, and Cannonau di Sorso-Sennori.

Veal

White wine with veal, however it is prepared, I find boring. Better a Cabernet from any of the northeastern regions, or a Veneto Merlot, or a Malbec.

Fish

Consider the intrinsic flavor intensity of the fish's flesh and that of the cooking method to which it is subjected. With freshwater fish—trout, perch, pike, whitefish—I like a fine but somewhat tart white, as light as possible if the fish is steamed, but more intense if it is grilled or served with a rich sauce. A representative range: Soave, Lugana, Erbaluce, Corvo, Gavi dei Gavi, Verdicchio, Rapitala', or Torgiano. With white-fleshed saltwater fish—striped bass, sea bass, porgy, red snapper, sole, halibut—that has been either steamed or grilled, a full white: Albana *secco,* Pinot Bianco or Grigio, Chardonnay, or Tocai Friulano. If it is fried, baked, or in a casserole: one of the lighter reds already mentioned in this connection on page 232. A similar choice of red wine would apply to dark-fleshed fish, to squid, to clams or mussels in soup, or any other fish soup. (The late Alberto Denti di Pirajno, one of Italy's most adventurous gastronomes, had an intriguing choice of wine for fish soup: Asti Spumante!) With salmon or sturgeon I would go for a light red with a bitter finish: St. Magdalener or Lago di Caldaro served no warmer than 55°F. With shrimp, lobster, or crab: Pinot Bianco del Collio or Montecarlo Bianco.

Cheese

With the exception of Parmigiano-Reggiano, cheese blurs the fine taste impressions that we look for in a great red wine. With most cheeses I prefer a firm, incisive white, such as Tocai or Fiano. With superripe cheeses, one of Italy's sherrylike wines: Vernaccia di Oristano, Malvasia di Bosa, or Marsala Vergine.

With some foods I find wine unpleasant: smoked fish or caviar, for example. With raw shellfish I don't find wine disagreeable, only superfluous: a raw oyster, clam, or sea urchin supplies its own delicious juice. To have wine with chocolate in any form is a waste of time, or at least of wine. And a great sweet wine is not half so fascinating with dessert as it is alone.

These suggestions express my preferences and are presented to the reader only as possible choices. There are alternatives beyond count, some of which, to another's palate, may be even more appealing. What is important is to make the palate do its work, inasmuch as no wine is ever "right" or "wrong" until our taste buds have discovered it as such for themselves.

Coupling wine with food is an expression of a person's style that is comparable to the way he chooses the colors, textures, and cut of his wardrobe. We should no more wish to slip another's taste over our own than to slip into someone else's clothes. What matters about style is not how closely it corresponds to canons of correctness. It is always correct when it is consistently and genuinely our own.

LETTING WINES BREATHE

The prevailing opinion in Italy is that red wines that have been aged in wood for a long time should be opened well in advance. Until recently, I agreed, but I have now come to the opposite view.

At the schools my wife and I have run in Bologna and Venice for several years, I have opened a few thousand bottles for our students. Following tradition, I used to leave some of them open for an hour or more before pouring them for the class. In time, I began to notice that when I presented the wine, the bouquet it had displayed when just opened had thinned out, and the vigor of its flavor had begun to flag.

I thereupon experimented with pairs of identical wines, opening one in advance and the other just a few minutes before tasting it. Although the wine that had breathed did taste mellower in some cases, it seemed to me that in nearly every instance it had less bouquet, less freshness, and less energy than the other.

Since contrary opinions do exist on the subject, my suggestion is that anyone seriously interested in aged, weighty Italian red wines may find it worth his while to experiment, as I have done, with one or more pairs of wines. So as not to tax too greatly one's objectivity, it is advisable to mark one of the labels for later identification and to mask both bottles before pouring.

My custom now is to open a Barolo, a Taurasi, or a similarly weighty red not more than thirty minutes before serving. All lighter wines I open just before pouring. If the wine has thrown off deposit and must be decanted. I place a saucer above the decanter and a few ice cubes over the saucer. This chills the air above the wine without noticeably cooling the wine itself and, by inhibiting the intake of oxygen, maintains the bouquet and flavor nearly intact.

All the airing a wine needs can be administered after it is served by swirling it vigorously in a suitably large glass.

A frequent observation is that wine seems to taste better as the meal progresses. I don't believe the air has anything to do with it, but rather that our taste buds, coated with food, are less irritated by astringency and sourness.

TEMPERATURE

Most people, Americans perhaps more than others, drink white wines too cold and reds too warm. Excessive cold blocks flavor; too much heat flattens it.

Practically all Italian whites should be consumed at not less than 46° to 48°F (8° to 9°C). A few of the fuller whites, such as those from Friuli, Piedmont's Arneis, Avellino's Fiano or Greco di Tufo, Tuscany's Vernaccia di San Gimignano, are better at 55°F (13°C). All light red wines are best served no warmer than 55°. The biggest red wines are perfect at 65°F (18°C). Sweet wines should be served the coldest, at 40°F (5°C).

When serving wine, the proper temperature is the one factor to which one should give the utmost consideration, for no other is so vital to its appreciation.

The Rules

How Italian Wine Production Is Regulated

D.O.C.

These initials, used throughout this book and in most references to Italian wine, stand for Denominazione di Origine Controllata, which may be translated as "controlled appellation of origin." The term was coined by a comprehensive wine statute adopted by Italy in 1963, modeled on the French *appellation contrôlée* laws.

Inasmuch as the D.O.C. statute has been credited with bringing Italian wines up to international standards of reliability, it is worth our while to examine briefly how it works and what assurances it offers the consumer.

The words *Denominazione di Origine Controllata* on a label signify that the wine in the bottle was produced from an approved single variety or blend of grapes, grown and vinified according to official guidelines, within a specific and limited territory.

Nearly five hundred wines bear D.O.C. appellations, but we need not be daunted by such a crowd of unfamiliar names. Once we have learned a few of them and understood how they are bestowed, the new ones that come our way will seem less strange. The most useful discovery we can make is that most D.O.C. appellations fall into one of two groups.

One group is composed of some of the oldest, and consequently some of the most familiar, names in Italian wine. Barolo, Chianti, Frascati, Soave, and Valpolicella are a few examples. In this group only one name appears, since that of the wine is identical with the name of the town, valley, or other geographic entity where it originates.

In the second group, there are two parts to the D.O.C. name. One part names the grape variety employed, and the other part names the restricted place of origin, although not necessarily in that sequence. Examples of this usage are Barbera D'Alba, Colli Berici Cabernet, Collio Pinot Bianco, Verdicchio dei Castelli di Jesi, Vernaccia di San Gimignano. In the above, Barbera, Cabernet, Pinot Bianco, Verdicchio, and Vernaccia are the grapes, and the names linked to them are the place, the two together forming the name of the wine. In those cases where the wine is a blend of grapes, only the color is identified, together with the place name, as in Bianco di Custoza, or Franciacorta Rosso. There is a much smaller third group composed of invented names that are neither geographic nor grape names, such as Botticino, Buttafuoco, Est! Est!! Est!!!, Gutturnio, and Sangue di Giuda. This category includes few classified wines—and none of great importance—but it is swollen by many non-D.O.C. bottlings, some of which are among the best in Italy. We'll discuss them in more detail a little further on.

The following examples of a red and a white, taken from the two major groups of classified wines described above, illustrate what stands behind a D.O.C. appellation and what requirements must be met to earn it.

Barolo

A red wine bearing this appellation must be made exclusively of the nebbiolo grape, grown on hilly vineyards, in a restricted territory that includes the town of Barolo in southern Piedmont. Barolo must reach a minimum of 13 percent alcohol, and it must be aged three years, two of them in wood, before it can be released. When qualified as *riserva,* it must be aged four years, and with five years' aging it becomes *riserva speciale.*

Collio Pinot Bianco

It is made exclusively from the pinot blanc grape grown only on sloping vineyards within the precisely mapped out limits of an area known as Collio in the region of Friuli in northeastern Italy. The wine must be dry, must be full-bodied, and must attain a minimum alcohol level of 12½ percent.

The wine law also regulates what is the maximum yield per acre for each appellation, how much must may be pressed from the grapes, what chemicals or other additives may be used in vinification and in what proportion, what minimum and maximum levels of acidity each wine must reach, and how the finished wine must look, smell, and taste.

In many ways, the Italian wine law is more severe than any other country's. If a vineyard's yield per acre is exceeded, it is assumed that the overall quality of the grapes has been diluted, and not only the excess but the entire crop is declassified. A lower ceiling than anywhere else is placed on the use of sulfur as a disinfectant. Fewer additives are permitted. Chaptalization, the French method of adding sugar to the must in order to raise the alcohol content of wine, is forbidden. French *appellation contrôlée* wines destined for domestic consumption are not required to state the percentage of alcohol by volume on the label. Italian D.O.C. wines must.

No more than one classified wine may be produced in a single appellation zone, whereas in France, for example, while a particular Burgundy may qualify as Chambertin, a lesser wine can still be entitled to the prestige of the appellation Bourgogne. In Piedmont, on the other hand, a great deal of wine is made from the fine nebbiolo grape, but only a small portion of it is allowed to bear a controlled appellation. The rest must be sold as unclassified Nebbiolo.

On the face of it, Italy's D.O.C. statute seems a formidable instrument for the application of standards of quality to what was once the most anarchic, and still is the most heterogeneous, production of wine on earth. A closer look reveals that, as with most laws, there is a gap between intent and effect.

It is true that to disqualify a vineyard's entire harvest because of overproduction is as severe as it is unprecedented. It is also true, however, that prescribed yields are extraordinarily permissive, and in areas where high-quality wines are made they exceed actual production.

It is true that Italy forbids its winemakers the use of sugar that is so liberally allowed the French and Germans. But it is also true that in many instances it permits the use of up to 15 percent concentrated musts made from strong southern wines. It is a practice that favors the South's lame economy, as much of Italian economic policy does, but it defeats the efforts to preserve the local character of those wines that the law was designed to protect. Fortunately, dedicated makers of fine wines decline this option, whose effects may be noted in the dull offerings of many cooperatives and commercially oriented wineries.

It is true that Italian producers, unlike their French colleagues, are

instructed on how long to age some of their red wines in wood. It is a
measure that was intended to shield the traditional character of Italy's big
reds from exploitative practices. But it forces producers to make wines
that are sometimes tarrier and more astringent than they and their customers would like. And in light vintages, which are not at all uncommon, it sentences short-lived wines to barrel and cellar aging they do not
need.

Its shortcomings notwithstanding, the D.O.C. statute has done as
much as can be expected of any law. In disciplining the use of hundreds
of wine names, it has brought order out of chaos. When we pick up a
bottle of D.O.C. wine, we can now assume that it is what it claims to
be, of the grapes and from the place its name declares. It is the same
assumption of authenticity we have long been accustomed to make about
French and German wines.

But authenticity, while it may carry implications of quality, is not
the same as quality. Those who have experienced disappointment with
classified growths from Burgundy or Bordeaux, or with *qualitätswein mit
prädikat* from Germany, already know that although laws can keep
winemakers reasonably honest, they can't compel them to make their
wine taste good. Excellence cannot be legislated. It proceeds from a
delicate collaboration between producer and consumer, generated by the
will of the first and nourished by the appreciation—in other words, the
readiness to pay the appropriate price—of the second.

D.O.C.G.,
THE GUARANTEED CONTROLLED APPELLATION

What we won't find among the classified names of Italian wines is the
equivalent of the French *cru* and the German *lage,* a recognized vineyard
where soil, exposure, microclimate, and local flora endow the wine made
on that land with distinctive character. It is not because they don't exist
that they haven't been officially acknowledged. Wherever vines are cultivated, there are plots capable of producing grapes of superior quality.
Italy's share of such plots is abundant, and their location is well known
to growers, producers, and even some bureaucrats. But to transform
common knowledge into an official classification of noble growths would
stir up more turbulence than the wobbly equilibrium of Italian wine
politics could withstand.

Instead of singling out growths of superior merit, Italy has devised a special classification that guarantees standards of quality for every producer in a designated appellation. This classification is known as Denominazione di Origine Controllata e Garantita, *"controlled and guaranteed appellation of origin,"* better known as D.O.C.G.

When a wine moves up from D.O.C. status to D.O.C.G., every producer of that wine must submit samples to an official tasting panel during varying stages of vinification and aging. A wine that clears all the hurdles is awarded a government seal to be placed over the bottle top that guarantees it has met the standards required of that appellation. The wines that do not meet D.O.C.G. requirements are declassified and can be sold only as table wine.

How well D.O.C.G. will work is far too early yet to know. The first wine to appear on the market with such a designation will be Vino Nobile di Montepulciano at the end of 1982. Others will be Barbaresco and Barolo in 1984 and Brunello di Montalcino in 1985. It will take more than one harvest bottled under D.O.C.G. supervision before one can begin to judge the results.

No one expects, however, that in taking the measure of an entire appellation, the examining commission can apply so fine a screen that only the finest examples will pass through. Those houses that are already making wine to self-imposed standards more exacting than those of the statute are counting not on the luster of a government guarantee, but on that of their own hard-earned reputations. But D.O.C.G. can still be a success, in those choice appellations it is designed to ennoble, if it nudges less meticulous producers up a few notches to higher levels of achievement.

VINO DA TAVOLA—UNCLASSIFIED WINES

In Italy, as in France and Germany, only a small proportion of total production bears a controlled appellation. The Italian proportion is about 12 percent. All the rest is known as *vino da tavola.* But, whereas in France and Germany such wine is indeed the common table wine its name implies, in Italy there are wines sold as plain *vino da tavola* that equal and sometimes surpass the finest of the D.O.C. appellations.

There are several reasons that so many exceptional Italian wines bear no official pedigree. There are growers who do not want to get entangled in the red tape that registering their vineyards for a designated appellation requires. Some are motivated by the ancestral reluctance, which most Italians share, to allow government intrusion into their affairs. Some prefer to promote their own coined trade name, rather than joining a multitude of producers competing for business with a wine bearing the same controlled name. Others make wine from grapes not approved for their area, such as cabernet sauvignon in Tuscany, for example, or pinot blanc in Apulia. Still others ignore official formulas that require the inclusion of white grapes in the Chianti blend or forbid the combination of merlot and cabernet in the Cabernet appellations of the Northeast.

Both D.O.C. and non-D.O.C. bottlings may, however, share the same grape names, since it is neither reasonable nor desirable to prohibit a producer from stating what grapes his wine is made from. But unclassified wines can link the name of the grape only to those place names that are not restricted by a controlled origin designation. For example, Barbera d'Asti is a controlled D.O.C. name for a wine made in a restricted area of Piedmont from the barbera grape. If, within that same area, a wine made from barbera does not for any reason meet D.O.C. requirements, it may still be called Barbera, but not d'Asti. The producer could, in such an instance, call it Barbera del Piemonte ("Barbera from Piedmont"), a generic and looser geographic indication.

Just as D.O.C. wines are a fraction of Italy's total production, elite unclassified wines are a small part of *vino da tavola* production. Most *vino da tavola* is plain indeed, much of it being sold in bulk, by the demijohn; and of this ordinary grade little is exported. Nevertheless, a few of Italy's unclassified wines are made by its most skilled and conscientious producers, exercising controls over grape selection, vinification, and aging that for scrupulousness are unsurpassed anywhere. Exploring the unclassified wines of Italy can be time well spent, for humbly cloaked as table wine go some of the country's noblest bottles.

VINO TIPICO

This is a new category adopted by the wine-producing countries of the Common Market. When it goes into effect in Italy, it will include many wines now labeled *vino da tavola*. It will be a classification a step below D.O.C., awarding recognition to wines that are made from approved grapes in traditional areas under more elastic controls but still conveying character typical of the zone of production.

CONSORTIUMS

A consortium—*consorzio* in Italian—is a voluntary association of producers that provides its members with technical assistance and some promotional support. Members must submit their wine for examination and approval to the consortium's laboratory and tasting panel, where standards sometimes more rigid than those of the D.O.C. law are applied. Participating producers are furnished a label with the *consorzio*'s emblem to wrap around the neck of their bottles. The best-known such emblem is probably Chianti Classico's black rooster.

Many consortiums, particularly the Chianti Classico, Chianti Putto, Asti Spumante, Barolo, and Barbaresco, render useful service to their members, and to some of them the government has delegated supervisory roles. They are more valuable to the producer than to the consumer. Several hundred wineries may belong to a *consorzio,* each with a different idea of what is good wine. And since the associations are voluntary, there are important, self-sufficient producers who choose not to belong. A consortium's emblem on the bottle is no guarantee of quality, nor is its absence a mark of infamy.

A Glossary of the More Common
Terms Used on Italian Wine Labels

WORDS INDICATING VINTAGE DATE

annata: year

vendemmia: harvest

TERMS RELATED TO APPELLATION STATUS
AND OTHER ATTRIBUTES

classico: produced in the older, traditional zone within a controlled appellation

Denominazione di Origine Controllata: Controlled Appellation of Origin

Denominazione di Origine Controllata e Garantita: Controlled and Guaranteed Appellation of Origin

riserva: the wine has undergone extra aging for a prescribed period that varies from wine to wine

riserva speciale: used on Barolo when it has undergone one more year's aging than a *riserva,* for a total of five years

superiore: the wine has at least 1 percent more alcohol than the minimum required and, usually, more aging

vino da tavola: unclassified table wine

V.Q.P.R.D. (Vini di Qualita' Prodotti in Regioni Delimitate): quality wines produced in delimited zones; a Common Market term qualifying all D.O.C. wines

BOTTLING TERMS

imbottigliato all'origine: bottled at the source (may be used only by estate-bottlers) *imbottigliato da:* bottled by (followed by the producer's name); does not denote estate-bottling

imbottigliato dal viticoltore: bottled by the grower (may be used only by a grower bottling his own wine)

imbottigliato nella zona di produzione: bottled in the production zone; not estate-bottled

TERMS DESCRIBING OR QUALIFYING THE PRODUCER

abbadia: abbey

azienda agricola: farm (may be used only if the wine is made from grapes grown and vinified on the property)

azienda vinicola: winery

azienda vitivinicola: grape-growing and winemaking company

cantina: cellar

cantina sociale: cooperative winery

casa vinicola: winery

cascina: farmhouse

castello: castle

convento: convent

ditta: firm, company

enotecnico: oenologist, winemaker

eredi: heirs

fattoria: farmstead

fratelli (f.lli): brothers

parroco: parish priest

podere: farm

produttore: producer

produttori riuniti: united producers

proprietà: property of

stabilimento: plant (as in bottling plant)

tenuta: estate

vigna or *vigneto* or *maso:* vineyard (term precedes the vineyard name and may be used only if the grapes from which the wine is made are actually grown on that property)

vignaiolo: grower

villa: country manor

viticoltore: grower

S.p.A.: Incorporated

WORDS DESCRIBING TASTE, COLOR, OR SPARKLE

abboccato: slightly sweet

amabile: sweet

asciutto: dry

cerasuolo: deep pink; darkest of the rosés

chiaretto: medium pink

dolce: decidedly sweet

fermentazione naturale: contains CO_2 produced naturally during fermentation

frizzante: lightly sparkling

liquoroso: fortified dessert wine

metodo champenois: sparkling wine fermented in the bottle by the champagne method

passito: sweet dessert wine made from partly shriveled grapes

rosato or rosé: light pink

rosso: red

secco: dry

spumante: sparkling

Three Examples
of Italian Labels

Example of a *vino da tavola,* an unclassified wine sold under a proprietary or coined name

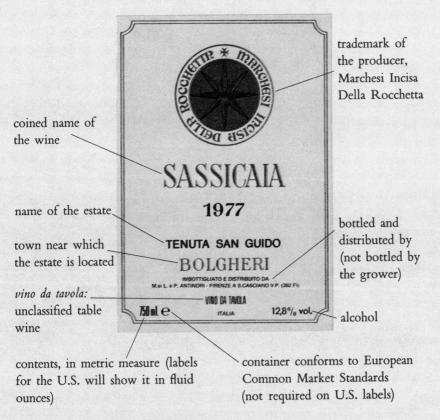

trademark of
the producer,
Marchesi Incisa
Della Rocchetta

coined name of
the wine

name of the estate

town near which
the estate is located

bottled and
distributed by
(not bottled by
the grower)

vino da tavola:
unclassified table
wine

alcohol

contents, in metric measure (labels
for the U.S. will show it in fluid
ounces)

container conforms to European
Common Market Standards
(not required on U.S. labels)

SASSICAIA
1977
TENUTA SAN GUIDO
BOLGHERI
IMBOTTIGLIATO E DISTRIBUITO DA
M.si L. e P. ANTINORI - FIRENZE A S.CASCIANO V.P. (382 FI)
VINO DA TAVOLA
750 mℓ ℮   ITALIA   12,8% vol.

Collio: name of
controlled appellation
zone, must be fol-
lowed by

"controlled
appellation of
origin" and

name of approved
grape used

town where farm
is located

alcohol

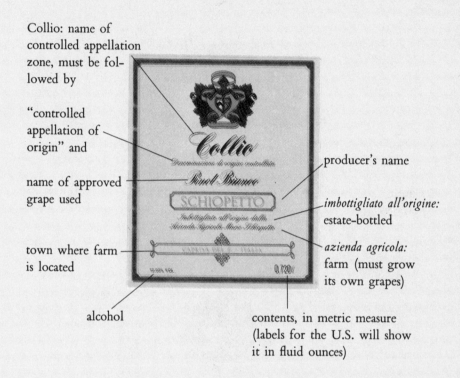

producer's name

imbottigliato all'origine:
estate-bottled

azienda agricola:
farm (must grow
its own grapes)

contents, in metric measure
(labels for the U.S. will show
it in fluid ounces)

Example of a D.O.C. (controlled appellation) wine in which the name
of the wine is composed of the controlled district name plus the name
of the approved grape variety from which it is made

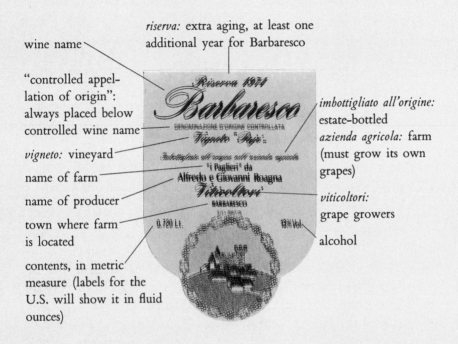

riserva: extra aging, at least one
additional year for Barbaresco

wine name

"controlled appel-
lation of origin":
always placed below
controlled wine name

vigneto: vineyard

name of farm

name of producer

town where farm
is located

contents, in metric
measure (labels for the
U.S. will show it in fluid
ounces)

imbottigliato all'origine:
estate-bottled

azienda agricola: farm
(must grow its own
grapes)

viticoltori:
grape growers

alcohol

Example of a D.O.C. (controlled appellation) wine in which the name
of the wine is the same as that of the locality where it originated

Italy's Controlled
Appellation Zones

The maps on pages 254-93 are intended to show, region by region, where Italy's D.O.C. production zones are located. They should also be used as reference to clarify the numerous geographic citations that appear throughout the text. In addition, accompanying the main text are eight topographic maps that focus on selected areas, illustrating through the use of relief the nature of their terrain. To help the reader place these areas, their exact location has been indicated on the appropriate regional map in this section.

Locating a specific D.O.C. zone by matching the graphic pattern in the keys to the one in the maps will, in many instances, require close attention. The territories of different appellations within the same region sometimes overlap or even coincide and, consequently, so do the symbols that identify them. The zones of two regions—Piedmont and Trentino-Alto Adige—have been distributed over more than one map in order to reduce the number of overlaps and improve legibility.

At times, the name of an appellation is identical to that of the only D.O.C. wine produced within it; for example, Chianti Classico. In such cases only one name appears next to the key. Sometimes, several different wines are entitled to the same controlled appellation, as for example, the reds and whites of the Collio. In those instances the appellation name is followed by the names of all the wines that are permitted to bear it.

In Italy, as in other countries with laws similar to D.O.C., wines carrying a controlled appellation name represent only a small part of all production. For each region, figures are given that show what proportion of their total production is D.O.C. However dry such figures may appear to be, they tell a revealing story about the geographic distribution, in Italy, of wine produced under strict controls. These statistics, which reflect the results of the 1979 and 1980 harvests, are derived from information supplied by the Italian Trade Commission in New York.

NOTE: The regional maps are arranged, according to Italian usage, in geographic rather than alphabetical order, zigzagging West to East and North to South, and concluding with the islands of Sicily and Sardinia. The only exceptions are Liguria and Abruzzi. For necessities of design, the first has been placed after Val d'Aosta instead of after Friuli-Venezia Giulia, and the second precedes Basilicata instead of Apulia.

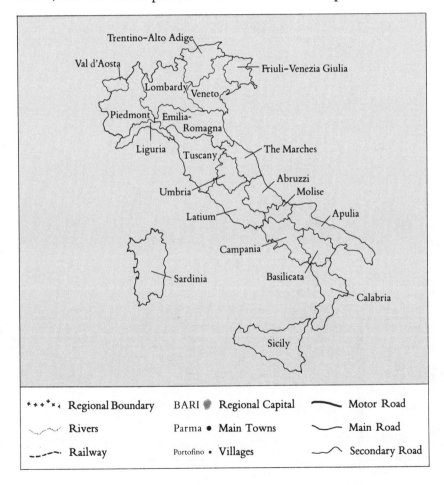

The above symbols are used in all the regional maps on the following pages.

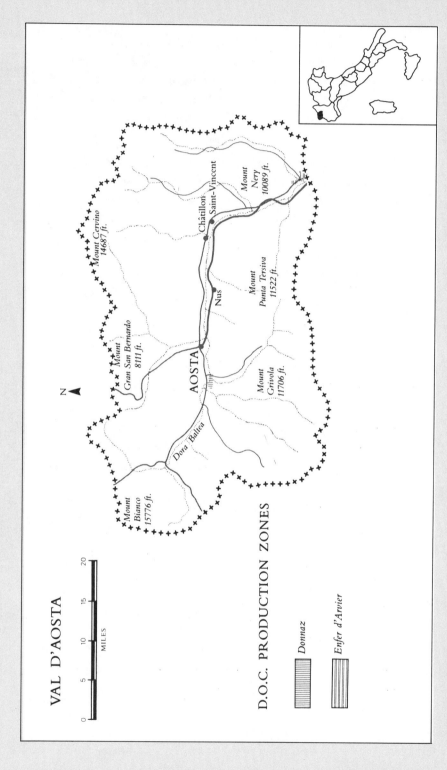

VAL D'AOSTA

MILES
0   5   10   15   20

N

Mount
Bianco
15776 ft.

Dora Baltea

Mount
Gran San Bernardo
8111 ft.

Mount Cervino
14687 ft.

AOSTA

Nus

Châtillon
Saint-Vincent

Mount Nery
10089 ft.

Mount
Grivola
11706 ft.

Mount
Punta Tersiva
11522 ft.

D.O.C. PRODUCTION ZONES

Donnaz

Enfer d'Arvier

D.O.C. bottlings are slightly above 2 percent of all wine made in Val d'Aosta, whose total production is the smallest of any Italian region.

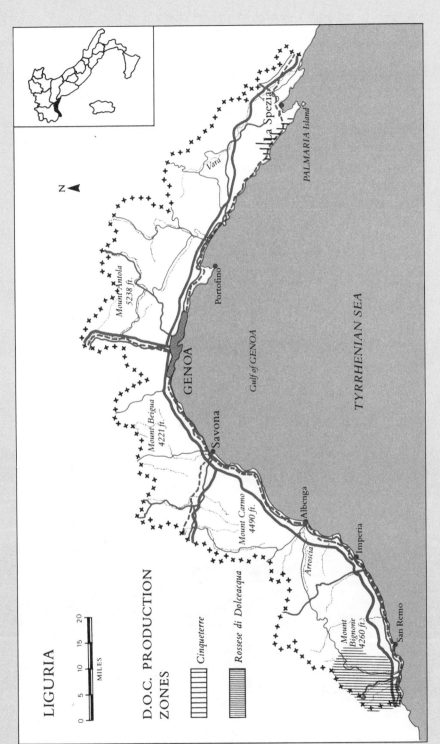

Ranks next to last both in overall production and in D.O.C. wines, which are but 1½ precent of its total.

PIEDMONT

With thirty-six D.O.C. appellations, Piedmont outstrips by far every other Italian region. In terms of quality and variety, it is the preeminent red wine area of Italy. Its total wine production, which can vary sharply, depending on the climate, usually places it seventh in the nation. The D.O.C. production is 22 percent of the total, well above the national average. Note that there are five maps here for Piedmont because it was impossible to present so many zones, which overlap, on a single map.

D.O.C. PRODUCTION ZONES

Boca

Bramaterra

Carema

Erbaluce di Caluso, or Caluso Passito

Fara

Gattinara

Ghemme

Lessona

Sizzano

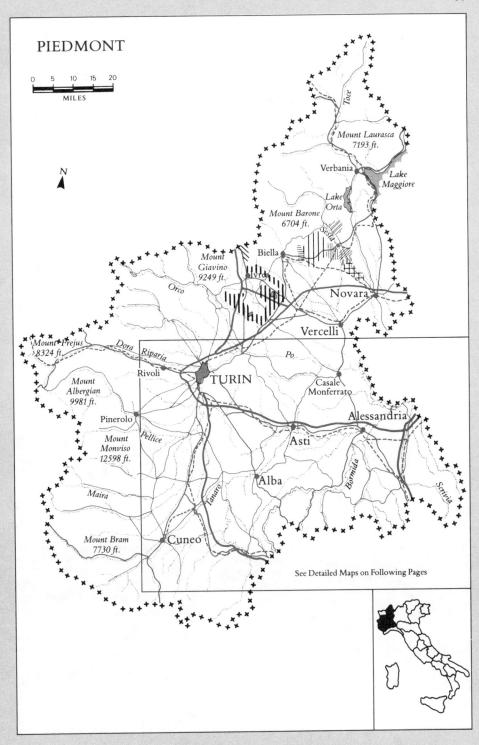

PIEDMONT 2

D.O.C. PRODUCTION ZONES

Barbera d'Alba

Barbera d'Asti

Barbera del Monferrato

Nebbiolo d'Alba

Rubino di Cantavenna

PIEDMONT 3

D.O.C. PRODUCTION ZONES

Asti Spumante, Moscato Naturale d'Asti, Moscato d'Asti Spumante

Freisa d'Asti

Freisa di Chieri

Grignolino d'Asti

Malvasia di Casorzo d'Asti

Malvasia di Castelnuovo Don Bosco

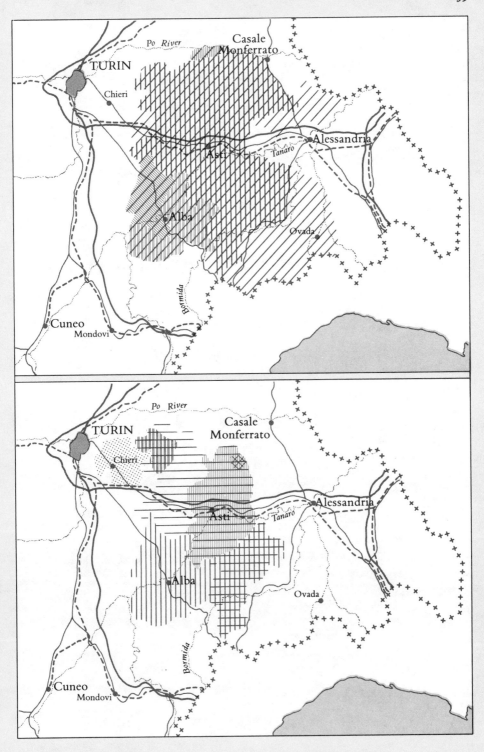

PIEDMONT 4

D.O.C. PRODUCTION ZONES

Barbaresco

Barolo

Colli Tortonesi
Barbera and Cortese

Dolcetto d'Alba

Dolcetto delle Langhe
Monregalesi

Dolcetto di Diano d'Alba

Dolcetto di Dogliani

PIEDMONT 5

D.O.C. PRODUCTION ZONES

Brachetto d'Acqui

Cortese dell'Alto Monferrato

Dolcetto d'Acqui

Dolcetto di Asti

Dolcetto di Ovada

Gavi or Cortese di Gavi

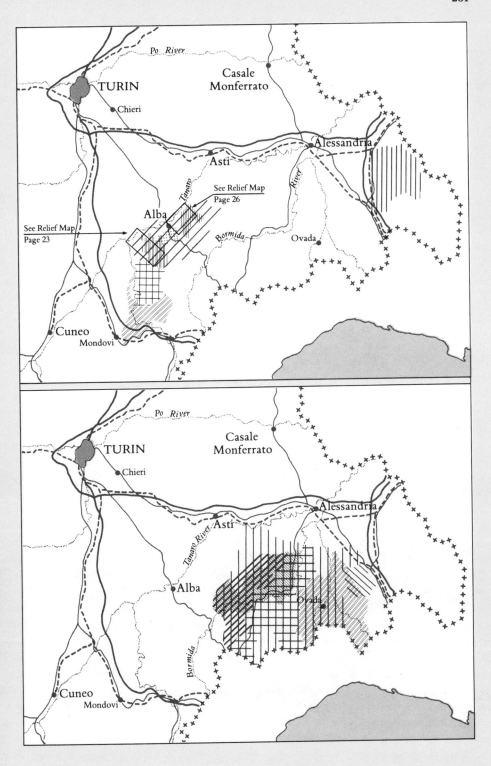

LOMBARDY

Hills, mountains, and lakeside plains give Lombardy's wine geography an exceptionally varied configuration. Although many different reds and whites are produced, the total quantity is moderate. Lombardy ranks eleventh among Italian regions. The percentage of D.O.C. production, however, is high, over 15 percent.

D.O.C. PRODUCTION ZONES

Botticino

Capriano del Colle
Bianco, Rosso

Cellatica

Colli Morenici del Garda
Bianco, Chiaretto, Rosato, Rubino

Franciacorta
Pinot Bianco, Rosso

Lugana

Oltrepò Pavese
Barbacarlo, Barbera, Bonarda, Buttafuoco,
Cortese, Moscato, Pinot (Bianco, Grigio,
Nero), Riesling (Italico, Renano), Rosso,
Sangue di Giuda

Riviera del Garda Bresciano
Chiaretto, Rosso

*Tocai di San Martino della
Battaglia*

Valcalepio
Bianco, Rosso

Valtellina
Valtellina, Valtellina Superiore
(Grumello, Inferno, Sassella,
Valgella), Sfurzàt or Sforzato

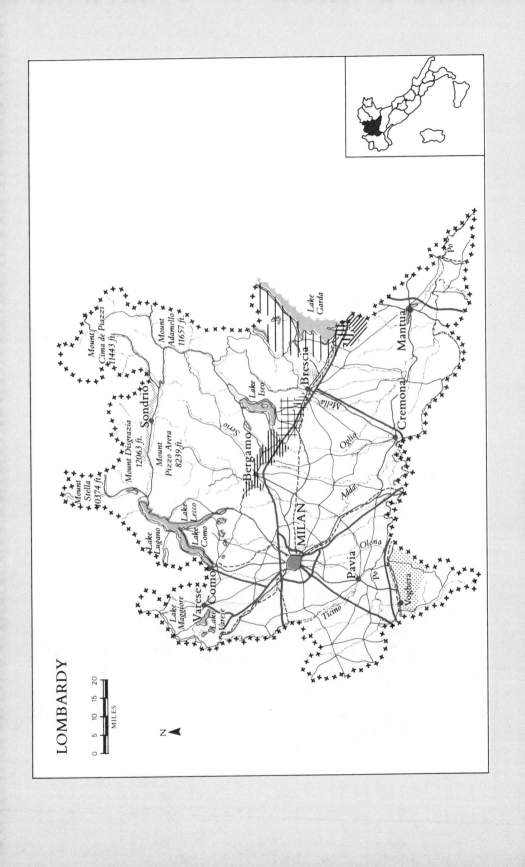

LOMBARDY

MILES
0   5   10   15   20

N

Mount
Cima de Piazzi
11443 ft

Mount
Adamello
11657 ft.

Lake
Garda

Mantua

Sondrio

Mount Disgrazia
12063 ft.

Mount
Pizzo Arera
8239 ft.

Serio

Lake
Iseo

Brescia

Cremona

Mella

Oglio

Po

Mount
Stella
10374 ft.

Lake
Lugano

Lake
Lecco

Lake
Como

Bergamo

Adda

MILAN

Olona

Pavia

Po

Voghera

Lake
Maggiore

Varese

Lake
Varese

Como

Ticino

TRENTINO–ALTO ADIGE

The Alto Adige, or northern half of this region, was once part of the Austrian Tyrol and to its German-speaking inhabitants is still known as the Südtirol. Here are produced some of Italy's most skillfully made wines. While Trentino–Alto Adige ranks only thirteenth in the nation in total production, an astounding 47 percent of its bottled wines carry D.O.C. designations. Note that there is more than one map here to encompass the numerous zones.

D.O.C. PRODUCTION ZONES

Alto Adige/Südtirol
Cabernet, Gewürztraminer, Lagrein, Malvasia/Malvasier, Merlot, Moscato, Giallo/ Goldenmuskateller, Moscato Rosa/Rosenmuskateller, Müller Thurgau, Pinot Bianco/ Weissburgunder, Pinot-Grigio/ Ruländer, Pinot Nero/ Blauburgunder, Riesling Renano/ Rheinriesling, Riesling Italico/ Welschriesling, Sauvignon, Schiava/Vernatsch, Sylvaner

Casteller

Trentino
Cabernet, Lagrein, Marzemino, Merlot, Moscato, Pinot Bianco, Pinot Nero, Riesling, Traminer Aromatico, Vin Santo

Valdadige/Etschtaler
Bianco, Rosso

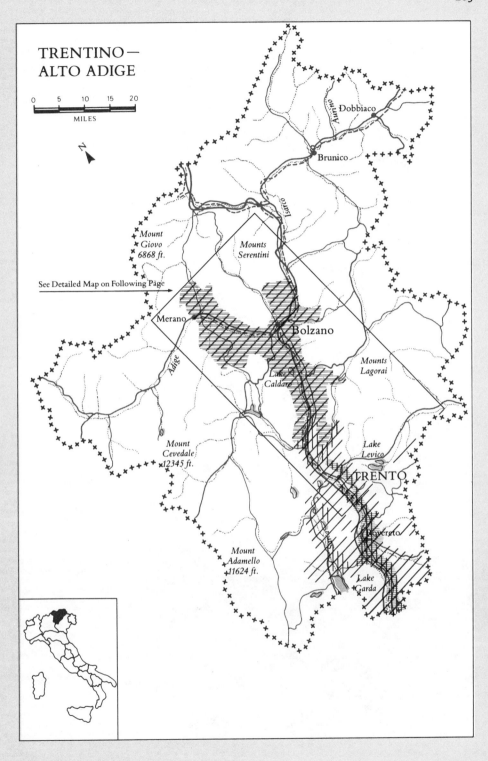

TRENTINO—
ALTO ADIGE

0   5   10   15   20
MILES

N

Mount
Giovo
×6868 ft.

Mounts
Serentini

Dobbiaco

Brunico

Aurino

Isarco

See Detailed Map on Following Page

Merano

Adige

Bolzano

Lake of
Caldaro

Mounts
Lagorai

Mount
Cevedale
×12345 ft.

Lake
Levico

TRENTO

Rovereto

Sarca

Mount
Adamello
×11624 ft.

Lake
Garda

TRENTINO–ALTO ADIGE 2

D.O.C. PRODUCTION ZONES

Caldaro

Colli di Bolzano/Bozner Leiten

Meranese di Collina/ Meraner

Santa Maddalena/St. Magdalener

Sorni
Bianco, Rosso, Rosato

Terlano/Terlaner
Riesling Italico/Welschriesling,
Riesling Renano/Rheinriesling,
Sauvignon, Sylvaner,
Terlano/Terlaner

Teroldego Rotaliano

Valle Isarco/Eisacktaler
Gewürztraminer,
Müller-Thurgau, Pinot Grigio/
Ruländer, Sylvaner, Veltliner

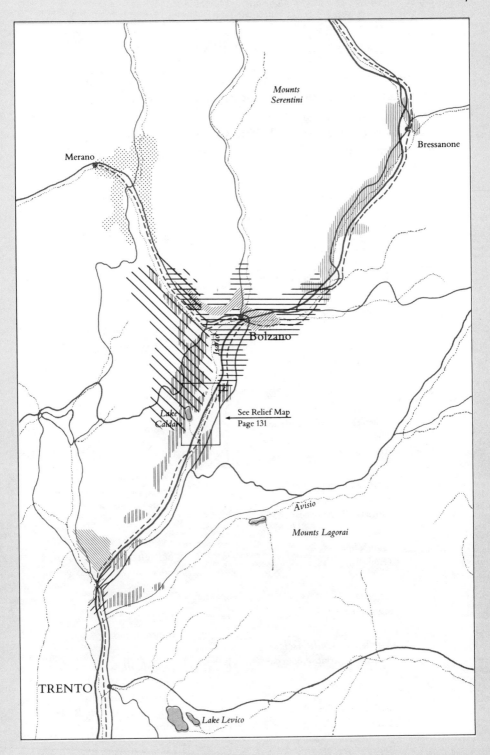

Mounts
Serentini

Bressanone

Merano

Bolzano

Isarco

Lake
Caldaro

See Relief Map
Page 131

Avisio

Mounts Lagorai

TRENTO

Lake Levico

VENETO

One of the most prolific Italian regions, the Veneto ranks third in the nation in total production. Two of its wines—Soave and Valpolicella—are among the most familiar names in wine in the world. D.O.C. wines account for 16 percent of the Veneto's total output, a far from negligible amount when one considers that nearly three hundred million gallons of wine are made here in a good year.

D.O.C. PRODUCTION ZONES

Bardolino
Bardolino, Bardolino Classico

Bianco di Custoza

Breganze
Bianco, Cabernet, Pinot Bianco, Pinot Nero, Rosso, Vespaiolo

Colli Berici
Cabernet, Garganega, Merlot, Pinot Bianco, Sauvignon, Tocai, Tocai Rosso

Colli Euganei
Bianco, Cabernet, Merlot, Moscato, Rosso, Tocai

Gambellara
Gambellara, Recioto, Vin Santo

Lugana
See also Lombardy

Montello e Colli Asolani
Cabernet, Merlot, Prosecco

Piave
Cabernet, Merlot, Tocai, Verduzzo

Pramaggiore
Cabernet, Merlot

Prosecco di Conegliano-Valdobbiadene, or Prosecco di Conegliano, or Prosecco di Valdobbiadene

Soave
Recioto di Soave, Soave, Soave Classico

Tocai di Lison
Largely coincides with Pramaggiore and extends into Friuli-Venezia Guilia

Tocai di S. Martino della Battaglia
Coincides with Lugana (see also Lombardy)

Valdadige
Bianco, Rosso

Valpolicella
Valpolicella, Valpolicella Classico, Valpolicella Valpantena, Recioto, Recioto Amarone

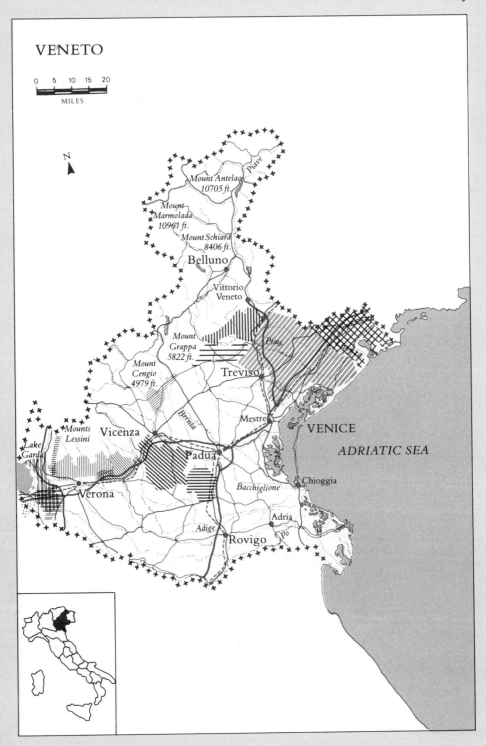

VENETO

0   5   10 15 20
MILES

N

Mount Antelao
10705 ft.

Piave

Mount
Marmolada
10961 ft.

Mount Schiara
8406 ft.

Belluno

Vittorio
Veneto

Mount
Grappa
5822 ft.

Piave

Mount
Cengio
4979 ft.

Treviso

Brenta

Mestre

Mounts
Lessini

Vicenza

VENICE

Lake
Garda

Padua

ADRIATIC SEA

Verona

Bacchiglione

Chioggia

Adige

Adria

Po

Rovigo

FRIULI–VENEZIA GIULIA

This largely hilly region on the Yugoslav border is the only one in Italy where white wines are held in greater esteem than the reds. Most of the varieties grown of both white and red grapes are of French origin, although the wine closest to the affections of its people, Tocai, is made from a purely local grape. Total production is small, ranking Friuli fourteenth among the regions. The D.O.C. proportion, on the other hand, is exceptionally high, 28 percent.

D.O.C. PRODUCTION ZONES

Aquileia
Cabernet, Merlot, Pinot Bianco,
Pinot Grigio, Refosco, Riesling
Renano, Tocai

Grave del Friuli
Cabernet, Merlot, Pinot Bianco,
Pinot Grigio, Refosco, Tocai,
Verduzzo

Collio Goriziano, or Collio
Bianco del Collio or Collio,
Cabernet Franc, Malvasia,
Merlot, Pinot Bianco, Pinot
Grigio, Riesling Italico,
Sauvignon, Tocai, Traminer

Isonzo
Cabernet, Malvasia Istriana,
Merlot, Pinot Bianco, Pinot
Grigio, Riesling Renano,
Sauvignon, Tocai, Traminer
Aromatico, Verduzzo

Colli Orientali del Friuli
Cabernet, Merlot, Picolit, Pinot
Bianco, Pinot Grigio, Pinot
Nero, Refosco, Ribolla,
Riesling Renano, Sauvignon,
Tocai, Verduzzo

Latisana
Cabernet, Merlot, Pinot Bianco,
Pinot Grigio, Refosco, Tocai,
Verduzzo

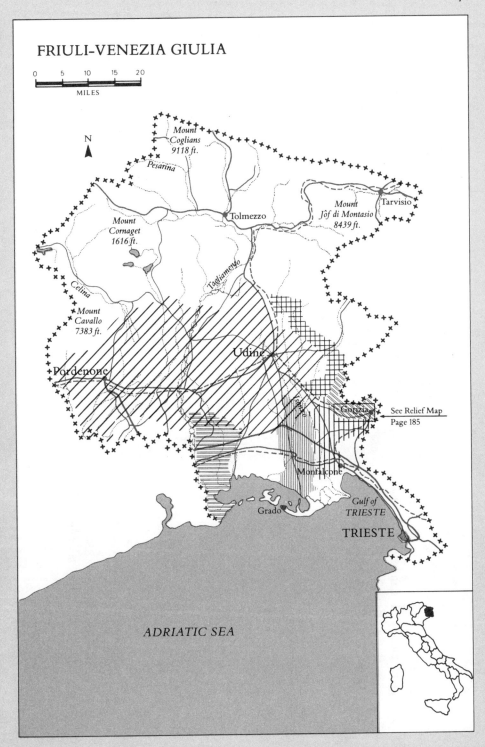

FRIULI-VENEZIA GIULIA

0   5   10   15   20
MILES

N

Mount
Coglians
9118 ft.

Pesarina

Tolmezzo

Mount
Jôf di Montasio
8439 ft.

Tarvisio

Mount
Cornaget
1616 ft.

Celina

Tagliamento

Mount
Cavallo
7383 ft.

Udine

Pordenone

Gorizia

See Relief Map
Page 185

Monfalcone

Gulf of
TRIESTE

Grado

TRIESTE

ADRIATIC SEA

EMILIA-ROMAGNA

The huge success of Lambrusco has helped boost Emilia-Romagna to the top spot in the list of Italy's most productive regions. Closer to home it is more admired for another red, Sangiovese di Romagna, and for a white, Albana. The large quantity of unclassified Lambrusco produced lowers its proportion of D.O.C. wines to a little less than 6 percent.

D.O.C. PRODUCTION ZONES

Monterosso Val d'Arda

Sangiovese di Romagna

Trebbiano di Romagna

Trebbianino Val Trebbia

Lambrusco di Sorbara

Lambrusco Gasparossa di Castelvetro

Lambrusco Reggiano

Lambrusco Salamino di Santa Croce

Albana di Romagna

Bianco di Scandiano

Colli Bolognesi—Monte San Pietro—Castelli Medioevali
Barbera, Bianco, Cabernet Sauvignon, Merlot, Pinot Bianco, Riesling Italico, Sauvignon

Gutturnio dei Colli Piacentini

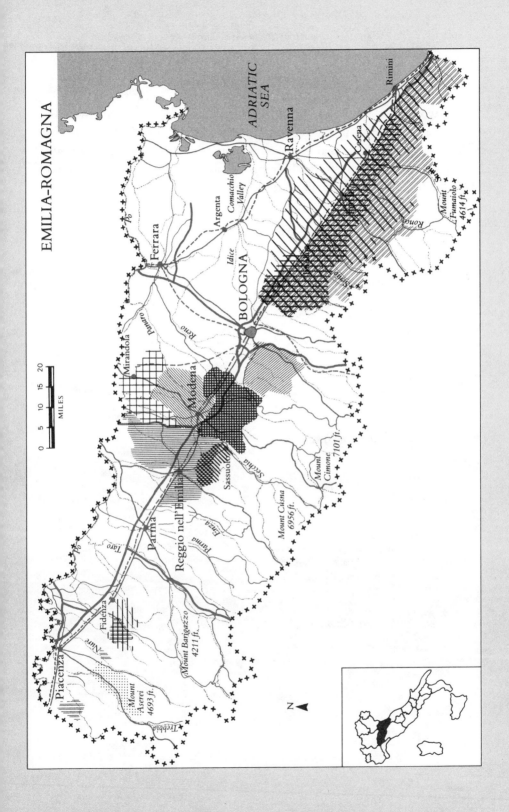

EMILIA-ROMAGNA

ADRIATIC
SEA

Rimini

Ravenna

Cesena

Forlì

Mount
Fumaiolo
4614 ft.

Po

Ferrara

Argenta

Comacchio
Valley

Idice

BOLOGNA

Reno

Mirandola

Panaro

Modena

Secchia

Mount Cimone
7101 ft.

Sassuolo

Mount Cusna
6956 ft.

Parma

Reggio nell'Emilia

Enza

Parma

Taro

Po

Piacenza

Fidenza

Nure

Mount Barigazzo
4211 ft.

Mount
Aserei
4693 ft.

Trebbia

MILES

0 5 10 15 20

N

TUSCANY

Two grapes dominate Tuscany's substantial production: sangiovese, responsible for all its D.O.C. reds, and trebbiano, principal source of its whites. Tuscany's total wine output ranks it sixth in the country, with over one hundred fifty million gallons in good years. The proportion of D.O.C. wines is an impressive 35 percent.

D.O.C. PRODUCTION ZONES

Bianco della Valdinievole

Bianco di Pitigliano

Bianco Vergine Val di Chiana

Brunello di Montalcino

Carmignano

Chianti
Colli Aretini, Colli Fiorentini,
Colline Pisane, Colline Senesi,
Montalbano, Rufina

Chianti Classico

Elba
Bianco, Rosso

Montecarlo

Montescudaio
Bianco, Rosso

Morellino di Scansano

Parrina
Bianco, Rosso

Rosso delle Colline Lucchesi

Vernaccia di San Gimignano

Vino Nobile di Montepulciano

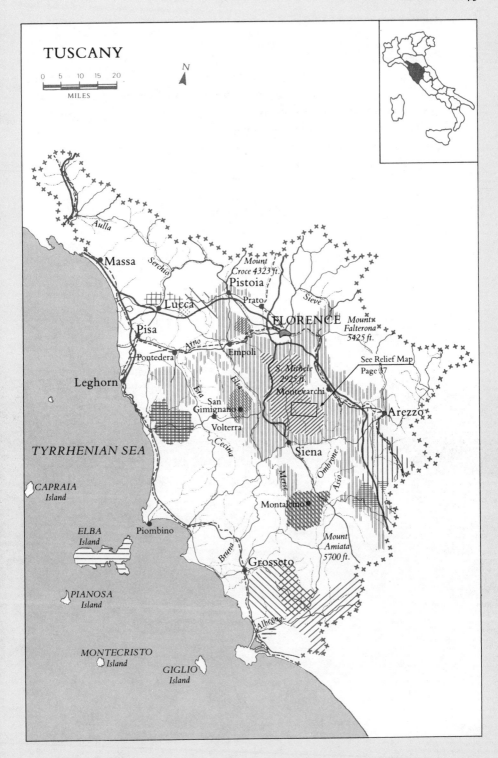

TUSCANY

0 5 10 15 20
MILES

N

Aulla

Massa

Serchio

Mount
Croce 4323 ft.

Pistoia

Prato

Sieve

Lucca

FLORENCE

Mount
Falterona
5425 ft.

Pisa

Arno

Empoli

Pontedera

See Relief Map
Page 37

Leghorn

Elsa

S. Michele
3925 ft.

Era

San
Gimignano

Montevarchi

Volterra

Arezzo

Cecina

TYRRHENIAN SEA

Siena

CAPRAIA
Island

Merse

Ombrone

Asso

Montalcino

ELBA
Island

Piombino

Bruna

Mount
Amiata
5700 ft.

PIANOSA
Island

Grosseto

MONTECRISTO
Island

Albegna

GIGLIO
Island

UMBRIA

Among the wines of Umbria, which on the whole are similar to the more modest of the Tuscan wines, those of the Torgiano appellation stand tall. Total production is one of the smallest in Italy, ranking Umbria sixteenth in the country. The D.O.C. proportion, however, is exceptional, having tripled during the past three years to reach the second-highest level in Italy, 36 percent.

D.O.C. PRODUCTION ZONES

Colli Altotiberini
Bianco, Rosso, Rosato

Colli del Trasimeno
Bianco, Rosso

Colli Perugini
Bianco, Rosso, Rosato

Orvieto

Orvieto Classico

Montefalco
Rosso, Sagrantino

Torgiano
Bianco, Rosso

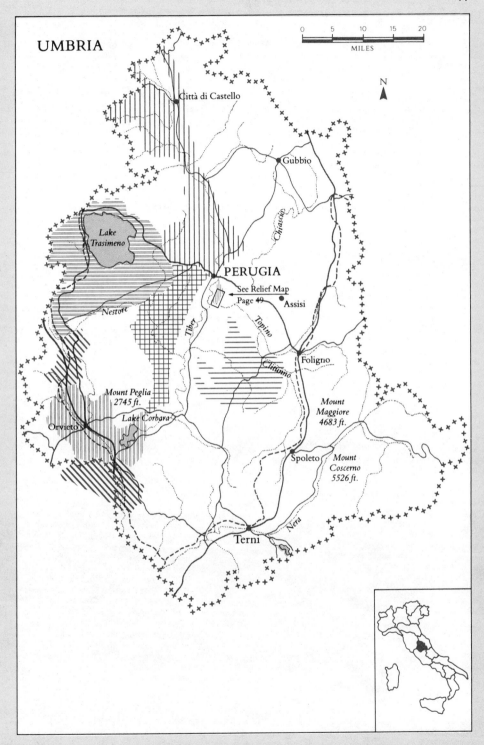

UMBRIA

Città di Castello

Gubbio

Chiascio

Lake Trasimeno

PERUGIA

See Relief Map
Page 49

Assisi

Nestore

Tiber

Topino

Clitunno

Foligno

Mount Peglia
2745 ft.

Lake Corbara

Orvieto

Mount
Maggiore
4683 ft.

Spoleto

Mount
Coscerno
5526 ft.

Nera

Terni

N

0   5   10   15   20
MILES

THE MARCHES

This central Adriatic region has made its greatest impact abroad with the product of a native grape, Verdicchio. Locally, a red—Rosso Conero—is far more abundant. Marches's production places it neatly in the middle of the national rankings: tenth. The D.O.C. proportion of it is substantially lower than the national average, 5½ percent.

D.O.C. PRODUCTION ZONES

Bianchello del Metauro

Bianco dei Colli Maceratesi

Falerio dei Colli Ascolani

Rosso Conero

Rosso Piceno

Sangiovese dei Colli Pesaresi

Verdicchio dei Castelli di Jesi

Verdicchio di Matelica

Vernaccia di Serrapetrona

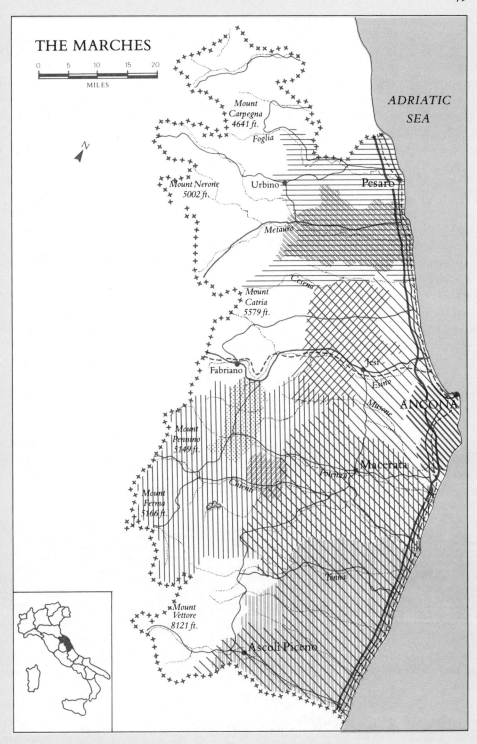

THE MARCHES

0 5 10 15 20
MILES

N

ADRIATIC SEA

Mount
Carpegna
4641 ft.

Foglia

Mount Nerone
5002 ft.

Urbino

Pesaro

Metauro

Cesena

Mount
Catria
5579 ft.

Fabriano

Jesi

Esino

Misone

ANCONA

Mount
Pennino
5149 ft.

Potenza

Macerata

Chienti

Mount
Ferma
5166 ft.

Mount
Vettore
8121 ft.

Tema

Ascoli Piceno

LATIUM

The flood of popular soft whites from the Castelli Romani zone and surrounding areas swells Latium's output, placing it fifth in Italy for total wine produced. Of this, only a little over 8 percent—decidedly less than the national average—is D.O.C.

D.O.C. PRODUCTION ZONES

Aleatico di Gradoli

Aprilia
Trebbiano, Merlot, Sangiovese

Cerveteri
Bianco, Rosso

Cesanese del Piglio, or Piglio

Cesanese di Olevano Romano, or Olevano Romano

Colli Albani

Colli Lanuvini

Cori
Bianco, Rosso

Est! Est!! Est!!! di Montefiascone

Frascati

Marino

Montecompatri Colonna

Orvieto

Velletri
Bianco, Rosso

Zagarolo

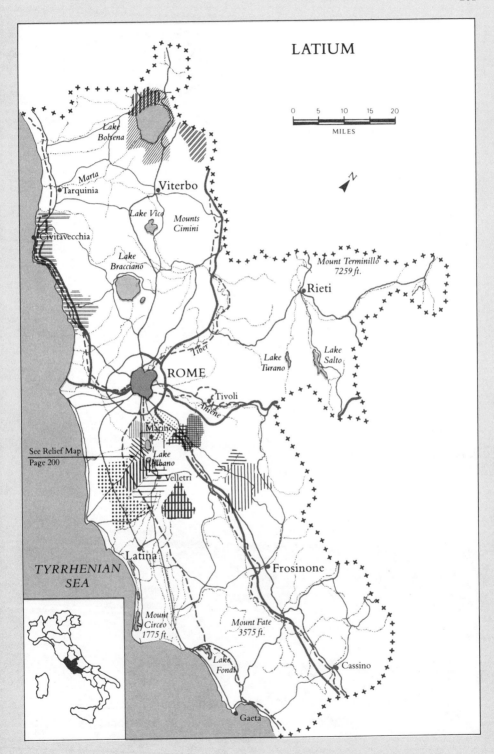

LATIUM

Lake
Bolsena

Marta
•Tarquinia
Viterbo

Lake Vico
Mounts
Cimini

Civitavecchia

Lake
Bracciano

0   5   10   15   20
MILES

N

Mount Terminillo
7259 ft.

Rieti

Tiber

Lake
Turano

Lake
Salto

ROME

Tivoli

Aniene

Marino

See Relief Map
Page 200

Lake
Albano

Velletri

TYRRHENIAN
SEA

Latina

Frosinone

Mount
Circeo
1775 ft.

Mount Fate
3575 ft.

Lake
Fondi

Cassino

Gaeta

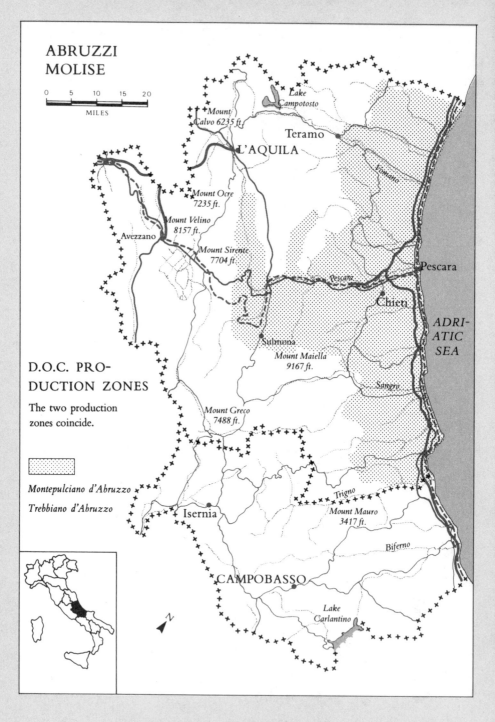

ABRUZZI
MOLISE

0 5 10 15 20
MILES

*Lake
Campotosto*

*Mount
Calvo 6235 ft.*

Teramo

L'AQUILA

Vomano

*Mount Ocre
7235 ft.*

*Mount Velino
8157 ft.*

Avezzano

*Mount Sirente
7704 ft.*

Pescara

Pescara

Chieti

ADRI-
ATIC
SEA

Sulmona

*Mount Maiella
9167 ft.*

Sangro

**D.O.C. PRO-
DUCTION ZONES**

The two production
zones coincide.

*Mount Greco
7488 ft.*

Montepulciano d'Abruzzo

Trebbiano d'Abruzzo

Trigno

Isernia

*Mount Mauro
3417 ft.*

Biferno

CAMPOBASSO

*Lake
Carlantino*

N

This region ranks eighth in total production, but only tenth in D.O.C.
wines, which account for only 8 percent of its gross output.

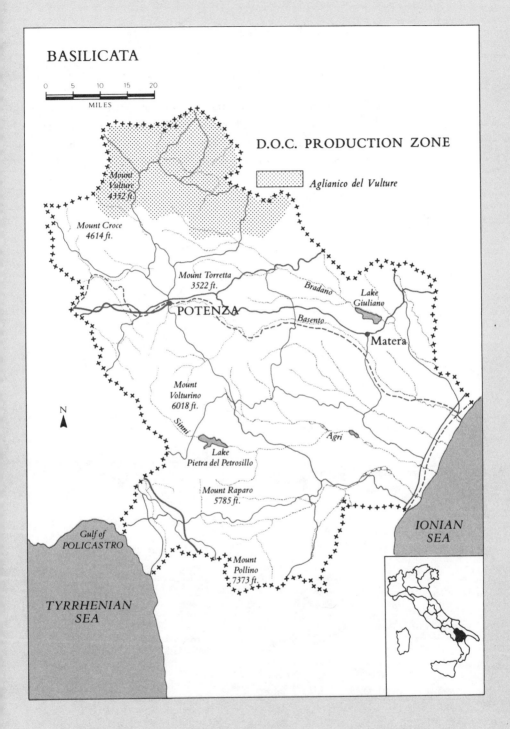

BASILICATA

0   5   10   15   20
MILES

D.O.C. PRODUCTION ZONE

Aglianico del Vulture

Mount
Vulture
4352 ft.

Mount Croce
4614 ft.

Mount Torretta
3522 ft.

Bradano

Lake
Giuliano

POTENZA

Basento

Matera

Mount
Volturino
6018 ft.

N

Sinni

Agri

Lake
Pietra del Petrosillo

Mount Raparo
5785 ft.

IONIAN
SEA

Gulf of
POLICASTRO

Mount
Pollino
7373 ft.

TYRRHENIAN
SEA

This area ranks next to last in total production: seventeenth. With only
one appellation, its D.O.C. wine proportion is 2½ percent.

APULIA

Apulian wine is the tonic whose color and alcohol have often strengthened the weaker but more famous reds of the North. The region's effort to establish itself as a source of light table wine rather than heavy blending wine is supported by the second highest number of controlled appellations in Italy. But, while production sometimes surpasses that of third-ranking Veneto, D.O.C. bottlings account for only 1.8 percent of the total.

D.O.C. PRODUCTION ZONES

Aleatico di Puglia
May be produced throughout
the region

Brindisi
Rosso, Rosato

Cacc'e mmitte di Lucera

Castel del Monte
Bianco, Rosso, Rosato

Copertino
Rosso, Rosato

Leverano
Bianco, Rosso, Rosato

Locorotondo

Martina, or Martina Franca

Matino
Rosso, Rosato

Moscato di Trani

Ostuni
Ostuni Bianco, Ostuni
Ottavianello

Primitivo di Manduria

Rosso Barletta

Rosso Canosa

Rosso di Cerignola

Salice Salentino
Rosso, Rosato

San Severo
Bianco, Rosso, Rosato

Squinzano
Rosso, Rosato

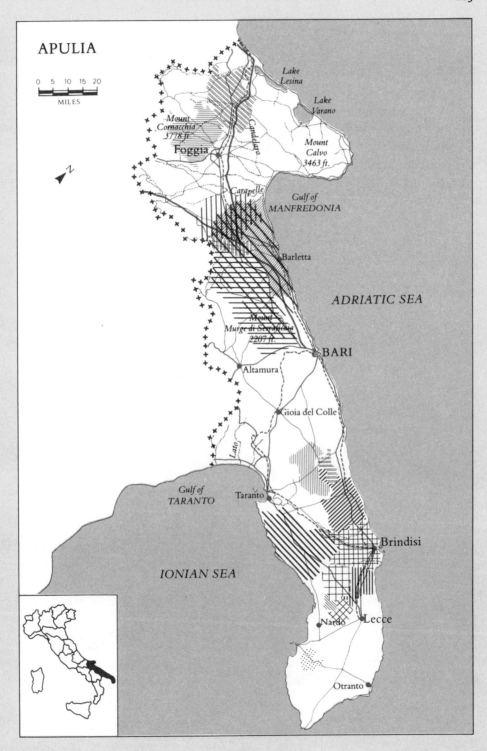

APULIA

0 5 10 15 20
MILES

N

Lake Lesina

Lake Varano

Mount Cornacchia 3778 ft.

Foggia

Mount Calvo 3463 ft.

Candelaro

Carapelle

Gulf of MANFREDONIA

Barletta

ADRIATIC SEA

Mount Murge di Serralunga 2207 ft.

BARI

Altamura

Gioia del Colle

Lato

Gulf of TARANTO

Taranto

Brindisi

IONIAN SEA

Nardò

Lecce

Otranto

CAMPANIA

Some of the best wines of antiquity were made here and the best of the South still are: the mountain-grown ones of the province of Avellino, Fiano, Greco di Tufo, and Taurasi. Campania is also distinguished, if that is the right word, by having the lowest percentage of D.O.C. wines in Italy, less than ½ percent. In total production it ranks ninth, with eighty million gallons.

D.O.C. PRODUCTION ZONES

Capri
Bianco, Rosso

Lacryma Christi del Vesuvio
Bianco, Rosso, Rosato

Fiano di Avellino

Solopaca
Bianco, Rosso

Greco di Tufo

Taurasi

Ischia
Bianco, Bianco Superiore, Rosso

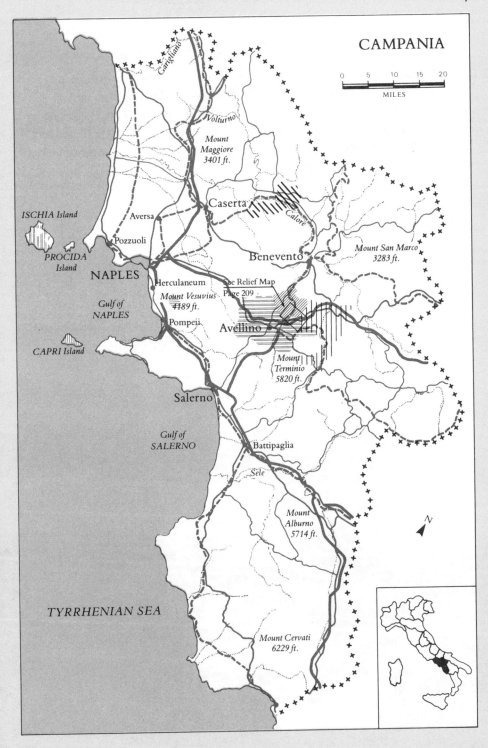

CAMPANIA

0   5   10   15   20
MILES

Garigliano

Volturno

Mount
Maggiore
3401 ft.

Caserta

Calore

ISCHIA Island

Aversa

Pozzuoli

PROCIDA
Island

Benevento

Mount San Marco
3283 ft.

NAPLES

Herculaneum

See Relief Map
Page 209

Mount Vesuvius
4189 ft.

Gulf of
NAPLES

Pompeii

Avellino

CAPRI Island

Mount
Terminio
5820 ft.

Salerno

Gulf of
SALERNO

Battipaglia

Sele

Mount
Alburno
5714 ft.

N

TYRRHENIAN SEA

Mount Cervati
6229 ft.

CALABRIA

Calabria, which for its ancient Greek colonizers was a source of prized wines, today ranks fifteenth both in total production and in D.O.C. wines. The proportion of the latter is 2½ percent. Only two wines have established a reputation beyond the region's borders—Cirò, a strong red, and Greco di Bianco, an extraordinary sweet wine which, unfortunately, is as scarce as it is great.

D.O.C. PRODUCTION ZONES

Cirò
Cirò Classico, Cirò Bianco, Rosso, Rosato

Greco di Bianco

Lamezia

Melissa
Bianco, Rosso

S. Anna di Isola di Capo Rizzuto

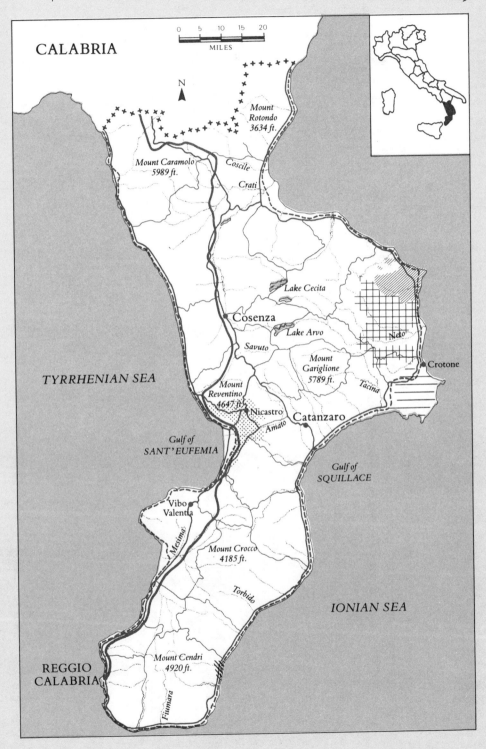

CALABRIA

0 5 10 15 20
MILES

N

Mount
Rotondo
3634 ft.

Mount Caramolo
5989 ft.

Coscile

Crati

Lake Cecita

Cosenza

Lake Arvo

Savuto

Neto

Mount
Gariglione
5789 ft.

Crotone

TYRRHENIAN SEA

Tacina

Mount
Reventino
4647 ft.

Nicastro

Catanzaro

Amato

Gulf of
SANT'EUFEMIA

Gulf of
SQUILLACE

Vibo
Valentia

Mesima

Mount Crocco
4185 ft.

Torbido

IONIAN SEA

REGGIO
CALABRIA

Mount Cendri
4920 ft.

Fiumara

SICILY

The vast Sicilian wine production—it is fourth in Italy—has only in recent years begun to include a significant quantity of sound, well-balanced wines that we can enjoy with meals. Much Sicilian wine travels north to be converted into vermouth or to France to replace the strong blending wines of Algeria. Indisputably great are its sweet wines and Marsala Vergine. D.O.C. production is a meager 4 percent of the total and does not include Sicily's most popular wines abroad, such as Corvo.

D.O.C. PRODUCTION ZONES

Alcamo

Cerasuolo di Vittoria

Etna
Bianco, Rosso, Rosato

Faro

Malvasia delle Lipari

Marsala

Moscato di Noto

Moscato di Pantelleria

Moscato di Siracusa

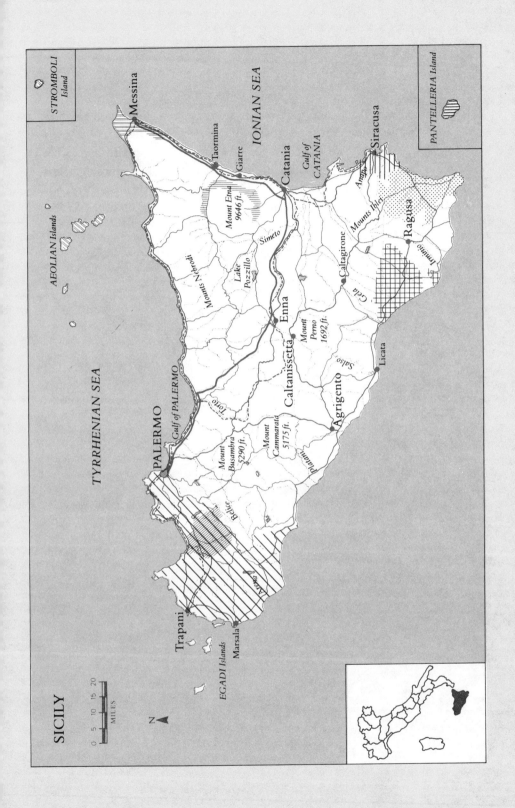

SICILY

STROMBOLI Island

PANTELLERIA Island

AEOLIAN Islands

TYRRHENIAN SEA

IONIAN SEA

Messina

Taormina

Giarre

Mount Etna 9646 ft.

Simeto

Mounts Nebrodi

Lake Pozzillo

Catania

Gulf of CATANIA

Mounts Iblei

Anapo

Siracusa

Ragusa

Caltagirone

Irminio

Enna

Mount Perno 1692 ft.

Gela

Caltanissetta

Salso

Licata

PALERMO

Gulf of PALERMO

Torto

Agrigento

Platani

Platani

Mount Busambra 5290 ft.

Mount Cammarata 5175 ft.

Belice

Trapani

Marsala

EGADI Islands

Verdura

MILES
0 5 10 15 20

N

SARDINIA

Sardinian wines are being transformed from the traditional high-alcohol, leaden potions of the past to fresh and easy-drinking wines. The island's greatest, however, are not those for table use, but its aperitif and sweet wines. Total production places Sardinia close to the lowest third of Italy's regions, but the proportion of D.O.C. wines is, at nearly 10 percent, not far from the national average, and above that of any region in the South.

D.O.C. PRODUCTION ZONES

Cagliari
Monica, Nasco, Moscato,
Malvasia, Girò, Nuragus

Campidano di Terralba

Cannonau Capo Ferrato

Cannonau di Sardegna
Rosso, Rosato
May be produced through-
out the island

**Cannonau Oliena, or
Nepente di Oliena**

Carignano del Sulcis
Rosso, Rosato

Malvasia di Bosa

Moscato di Sorso–Sennori

Vermentino di Gallura

Vernaccia di Oristano

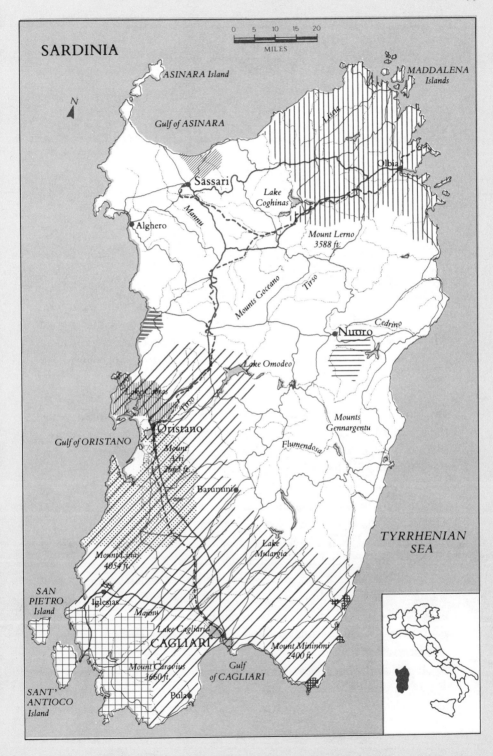

SARDINIA

ASINARA Island

MADDALENA
Islands

N

Gulf of ASINARA

Sassari

Lake
Coghinas

Olbia

Alghero

Mannu

Mount Lerno
3588 ft.

Mounts Goceano

Tirso

Cedrino

Nuoro

Lake Omodeo

Lago Oras

Tirso

Oristano

Mounts
Gennargentu

Gulf of ORISTANO

Mount
Arci
2612 ft.

Flumendosa

Barumini

Lake
Mulargia

TYRRHENIAN
SEA

Mount Linas
4054 ft.

SAN
PIETRO
Island

Iglesias

Mannu

Lake Cagliari

CAGLIARI

Mount Minimmi
2400 ft.

SANT'
ANTIOCO
Island

Mount Carbonis
3660 ft.

Pula

Gulf
of CAGLIARI

0   5   10   15   20
MILES

How to Shop for Italian Wine

When talk turns to Italian wines, the most common questions are, "How do I go about buying them? How do I know if a shop carries a good selection?" I'd like to reply, "Use my book." Much as I think that is good advice, and mutually beneficial to boot, I can't expect those who follow it to commit my text to memory or to carry the tome whenever they want a bottle.

To be sure, no one can be a discriminating buyer of wine or of anything else who is not armed with some knowledge, particularly when the arsenal of facts becomes powered with experience. But first, however, there are some basic strategies that help one divine, when browsing through a shop, what prizes it may, or may not, yield.

To begin with, see how Italian wines are displayed. If they are relegated to an obscure corner, possibly sharing a shelf with equally neglected bottles from Spain or Chile, you are about to deal with a merchant who does not have a high regard for Italy's wine. No treasures are likely to be found here—except by accident.

Similarly, an emphasis on 1½-liter bottles at bargain prices can be a warning. There is nothing wrong with offering attractively priced jug wines. Some of them may even be good. But when there is only a scanty assortment of other bottlings beyond these, the store is evidently focusing on price rather than quality.

If you find what appears to be a varied assortment, look for evidence of how carefully the selection has been assembled. How are such premier reds as Barolo and Barbaresco represented? Is there a variety of each, with possibly a choice of single vineyard bottlings? Is there more than one vintage? Good examples of these wines are never inexpensive. If the ones you see are under $10.00, be wary. When you pay too little, you may be paying too much.

Dolcetto and Barbera are among Italy's most satisfying reds. Does the store have them? The whites from Friuli, made from such grape varieties as Tocai, Ribolla, and Pinot Bianco, and carrying the appellations Collio or Colli Orientali, are often the fullest, richest white wines of Italy. Are they included? Is there a Gavi, the delicate Piedmontese white, or Fiano, the extraordinary, if costly, white from Avellino?

Does the selection of Chiantis balance the standard versions with a choice of the more powerful, longer-lived *riservas*? Alongside these Tuscan reds, are there any of the premium proprietary estate wines of Central Italy, such as Brusco dei Barbi, Pergole Torte, Tignanello, or Rubesco Riserva?

In addition to the ubiquitous Soave and Valpolicella, do you find the less common, but often more appealing, Lugana and Merlot?

One of the meatiest, most intense red wines on earth is Amarone. It is produced from partly shriveled berries grown in Valpolicella's choicest plots. It cannot be made well at low cost, but cheap versions are nonetheless available. If the store's offering is modestly priced, its concept of quality will be equally modest.

There are some Italian shippers who specialize in commercial grade wines from different districts. If you find a variety of wines from more than one area all bearing the same shipper's label, you know that the merchant is simplifying the process of selection for himself while reducing the choices available to you.

It is not necessary or desirable for a store to carry only rare and expensive wines. What matters is that wines in all price categories reflect a merchant's interest in good Italian wine and an appreciation of its variety and value.

In looking at the store's assortment you should try to form a sense of the person who put it together. If this sense reveals someone who has not merely ordered but chosen his wines, you should ask to talk to him. A good merchant is responsive to his customer's interests. If he does not have something you want in stock, he can probably order it for you, or its equivalent. You will find that you have much to talk about: vintages, producers, proprietary wines versus controlled appellation wines, wines to lay down, wines to drink soon. The subject of Italian wine is inexhaust-ible. And as you talk you may discover that the best way to buy wine is to find someone you can buy from.

Bibliography

Adams, Leon D. *Commonsense Book of Wine.* Boston: Houghton Mifflin Company, 1975.

Ambrois, Umberto. *Roero: Vite e Vino.* Cavallermaggiore: Gribaudo, 1978.

Amerine, Maynard A.; Pangborn, Rose Marie; and Roessler, Edward B. *Principles of Sensory Evaluation of Food.* New York: Academic Press, 1965.

Amerine, Maynard A., and Roessler, Edward B. *Wines: Their Sensory Evaluation.* San Francisco: W. H. Freeman & Company, 1976.

Amerine, Maynard A., and Singleton, Vernon L. *Wine: An Introduction for Americans.* Berkeley and Los Angeles: University of California Press, 1965.

Anderson, Burton. *Vino.* Boston: Little, Brown & Co., 1980.

Barbero, Giovanni. *Codice del Vino,* 5th ed. Rome: Luigi Scialpi, 1977. 1st supp., 1977; 2d and 3d supps., 1978; 4th and 5th supps., 1979; 6th supp.,: 1980.

Beniscelli, Giannetto. *La Liguria del Buon Vino.* Genoa: SIAG, 1978.

Bespaloff, Alexis. "A Corking New Wine Theory," *New York Magazine,* May 23, 1977: pp. 43-45.

———. *The New Signet Book of Wine: A Complete Introduction.* New York: New American Library, 1980.

Biagi, Gianni; Roversi, Giancarlo; and Santi, Renzo. *Monte San Pietro: Fulcro delle Colline Occidentali Bolognesi.* Bologna: Luigi Parma, 1974.

Biondo, Enzo, and Fazzi, Sandro. *Le Strade del Vino in Sardegna.* Cagliari: S.VI.SA., 1980.

Bocci, Zeffiro. *I Vini Veneti: A Denominazione di Origine Controllata.* Verona: Espro, 1980.

Bolognesi, Gianfranco. *Il Calice dell'Ospitalità: Andar per Vini in Romagna: Il Forlivese.* Forlì: Editrice Forlivese, 1978.

Bonacina, Gianni. *Lo Stivale in Bottiglia: Piccola Enciclopedia dei 3811 Vini Italiani.* Brescia: Edizioni AEB, 1978.

Bosi, Enrico. *Atlante del Chianti Classico.* Florence: La Meridiana, 1972.

————. *Atlante del Chianti Putto.* Florence: Sansoni, 1976.

Broadbent, J. M. *Wine Tasting.* London: Wine & Spirit Publications, 1968.

Bruni, Bruno. *Vini Italiani: Portanti una Denominazione di Origine.* Bologna: Edagricole, 1970.

Confezionatori del Chianti Classico Gallo Nero. Florence: Consorzio Chianti Classico, 1980.

Cosmo, Italo, et al. *Principali Vitigni da Vino Coltivati in Italia.* Rome: Ministero dell'Agricoltura e delle Foreste, vol. 1, 1960; vol. 2, 1962; vol. 3, 1964; vol. 4, 1965; vol. 5, 1966.

de Petro, Salvatore. *Vini di Puglia.* Bari: Edizioni Puglia Agricola, 1976.

Di Corato, Riccardo. *2214 Vini d'Italia.* Milan: Sonzogno, 1975.

Dolcini, Alteo; Simoni, Tommaso; and Fonta, Gian Franco. *La Romagna dei Vini.* Bologna: Alfa, 1967.

Ducati, Silvio, and Tonon, Ferdinando. *La Strada del Vino: Itinerari Viticoli nel Trentino.* Trento: Assessorato Provinciale all'Agricoltura e Foreste, n.d.

Flower, Raymond. *Chianti: The Land, the People and the Wine.* New York: Universe Books, 1979.

Garoglio, Pier Giovanni. *Enciclopedia Vitivinicola Mondiale.* Vol. 1. Milan: Edizioni Scientifiche U.I.V., 1973.

Gavotti, Giuseppe. *Cucina e Vini di Liguria.* Savona: Sabatelli, 1973.

Giovannini, A., and Tafner, S. *Atlante dei Vini del Trentino.* Florence: Sansoni, 1974.

Grossi, Spartaco. *Guida dei Vini d'Italia.* Milan: Bietti, 1973.

Grossman, Harold J. *Grossman's Guide to Wines, Beers and Spirits.* 6th ed. Revised by Harriet Lembeck. New York: Charles Scribner's Sons, 1977.

Il Chianti Classico. Florence: Consorzio Vino Chianti Classico, 1974.

I Vini dell'Emilia Romagna [periodical]. Bologna: vol. 1, April/June 1973;

vol. 2, July/September 1973; vol. 3, October/December 1973; vol. 4, December 1973; vol. 5, March 1974.

I Vini di Valtellina [periodical]. Sondrio: Camera di Commercio, no. 4, April 1972.

Johnson, Hugh. *Wine.* Rev. ed. New York: Simon and Schuster, 1974.

————.*The World Atlas of Wine.* New York: Simon and Schuster, 1971.

Leglise, Max. *Une Initiation à la Dégustation des Grands Vins.* Lausanne: Divo, 1976.

Madau, Gianluigi. *La Composizione del Vino Vermentino Prodotto nella Sardegna Settentrionale.* Sassari: Gallizzi, 1977.

————. *Qualche Considerazione sui Vini dell'Ogliastra.* Sassari: Gallizzi, 1977.

Mazzei, A. *L'Arte di Fare il Vino.* Rome: Reda, 1976.

Molino, Rodolfo. *Guida ai Vini d'Abruzzo.* Bologna: Edagricole, 1977.

Ordine dei Cavalieri del Tartufo e dei Vini di Alba. *I Grandi Vini de l'Albese.* Turin: Toso, 1977.

Pallotta, Umberto; Amati, Aureliano; and Minguzzi, Attile. *Lezioni di Enologia.* Bologna: Cooperativa Libraria Universitaria, 1977.

Paronetto, Lamberto. *Il Magnifico Chianti.* Verona: Enostampa, 1967.

————. *Verona Antica Terra di Vini Pregiati.* Verona: Fiorini, 1977.

Pellucci, Emanuele. *Brunello di Montalcino.* Florence: English version, privately printed, 1981.

Ratti, Renato. *Civiltà del Vino.* Rome: Luigi Scialpi, 1973.

————. *Guida ai Vini del Piemonte.* Turin: EDA, 1977.

————. *Manuale del Bevitore Saggio.* Rome: Luigi Scialpi, 1974.

Ravegnani, Adriano. *I 100 Vini d'Italia.* Milan: Longanesi & C., 1979.

————. *I Vini dell'Oltrepò Pavese.* Milan: Gabriele Mazzotta, 1974.

————. *I Vini di Sardegna.* Milan: Longanesi & C., 1976.

Ray, Cyril. *The Wines of Italy.* Middlesex, England: Penguin Books, 1971.

Roncarati, Bruno. *Viva Vino: D.O.C. Wines of Italy.* London: Wine & Spirit Publications, 1976.

Schneider, Steven J. *The International Album of Wine.* New York: Holt, Rinehart & Winston, 1977.

Schoonmaker, Frank. *Encyclopedia of Wine.* 7th ed. Revised by Julius Wile. New York: Hastings House, 1978.

Soldati, Mario. *Vino al Vino.* Milan: Arnoldo Mondadori, 1969. *Vino al Vino: seconda serie* Milan: Arnoldo Mondadori, 1971. *Vino al Vino: terzo viaggio* Milan: Arnoldo Mondadori, 1976.

Spagnolli, Francesco. "Il Vino Santo del Trentino," *L'Enotecnico,* vol. 12, no. 5 (May 1976): pp. 11–15.

Tingey, Nancy. *Wine Roads of Italy.* London: Charles Letts & Co., 1977.

Veronelli, Luigi. *Catalogo Bolaffi dei Vini Bianchi d'Italia.* Turin: Giulio Bolaffi, 1979.

———. *Catalogo Bolaffi dei Vini Rossi d'Italia.* Turin: Giulio Bolaffi, 1980.

Vodret, Antonio. "Problemi Enologici della Sardegna con Particolare Riferimento ai Vini da Tavola." *Industrie Agrarie,* vol. 10 (January/February 1972), pp. 15–19.

Vodret, Francesco Luigi. *Ricerche sui Vini Fini della Sardegna.* Cagliari: Pietro Valdès, 1928.

Wagner, Philip M. *Grapes into Wine.* New York: Alfred A. Knopf, 1976.

Index

A

A NOTE ABOUT THE AUTHOR

Victor Hazan was born in Italy and came to the United States in his youth. He
has collaborated with his wife, Marcella Hazan, on the translation of her
cookbooks into English, and since 1976 he has conducted the wine lecture and
tasting classes at the Hazans' School for Italian Cooking in Bologna.
He has published articles on wine in *Food & Wine, Cooking,* and
Travel & Leisure. Mr. Hazan and his wife divide their time
between New York City and Bologna and Venice.

A NOTE ON THE TYPE

The text of this book was set via computer-driven cathode ray tube in a
digitized version of Bembo, the well-known monotype face. The original cut-
ting of Bembo was made by Francesco Griffo of Bologna only a few years after
Columbus discovered America. It was named for Pietro Bembo, the celebrated
Renaissance writer and humanist scholar who was made a cardinal and served as
secretary to Pope Leo X. Sturdy, well-balanced, and finely proportioned, Bembo
is a face of rare beauty. It is, at the same time, extremely legible in all of its sizes.
Composed by The Haddon Craftsmen, Inc., Scranton, Pennsylvania
Printed and bound by The Murray Printing Company,
Westford, Massachusetts
Maps by Maria Grazia Piancastelli
Design by Joe Marc Freedman